Using Mplus for Structural Equation Modeling

Second Edition

*For Debra, for her unending
patience as I run "just one more analysis."*

Using Mplus for Structural Equation Modeling

A Researcher's Guide

Second Edition

E. Kevin Kelloway

Saint Mary's University

SAGE

Los Angeles | London | New Delhi
Singapore | Washington DC

SAGE

Los Angeles | London | New Delhi
Singapore | Washington DC

FOR INFORMATION:

SAGE Publications, Inc.
2455 Teller Road
Thousand Oaks, California 91320
E-mail: order@sagepub.com

SAGE Publications Ltd.
1 Oliver's Yard
55 City Road
London EC1Y 1SP
United Kingdom

SAGE Publications India Pvt. Ltd.
B 1/I 1 Mohan Cooperative Industrial Area
Mathura Road, New Delhi 110 044
India

SAGE Publications Asia-Pacific Pte. Ltd.
3 Church Street
#10-04 Samsung Hub
Singapore 049483

Acquisitions Editor:	Helen Salmon
Assistant Editor:	Katie Guarino
Editorial Assistant:	Anna Villarruel
Project Editor:	Bennie Clark Allen
Production Editor:	Stephanie Palermini
Copy Editor:	Jim Kelly
Typesetter:	C&M Digitals (P) Ltd.
Proofreader:	Sally Jaskold
Indexer:	Jeanne Busemeyer
Cover Designer:	Candice Harman
Marketing Manager:	Nicole Elliott

Copyright © 2015 by SAGE Publications, Inc.

All rights reserved. No part of this book may be reproduced or utilized in any form or by any means, electronic or mechanical, including photocopying, recording, or by any information storage and retrieval system, without permission in writing from the publisher.

Printed in the United States of America

Library of Congress Cataloging-in-Publication Data

Kelloway, E. Kevin, author.
  Using Mplus for structural equation modeling : a researcher's guide / E. Kevin Kelloway, Saint Mary's University. — Second edition.
    pages cm
  Revision of: Using LISREL for structural equation modeling. 1998.
  Includes bibliographical references and indexes.
  ISBN 978-1-4522-9147-5 (pbk. : alk. paper)

1. Mplus. 2. LISREL (Computer file) 3. Structural equation modeling—Data processing. 4. Social sciences—Statistical methods. I. Title.

QA278.3.K45 2015

519.5′3—dc23   2014008154

This book is printed on acid-free paper.

14 15 16 17 18 10 9 8 7 6 5 4 3 2 1

Brief Contents

Acknowledgments	viii
About the Author	ix
Chapter 1: Introduction	1
Chapter 2: Structural Equation Models: Theory and Development	5
Chapter 3: Assessing Model Fit	21
Chapter 4: Using Mplus	37
Chapter 5: Confirmatory Factor Analysis	52
Chapter 6: Observed Variable Path Analysis	94
Chapter 7: Latent Variable Path Analysis	129
Chapter 8: Longitudinal Analysis	151
Chapter 9: Multilevel Modeling	185
References	225
Index	231

Detailed Contents

Acknowledgments	viii
About the Author	ix
Chapter 1: Introduction	1
Why Structural Equation Modeling?	2
The Remainder of This Book	4
Chapter 2: Structural Equation Models: Theory and Development	5
The Process of Structural Equation Modeling	6
Model Specification	7
Identification	13
Estimation and Fit	15
Choice of Estimators	16
Sample Size	16
Model Modification	17
Chapter 3: Assessing Model Fit	21
Absolute Fit	22
Comparative Fit	26
Parsimonious Fit	29
Nested Model Comparisons	30
Model Respecification	34
Toward a Strategy for Assessing Model Fit	35
Chapter 4: Using Mplus	37
The Data File	37
The Command File	39
Specify the Data	39
Specify the Analysis	41
Specify the Output	42
Putting It All Together: Some Basic Analyses	42
Regression Analysis	42
The Standardized Solution in Mplus	47
Logistic Regression	47

Chapter 5: Confirmatory Factor Analysis	52
Model Specification	52
From Pictures to Mplus	54
In the Background	55
Identification	56
Estimation	57
Assessment of Fit	69
Model Modification	70
Item Parceling	70
Exploratory Structural Equation Models	71
Sample Results Section	89
Results	90
Exploratory Analysis	90
Chapter 6: Observed Variable Path Analysis	94
Model Specification	94
From Pictures to Mplus	95
Alternative Models	96
Identification	97
Estimation	97
Fit and Model Modification	97
Mediation	106
Using Equality Constraints	115
Multisample Analysis	120
Chapter 7: Latent Variable Path Analysis	129
Model Specification	129
Alternative Model Specifications	130
Model Testing Strategy	130
Sample Results	148
Chapter 8: Longitudinal Analysis	151
Measurement Equivalence Across Time	151
Latent Growth Curves	170
Cross-Lagged Models	176
Chapter 9: Multilevel Modeling	185
Multilevel Models in Mplus	187
Conditional Models	195
Random-Slope Models	211
Multilevel Modeling and Mediation	217
References	225
Index	231

Acknowledgments

SAGE and the author gratefully acknowledge feedback from the following reviewers:

- Alan C. Acock, Oregon State University
- Kevin J. Grimm, University of California, Davis
- George Marcoulides, University of California, Santa Barbara
- David McDowall, University at Albany—SUNY
- Rens van de Schoot, Universiteit Utrecht

Data files and code used in this book are available on an accompanying website at **www.sagepub.com/kellowaydata**

About the Author

E. Kevin Kelloway is the Canada Research Chair in Occupational Health Psychology at Saint Mary's University. He received his PhD in organizational psychology from Queen's University (Kingston, ON) and taught for eight years at the University of Guelph. In 1999, he moved to Saint Mary's University, where he also holds the position of professor of psychology. He was the founding director of the CN Centre for Occupational Health and Safety and the PhD program in business administration (management). He was also a founding principal of the Centre for Leadership Excellence at Saint Mary's. An active researcher, he is the author or editor of 12 books and over 150 research articles and chapters. He is a fellow of the Association for Psychological Science, the Canadian Psychological Association, and of Society for Industrial and Organizational Psychology. Dr. Kelloway will be President of the Canadian Psychological Association in 2015–2016, and is a Fellow of the International Association of Applied Psychology.

1

Introduction

A couple of years ago I noticed a trend. I am a subscriber to RMNET, the list server operated by the Research Methods Division of the Academy of Management. Members of the division frequently post questions about analytic issues and receive expert advice. "How do I do confirmatory factor analysis with categorical variables?" "How do I deal with a binary outcome in a structural equation model?" "How I can I test for multilevel mediation?" The trend I noticed was that with increasing frequency, the answer to these, and many other, questions was some variant of "Mplus will do that." Without having ever seen the program, I began to think of Mplus as some sort of analytic Swiss Army knife with a tool for every occasion and every type of data.

As I became more immersed in Mplus, I recognized that, in fact, this perception was largely correct. Now in its seventh version, Mplus can do just about every analysis a working social scientist might care to undertake. Although there are many structural equation modeling programs currently on the market, most require data that are continuous. Mplus allows the use of binary, ordinal, and censored variables in various forms of analysis. If that weren't enough, Mplus incorporates some forms of analysis that are not readily accessible in other statistical packages (e.g., latent class analysis) and allows the researcher to implement new techniques, such as exploratory structural equation modeling, that are not available elsewhere. Moreover, the power of Mplus, in my opinion, lies in its ability to combine different forms of analysis. For example, Mplus will do logistic regression. It will also do multilevel regression. Therefore, you can also do multilevel logistic regression. Few, if any, other programs offer this degree of flexibility.

After using and teaching the program for a couple of years, I was struck with a sense of déjà vu. Despite all its advantages, Mplus had an archaic interface requiring knowledge of a somewhat arcane command language. It operated largely as a batch processor: The user created a command file that defined the data and specified the analysis. The programming could be finicky about punctuation and syntax, and of course, the manual (although incredibly comprehensive) was little more than technical documentation and sample program files. In short, the Mplus of 2013 was the LISREL of the late 1990s. Indeed, in perhaps the ultimate irony, as I was in the midst of writing a book about the text-based Mplus, its developers came out with a graphical interface: exactly what happened when I wrote a book about LISREL!

Recognizing that researchers needed to be able to access structural equation modeling techniques, in 1998 I wrote a book that introduced the logic of structural equation modeling and introduced the reader to the LISREL program (Kelloway, 1998). This volume is an update of that original book. My goal this time around was to provide the reader with an introduction to the use of Mplus for structural equation modeling. As in the original book, I have tried to avoid the features of Mplus that are implementation dependent. For example, the diagrammer (i.e., the graphical interface) works differently on a Mac than it does on a Windows-based system. Similarly, the plot commands are implemented for Windows-based machines but do not work on a Mac. I have eschewed these features in favor of a presentation that relies on the Mplus code that will work across implementations.

Although this version of the book focuses on Mplus, I also hoped to introduce new users to structural equation modeling. I have updated various sections of the text to reflect advances in our understanding of various modeling issues. At the same time, I recognize that this is very much an introduction to the topic, and there are many other varieties of structural equation models and applications of Mplus the user will want to explore.

Why Structural Equation Modeling?

Why is structural equation modeling so popular? At least three reasons immediately spring to mind. First, social science research commonly uses measures to represent constructs. Most fields of social science research have a corresponding interest in measurement and measurement techniques. One form of structural equation modeling deals directly with how well our measures reflect their intended constructs. Confirmatory factor analysis, an application of structural equation modeling, is both more rigorous and more parsimonious than the "more traditional" techniques of exploratory factor analysis.

Moreover, unlike exploratory factor analysis, which is guided by intuitive and ad hoc rules, structural equation modeling casts factor analysis in the tradition of hypothesis testing, with explicit tests of both the overall quality of the factor solution and the specific parameters (e.g., factor loadings) composing the model. Using structural equation modeling techniques, researchers can explicitly examine the relationships between indicators and the constructs they represent, and this remains a major area of structural equation modeling in practice (e.g., Tomarken & Waller, 2005).

Second, aside from questions of measurement, social scientists are principally interested in questions of prediction. As our understanding of complex phenomena has grown, our predictive models have become more and more complex. Structural equation modeling techniques allow the specification and testing of complex "path" models that incorporate this sophisticated understanding. For example, as research accumulates in an area of knowledge, our focus as researchers increasingly shifts to mediational relationships (rather than simple bivariate prediction) and the causal processes that give rise to the phenomena of interest. Moreover, our understanding of meditational relationships and how to test for them has changed (for a review, see James, Mulaik, & Brett, 2006), requiring more advanced analytic techniques that are conveniently estimated within a structural equation modeling framework.

Finally, and perhaps most important, structural equation modeling provides a unique analysis that simultaneously considers questions of measurement and prediction. Typically referred to as "latent variable models," this form of structural equation modeling provides a flexible and powerful means of simultaneously assessing the quality of measurement and examining predictive relationships among constructs. Roughly analogous to doing a confirmatory factor analysis and a path analysis at the same time, this form of structural equation modeling allows researchers to frame increasingly precise questions about the phenomena in which they are interested. Such analyses, for example, offer the considerable advantage of estimating predictive relationships among "pure" latent variables that are uncontaminated by measurement error. It is the ability to frame and test such questions to which Cliff (1983) referred when he characterized structural equation modeling as a "statistical revolution."

As even this brief discussion of structural equation modeling indicates, the primary reason for adopting such techniques is the ability to frame and answer increasingly complex questions about our data. There is considerable concern that the techniques are not readily accessible to researchers, and James and James (1989) questioned whether researchers would invest the time and energy to master a complex and still evolving form of analysis. Others have extended the concern to question whether the "payoff" from using structural equation modeling techniques is worth mastering a sometimes esoteric and complex literature (Brannick, 1995). In the interim, researchers have answered these questions with an unequivocal "yes." Structural equation modeling techniques continue to predominate in many areas of research (Hershberger, 2003; Tomarken & Waller, 2005; Williams, Vandenberg, & Edwards, 2009), and a knowledge of structural equation modeling is now considered part of the working knowledge of most social science researchers.

The goal of this book is to present a researcher's approach to structural equation modeling. My assumption is that the knowledge requirements of using structural equation modeling techniques consist primarily of (a) knowing the kinds of questions structural equation modeling can help you answer, (b) knowing the kinds of assumptions you need to make (or test) about your data, and (c) knowing how the most common forms of analysis are implemented in the Mplus environment. Most important, the goal of this book is to assist you in framing and testing research questions using Mplus. Those with a taste for the more esoteric mathematical formulations are referred to the literature.

The Remainder of This Book

The remainder of this book is organized in three major sections. In the next three chapters, I present an overview of structural equation modeling, including the theory and logic of structural equation models (Chapter 2), assessing the "fit" of structural equation models to the data (Chapter 3), and the implementation of structural equation models in the Mplus environment (Chapter 4). In the second section of the book, I consider specific applications of structural equation models, including confirmatory factor analysis (Chapter 5), observed variable path analysis (Chapter 6), and latent variable path analysis (Chapter 7). For each form of model, I present a sample application, including the source code, printout, and results section. Finally, in the third section of the book, I introduce some additional techniques, such as analyzing longitudinal data within a structural equation modeling framework (Chapter 8) and the implementation and testing of multilevel analysis in Mplus (Chapter 9).

Although a comprehensive understanding of structural equation modeling is a worthwhile goal, I have focused in this book on the most common forms of analysis. In doing so, I have "glossed over" many of the refinements and types of analyses that can be performed within a structural equation modeling framework. When all is said and done, the intent of this book is to give a "user-friendly" introduction to structural equation modeling. The presentation is oriented to researchers who want or need to use structural equation modeling techniques to answer substantive research questions.

Data files and code used in this book are available on an accompanying website at **www.sagepub.com/kellowaydata**

2

Structural Equation Models

Theory and Development

To begin, let us consider what we mean by the term *theory*. Theories serve many functions in social science research, but most would accept the proposition that theories explain and predict behavior (e.g., Klein & Zedeck, 2004). At a more basic level, a theory can be thought of as an explanation of why variables are correlated (or not correlated). Of course, most theories in the social sciences go far beyond the description of correlations to include hypotheses about causal relations, boundary conditions, and the like. However, a necessary but insufficient condition for the validity of a theory would be that the relationships (i.e., correlations or covariances) among variables are consistent with the propositions of the theory.

For example, consider Fishbein and Ajzen's (1975) well-known theory of reasoned action. In the theory (see Figure 2.1), the best predictor of behavior is posited as being the intention to perform the behavior. In turn, the intention to perform the behavior is thought to be caused by (a) the individual's attitude toward performing the behavior and (b) the individual's subjective norms about the behavior. Finally, attitudes toward the behavior are thought to be a function of the individual's beliefs about the behavior. This simple presentation of the theory is sufficient to generate some expectations about the pattern of correlations between the variables referenced in the theory.

If the theory is correct, one would expect that the correlation between behavioral intentions and behavior and the correlation between beliefs and attitudes should be stronger than the correlations between attitudes and behavior and between subjective norms and behavior. Correspondingly, the correlations between beliefs and behavioral intentions and beliefs and behavior should be the weakest correlations. With reference to Figure 2.1, the general

Figure 2.1

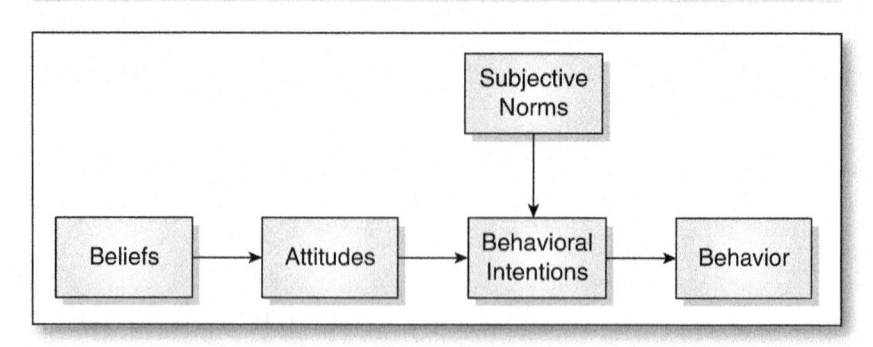

[Diagram: Beliefs → Attitudes → Behavioral Intentions → Behavior, with Subjective Norms → Behavioral Intentions]

principle is that if the theory is correct, then direct and proximal relationships should be stronger than more distal relationships.

As a simple test of the theory, one could collect data on behavior, behavioral intentions, attitudes, subjective norms, and beliefs. If the theory is correct, one would expect to see the pattern of correlations described above. If the actual correlations do not conform to the pattern, one could reasonably conclude that the theory was incorrect (i.e., the model of reasoned action did not account for the observed correlations).

Note that the converse is not true. Finding the expected pattern of correlations would not imply that the theory is right, only that it is plausible. There might be other theories that would result in the same pattern of correlations (e.g., one could hypothesize that behavior causes behavioral intentions, which in turn cause attitudes and subjective norms). As noted earlier, finding the expected pattern of correlations is a necessary but not sufficient condition for the validity of the theory.

Although the above example is a simple one, it illustrates the logic of structural equation modeling. In essence, structural equation modeling is based on the observations that (a) every theory implies a set of correlations and (b) if the theory is valid, it should be able to explain or reproduce the patterns of correlations found in the empirical data.

The Process of Structural Equation Modeling

The remainder of this chapter is organized according to a linear "model" of structural equation modeling. Although linear models of the research process are notoriously suspect (McGrath, Martin, & Kukla, 1982) and may not reflect actual practice, the heuristic has the advantage of drawing attention to the major concerns, issues, and decisions involved in developing and evaluating structural equation modeling. It is now common (e.g., Meyers, Gamst, & Guarino, 2006) to discuss structural equation modeling according to Bollen and Long's (1993, pp. 1–2) five stages characteristic of most applications of structural equation modeling:

1. model specification,
2. identification,
3. estimation,
4. testing fit, and
5. respecification.

For presentation purposes, I will defer much of the discussion of testing fit until the next chapter.

MODEL SPECIFICATION

Structural equation modeling is inherently a confirmatory technique. That is, for reasons that will become clear as the discussion progresses, the methods of structural equation modeling are ill suited for the exploratory identification of relationships. Rather, the foremost requirement for any form of structural equation modeling is the a priori specification of a model. The propositions composing the model are most frequently drawn from previous research or theory, although the role of informed judgment, hunches, and dogmatic statements of belief should not be discounted. However derived, the purpose of the model is to explain why variables are correlated in a particular fashion. Thus, in the original development of path analysis, Sewall Wright focused on the ability of a given path model to reproduce the observed correlations (see, e.g., Wright, 1934). More generally, Bollen (1989, p. 1) presented the fundamental hypothesis for structural equation modeling as

$$\Sigma = \Sigma(\Theta),$$

where Σ is the observed population covariance matrix, Θ is a vector of model parameters, and $\Sigma(\Theta)$ is the covariance matrix implied by the model. When the equality expressed in the equation holds, the model is said to "fit" the data. Thus, the goal of structural equation modeling is to explain the patterns of covariance observed among the study variables.

In essence, then, a model is an explanation of why two (or more) variables are related (or not). In undergraduate statistics courses, we often harp on the observation that a correlation between X and Y has at least three possible interpretations (i.e., X causes Y, Y causes X, or X and Y are both caused by a third variable Z). In formulating a model, you are choosing one of these explanations, in full recognition of the fact that either of the remaining two might be just as good, or better, an explanation.

It follows from these observations that the "model" used to explain the data cannot be derived from those data. For any covariance or correlation matrix, one can always derive a model that provides a perfect fit to the data. Rather, the power of structural equation modeling derives from the attempt to assess the fit of theoretically derived predictions to the data.

It might help at this point to consider two types of variables. In any study, we have variables we want to explain or predict. We also have variables we think will offer the explanation or prediction we desire. The former are known as *endogenous* variables, whereas the latter are *exogenous* variables. Exogenous variables are considered to be the starting points of the model. We are not interested in how the exogenous variables came about. Endogenous variables may serve as both predictors and criteria, being predicted by exogenous variables and predicting other endogenous variables. A model, then, is a set of theoretical propositions that link the exogenous variables to the endogenous variables and the endogenous variables to one another. Taken as a whole, the model explains both what relationships we expect to see in the data and what relationships we do not expect to emerge.

It is worth repeating that the fit of a model to data, in itself, conveys no information about the validity of the underlying theory. Rather, as previously noted, a model that "fits" the data is a necessary but not sufficient condition for model validity.

The conditions necessary for causal inference were recently reiterated by Antonakis, Bendahan, Jacquart, and Lalive (2010) as comprising (a) association (i.e., for X to cause Y, X and Y must be correlated), (b) temporal order (i.e., for X to cause Y, X must precede Y in time), and (c) isolation (the relationship between X and Y cannot be a function of other causes).

Figure 2.2

Path diagrams. Most frequently, the structural relations that form the model are depicted in a path diagram in which variables are linked by unidirectional arrows (representing causal relations) or bidirectional curved arrows (representing noncausal, or correlational, relationships).[1] Consider three variables X, Y, and Z. A possible path diagram depicting the relationships among the three is given in Figure 2.2.

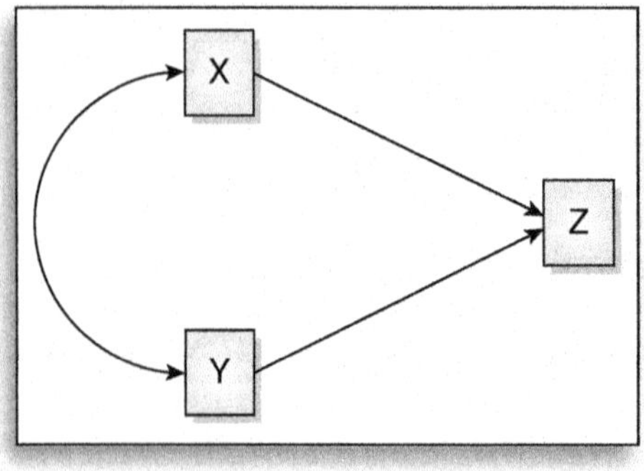

The diagram presents two exogenous variables (X and Y) that are assumed to be correlated (curved arrow). Both variables are presumed to cause Z (unidirectional arrows).

Now consider adding a fourth variable, Q, with the hypotheses that Q is caused by both X and Z, with no direct effect of Y on Q. The path diagram representing these hypotheses is presented in Figure 2.3.

Three important assumptions underlie path diagrams. First, it is assumed that all of the proposed causal relations are linear. Although there are ways of estimating nonlinear relations in structural equation modeling, for the most part we are concerned only with linear relations. Second, path diagrams are assumed to represent all the causal relations between the variables. It is just as important to specify the causal relationships that do exist as it is to specify the relationships that do not. Finally, path diagrams are based on the assumption of causal closure; this is the assumption that all causes of the variables in the model are represented in the model. That is, any variable thought to cause two or more variables in the model should in itself be part of the model. Failure to actualize this assumption results in misleading and often inflated results (which economists refer to as specification error). In general, we are striving for the most parsimonious diagram that (a) fully explains why variables are correlated and (b) can be justified on theoretical grounds.

Finally, it should be noted that one can also think of factor analysis as a path diagram. The common factor model on which all factor analyses are based states that the responses to an individual item are a function of (a) the trait that the item is measuring and (b) error. Another way to phrase this is that the observed variables (items) are a function of both common factors and unique factors.

For example, consider the case of six items that are thought to load on two factors (which are oblique). Diagrammatically, we can represent this model as shown in Figure 2.4. Note that this is the conceptual model we have

Figure 2.3

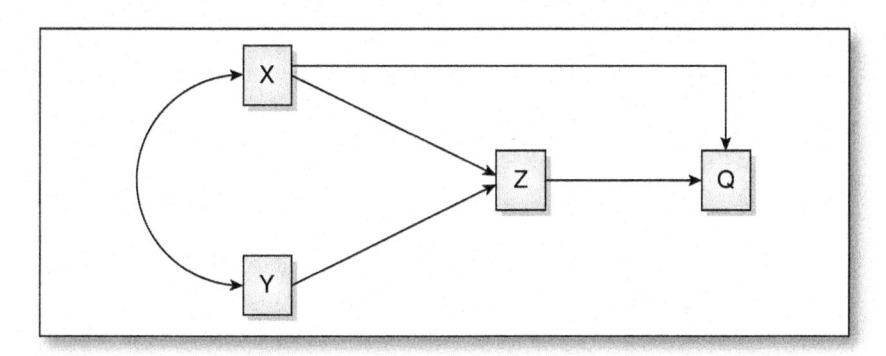

Figure 2.4

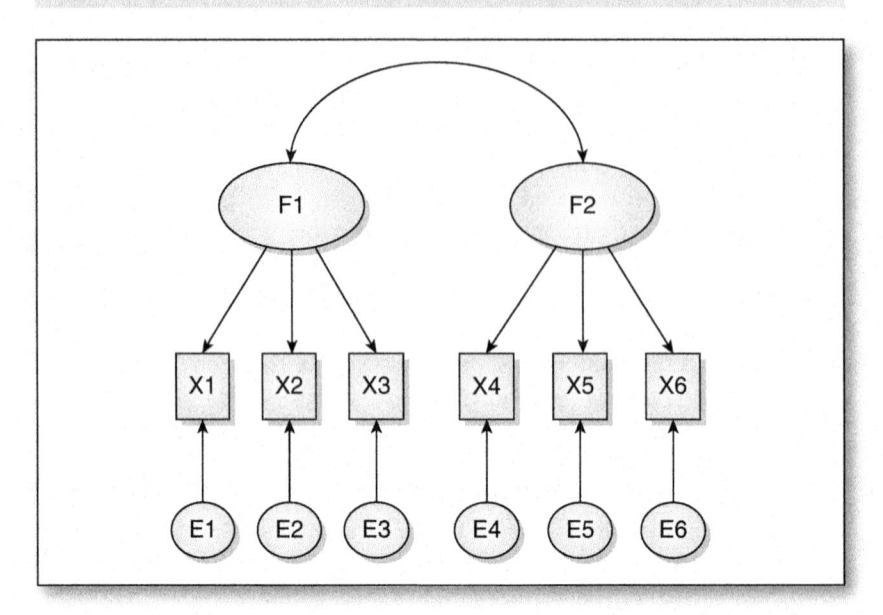

when planning a factor analysis. As will be explained in greater detail later, the model represents the confirmatory factor analysis model, not the model commonly used for exploratory factor analysis.

In the diagram, F1 and F2 are the two common factors. They are also referred to as *latent variables* or unobserved variables because they are not measured directly. Note that it is common to represent latent variables in ovals or circles. X1 ... X6 are the *observed* or *manifest variables* (test items, sometimes called indicators), whereas E1 ... E6 are the residuals (sometimes called unique factors or error variances). Thus, although most of this presentation focuses on path diagrams, all the material is equally relevant to factor analysis, which can be thought of as a special form of path analysis.

Converting the path diagram to structural equations. Path diagrams are most useful in depicting the hypothesized relations because there is a set of rules that allow one to translate a path diagram into a series of structural equations. The rules, initially developed by Wright (1934), allow one to write a set of equations that completely define the observed correlations matrix.

The logic and rules for path analysis are quite straightforward. The set of arrows constituting the path diagram include both simple and compound paths. A *simple path* (e.g., $X \rightarrow Y$) represents the direct relationship between two variables (i.e., the regression of Y on X). A compound path (e.g., $X \rightarrow Y \rightarrow Z$) consists of two or more simple paths. The value of a compound path is the product of all the simple paths constituting the compound path. Finally, and most important for our purposes, the correlation between any two variables is the sum of the simple and compound paths linking the two variables.

Given this background, Wright's (1934) rules for decomposing correlations are these:

1. After going forward on an arrow, the path cannot go backward. The path can, however, go backward as many times as necessary prior to going forward.
2. The path cannot go through the same construct more than once.
3. The path can include only one curved arrow.

Consider, for example, three variables, A, B, and C. Following psychological precedent, I measure these variables in a sample of 100 undergraduates and produce the following correlation matrix:

	A	B	C
A	1.00		
B	.50	1.00	
C	.65	.70	1.00

I believe that both A and B are causal influences on C. Diagrammatically, my model might look like the model shown in Figure 2.5.

Following the standard rules for computing path coefficients, I can write a series of structural equations to represent these relationships. By solving for the variables in the structural equations, I am computing the path coefficients (the values of the simple paths):

$c = .5$

$a + cb = .65$ (2.1)

$b + ca = .70$ (2.2)

Figure 2.5

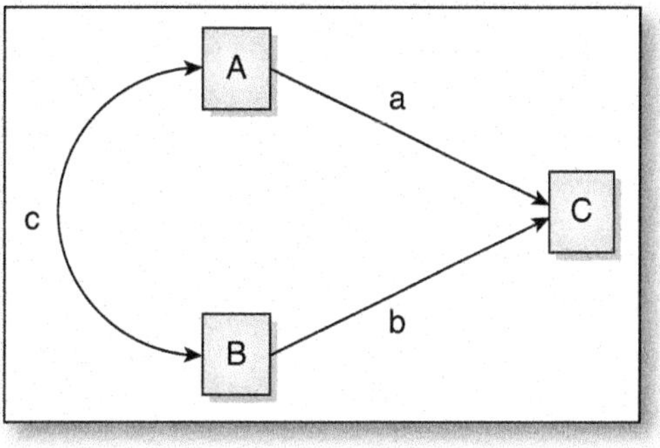

Note that three equations completely define the correlation matrix. That is, each correlation is thought to result from the relationships specified in the model. Those who still recall high school algebra will recognize that I have three equations to solve for three unknowns; therefore, the solution is straightforward. Because I know the value of c (from the correlation matrix), I begin by substituting c into Equations 2.1 and 2.2. Equation 2.1 then becomes

$$a + .5b = .65, \qquad (2.1.1)$$

and Equation 2.2 becomes

$$b + .5a = .70. \qquad (2.2.1)$$

To solve the equations, one can multiply Equation 2.2.1 by 2 (resulting in Equation 2.2.2) and then subtract Equation 2.1.1 from the result:

$$2b + a = 1.4 \qquad (2.2.2)$$
$$-.5b + a = .65 \qquad (2.1.1)$$
$$= 1.5b = .75. \qquad (2.3)$$

From Equation 2.3, we can solve for b: $b = .75/1.5 = .50$. Substituting b into either Equation 2.2.1 or Equation 2.1.1 results in $a = .40$. Thus, the three path values are $a = .40$, $b = .50$, and $c = .50$.

These numbers are standardized partial regression coefficients or beta weights and are interpreted exactly the same as beta weights derived from multiple regression analyses. Indeed, a simpler method to derive the path coefficients a and b would have been to use a statistical software package to conduct an ordinary least squares regression of C on A and B. The important point is that any model implies a set of structural relations among the variables. These structural relations can be represented as a set of structural equations and, in turn, imply a correlation (or covariance) matrix.

Thus, a simple check on the accuracy of the solution is to work backward. Using the estimates of structural parameters, we can calculate the correlation matrix. If the matrix is the same as the one we started out with, we have reached the correct solution. Thus,

$$c = .50,$$
$$a + cb = .65,$$
$$b + ca = .70,$$

and we have calculated that $b = .50$ and $a = .40$. Substituting into the second equation above, we get $.40 + .50 \times .50 = .65$, or $.40 + .25 = .65$. For the second equation, we get $.50 + .50 \times .40 = .70$, or $.50 + .20 = .70$. In this case, our model was able to reproduce the correlation matrix. That is, we were able to find a set of regression or path weights for the model that can replicate the original, observed correlations.

IDENTIFICATION

As illustrated by the foregoing example, application of structural equation modeling techniques involves the estimation of unknown parameters (e.g., factor loadings or path coefficients) on the basis of observed covariances or correlations. In general, issues of identification deal with whether a unique solution for a model (or its component parameters) can be obtained (Bollen, 1989). Models and/or parameters may be underidentified, just-identified, or overidentified (Pedhazur, 1982).

In the example given above, the number of structural equations composing the model exactly equals the number of unknowns (i.e., three unknowns and three equations). In such a case, the model is said to be *just-identified* (because there is just one correct answer). A just-identified model will always provide a unique solution (i.e., set of path values) that will be able to perfectly reproduce the correlation matrix. A just-identified model is also referred to as a "saturated" model (Medsker, Williams, & Holahan, 1994). One common just-identified or saturated model is the multiple regression model. As we will see in Chapter 4, such models provide a perfect fit to the data (i.e., perfectly reproduce the correlation matrix).

A necessary, but insufficient, condition for the identification of a structural equation model is that one cannot estimate more parameters than there are unique elements in the covariance matrix. Bollen (1989) referred to this as the "t rule" for model identification. Given a $k \times k$ covariance matrix (where k is the number of variables), there are $k \times (k-1)/2$ unique elements in the covariance matrix. Attempts to estimate exactly $k \times (k-1)/2$ parameters results in the just-identified or saturated (Medsker et al., 1994) model. Only one unique solution is obtainable for the just-identified model, and the model always provides a perfect fit to the data.

When the number of unknowns exceeds the number of equations, the model is said to be *underidentified*. This is a problem because the model parameters cannot be uniquely determined; there is no unique solution. Consider, for example, the solution to the equation $X + Y = 10$. There are no two unique values for X and Y that solve this equation (there is, however, an infinite number of possibilities).

Last, and most important, when the number of equations exceeds the number of unknowns, the model is *overidentified*. In this case, it is possible that there is no solution that satisfies the equation, and the model is falsifiable. This is, of course, the situation that lends itself to hypothesis testing. As implied by the foregoing, the question of identification is largely, although not completely, determined by the number of estimated parameters (Bollen, 1989).

The ideal situation for the social scientist is to have an overidentified model. If the model is underidentified, no solution is possible. If the model is just-identified, there is one set of values that completely fit the observed correlation matrix. That matrix, however, also contains many sources of error (e.g., sampling error, measurement error). In an overidentified model, it is possible to falsify a model, that is, to conclude that the model does not fit the data. We always, therefore, want our models to be overidentified.

Although it is always possible to "prove" that your proposed model is overidentified (for examples, see Long, 1983a, 1983b), the procedures are cumbersome and involve extensive calculations. Overidentification of a structural equation model is achieved by placing two types of restrictions on the model parameters to be estimated.

First, researchers assign a direction to parameters. In effect, positing a model on the basis of one-way causal flow restricts half of the posited parameters to be zero. Models incorporating such a one-way causal flow are known as *recursive models*. Bollen (1989) pointed out that recursiveness is a sufficient condition for model identification. That is, as long as all the arrows are going in the same direction, the model is identified. Moreover, in the original formulation of path analysis, in which path coefficients are estimated through ordinary least squares regression (Pedhazur, 1982), recursiveness is a required property of models. Recursive models, however, are not a necessary condition for identification, and it is possible to estimate identified nonrecursive models (i.e., models that incorporate reciprocal causation) using programs such as Mplus.

Second, researchers achieve overidentification by setting some parameters to be fixed to predetermined values. Typically, values of specific parameters are set to zero. Earlier, in the discussion of model specification, I made the point that it is important for researchers to consider (a) which paths will be in the model and (b) which paths are not in the model. By "not in the model," I am referring to the setting of certain paths to zero. For example, in the theory of reasoned action presented earlier (see Figure 2.1), several potential paths (i.e., from attitudes to behavior, from norms to behavior, from beliefs to intentions, from beliefs to norms, and from beliefs to behavior) were set to zero to achieve overidentification. Had these paths been included in the model, the model would have been just-identified.

ESTIMATION AND FIT

If the model is overidentified, then, by definition, there is an infinite number of potential solutions. Moreover, given moderately complex models, solving the structural equations by hand would quickly become a formidable problem. Indeed, the growing popularity of structural equation modeling is probably most attributable to the availability of software packages such as Mplus that are designed to solve sets of structural equations.

Mplus solves these equations (as do most similar programs) by using numerical methods to estimate parameters. In particular, Mplus solves for model parameters by a process of iterative estimation. To illustrate the process of iterative estimation, consider a common children's guessing game.

When I was a boy, we played a game called hot, hotter, hottest. In one version of the game, one child would pick a number and another child would attempt to guess the number. If the guess was close, the guesser was "getting hotter." If the guess was way off, the guesser was "getting colder." By a simple process of informed trial and error, you could almost always guess the number.

This is precisely the process Mplus uses to estimate model parameters. The program starts by taking a "guess" at the parameter values. It then calculates the implied covariance matrix (the covariance matrix that would result from that set of model parameters). The implied covariance matrix is then compared with the observed covariance matrix (i.e., the actual data) to see how "hot" the first guess was. If the guess was right (i.e., if the implied and actual covariance matrices are very similar), the process stops. If the guess was wrong, Mplus adjusts the first guess (the starting values) and checks again. This process of iterative estimation continues until some fitting criterion has been achieved (the solution is "red hot").

How does Mplus know when it is "red hot," that is, when the correct answer is obtained? In general, the user specifies a fitting criterion (a mathematical function) that the program tries to minimize. For the most part, structural equation modeling will use the maximum likelihood method of estimation. Although the specifics of the fitting equations are not important for our purposes, it is important to note that each criterion attempts to minimize the differences between the implied and observed covariance matrices. When the observed and predicted covariance matrices are exactly the same, the criteria will equal zero. Conversely, when the matrices are different, the value of the fitting function gets larger. Thus, the goal of the iterative estimation procedure used by Mplus is to minimize the fitting function specified by the user.

Because of the complexity of the subject, we will defer further discussion of assessing model fit until the next chapter. Three additional issues regarding model estimation should be noted, however: the choice of estimators, the choice of data type, and sample-size requirements.

Choice of Estimators

By far the most popular choice of estimators in structural equation modeling is maximum likelihood, and this is the default in Mplus. Maximum likelihood estimators are known to be consistent and asymptotically efficient in large samples (Bollen, 1989). The popularity of these methods, however, is more likely attributable to the fact that (under certain conditions) the minimum of the fitting criterion multiplied by $N - 1$ (where N is the number of observations) is distributed as χ^2. For maximum likelihood estimation, if we have a large sample and are willing to assume (or show) that the observed variables are multivariate normal, then the chi-square test is reasonable.

Mplus also implements the MLR and MLM estimators, both versions of maximum likelihood that are appropriate for data that do not meet the assumption of multivariate normality. MLM provides the Satorra-Bentler (Satorra & Bentler, 2001) χ^2 corrected value, which is robust to the violation of multivariate normality in addition to other robust fit indices. MLR is an extension of MLM that allows for missing data. For the most part, Mplus will choose the correct estimator for the type of data and analysis you specify. However, Byrne (2012) suggested an interesting strategy for those concerned about multivariate normality. That is, one can simply run the model using maximum likelihood estimation and then run it using the MLM estimator and compare the results. If the data are multivariate normal, there will be little difference in the fit statistics generated by each method. If there are substantial differences, this indicates a violation of the normality assumption, and one should report the MLM solution.

Other estimators are available in Mplus and may be used for different types of models and data. For example, the weighted least squares estimator is available for use with categorical data, and Bayesian estimators are used with very complex models. Again, although researchers may have specific reasons to choose a particular estimator, the Mplus program will typically choose the most appropriate estimator for your type of data and analysis.

Sample Size

Although it may not have been obvious up until this point, structural equation modeling is very much a large-sample technique. Both the estimation methods (e.g., maximum likelihood) and tests of model fit (e.g., the chi-square test) are based on the assumption of large samples. On the basis of reviews of simulation studies (e.g., Boomsma & Hoogland, 2001), Tomarken and Waller (2005) suggested a minimum sample size of 200 observations for simple models. For example, it is commonly recommended that models incorporating latent variables require a sample size of at least 100 observations, although parameter estimates may be inaccurate in samples of less than 200 (Marsh, Balla, & MacDonald, 1988). Boomsma (1983) recommended a sample size of approximately 200 for models of moderate complexity. Taking a somewhat different approach, Bentler and Chou (1987) suggested that the ratio of sample size to estimated parameters be between 5:1 and 10:1 (similar to frequently cited guidelines for regression analyses, e.g., Tabachnick & Fidell, 1996).

An alternative approach to determining the required sample size for structural equation models is to do a power analysis. Soper (2013) offers an online calculator to determine sample size on the basis of the anticipated effect size, numbers of observed and latent variables, and desired power (an implementation of the guidelines found in Westland, 2010). Other authors have provided code (e.g., in R or SAS) that implement various power routines; these programs typically must be downloaded and run in the appropriate software environment. For example, an online implementation of MacCallum, Browne, and Sugawara's (1996) power analysis can be found at http://www.unc.edu/~rcm/power/power.htm (retrieved December 14, 2013). Preacher and Coffman (2006) provide a calculator for power based on the root mean square error of approximation (see also Schoemann, Preacher, & Coffman, 2010). A collection of programs that implement power routines on the basis of Kim (2005) and the work of MacCallum and colleagues (MacCallum, Browne, & Cai, 2006; MacCallum et al., 1996; MacCallum & Hong, 1997) can be found at http://timo.gnambs.at/en/scripts/powerforsem (retrieved February 10, 2014).

In the current context, a useful way to generate sample-size estimates when testing a model is to use the capacity of Mplus analysis for Monte Carlo analysis (see Muthén & Muthén, 2002). In a Monte Carlo analysis, the researcher generates a set of hypothesized population parameters. Data are randomly generated to replicate those parameters, and the program then repeatedly samples from these population data. Finally, the estimates are averaged across samples. Muthén and Muthén (2002) provided examples of how this method can be used to estimate the power of specific parameter tests in the model. The programs and examples used in their article can be found at http://www.statmodel.com.

MODEL MODIFICATION

Perhaps no aspect of structural equation modeling techniques is more controversial than the role of model respecification. The goal of model respecification is to improve either the parsimony or the fit of a model (MacCallum, 1986). Thus, respecification typically consists of one of two forms of model modification. First, researchers may delete nonsignificant paths from their models in a "theory-trimming" (Pedhazur, 1982) approach. Second, researchers may add paths to the model on the basis of the empirical results.

Although model respecification frequently is included in descriptions of the modeling process (e.g., Bollen & Long, 1993), there are several problems with specification searches. Perhaps most important, the available data suggest that specification searches typically do not retrieve the actual model (MacCallum, 1986). Moreover, because specification searches are conducted post hoc and are empirically rather than theoretically derived, model modifications based on such searches must be validated on an independent sample. As James and James (1989) pointed out, it is perfectly acceptable to modify a model and assess the fit of the model on the basis of data from one sample; it is the interpretation of such model modifications that is suspect. When models are modified and reassessed on the same data, parameters added to or deleted from the model cannot be said to be confirmed.

Aside from the exploratory nature of model respecifications, there is considerable doubt about the meaning of parameters added to a model on the basis of a specification search. Certainly, there are examples in the literature (and in my own work; see Barling, Kelloway, & Bremermann, 1991) of adding substantively uninterpretable parameters (e.g., covariances among error terms) to a model to improve the fit of the model. Such parameters have been termed "wastebasket" parameters (Browne, 1982), and there is little justification for their inclusion in structural models (Kelloway, 1995, 1996).

It is tempting to conclude, as I have previously (Kelloway, 1996), that parameters that can be assigned a substantive meaning are "legitimate" additions to a structural model during a specification search. Steiger (1990) pointed to the flaw in this conclusion when he questioned, "What percentage of researchers would find themselves unable to think up a 'theoretical justification' for freeing a parameter? In the absence of empirical information to the contrary, I assume that the answer... is 'near zero' " (p. 175).

Although replication of model modifications on an independent sample is commonly recognized to be an appropriate strategy, it should be noted that there are also problems with this strategy. Perhaps most important, because the empirically driven respecification of model parameters capitalizes on chance variations in the data, the results of such replication efforts may be inconsistent (MacCallum, Roznowski, & Necowitz, 1992). Thus, there are both conceptual and empirical problems with the practice of respecifying models, and, at best, such respecifications provide limited information.

So what do you do if your model doesn't fit the data? One solution to an ill-fitting model is to simply stop testing and declare the theory that guided model development to be wrong. This approach has the advantage of conforming to a classical decision-making view of hypothesis testing; that is, you have a hypothesis, you perform a test, and you either accept or reject the hypothesis. The disadvantage of this approach is, of course, that one does not gain any insight into what the "correct" (or at least one plausible) theory might be. In particular, there is information in the data you have collected that you may not be using to its fullest advantage.

A second approach to an ill-fitting model is to use the available information to try to generate a more appropriate model. This is the "art" of model modification: changing the original model to fit the data. Although model modification is fraught with perils, I do not believe anyone has ever "gotten it right" on the first attempt at model fitting. Thus, the art of model fitting is to understand the dangers and try to account for them when you alter your model on the basis of empirical observations.

The principal danger in post hoc model modification is that this procedure is exploratory and involves considerable capitalization on chance. Thus, you might add a path to a model to make it fit the data, only to find that you have capitalized on chance variation within your sample, and the results will never be replicated in another sample. There are at least two strategies for minimizing this problem.

First, try to make model modifications that have some semblance of theoretical consistency (bearing in mind Steiger's [1990] comments about our ability to rationalize). If there are 20 studies suggesting that job satisfaction and job performance are unrelated, do not hypothesize a path between satisfaction and performance just to make your model fit. Second, as with any scientific endeavor, models are worthwhile only when they can be replicated in another sample. Post hoc modifications to a model should always be (a) identified as such and (b) replicated in another sample.[2]

There is another, potentially more controversial, approach to model testing and specification. Rather than beginning with a well-developed theory that we either do not modify or modify only with the most conservative approach, an alternative would be to begin with a loose commitment, or none at all, to a model and let the data guide us to the most appropriate model. Although vaguely heretical, this approach is similar to the classic "grounded theory" (Glaser & Strauss, 1967) approach in qualitative data analysis, in which one begins without preconceptions and lets the theory emerge from the data. At risk of offending the sensibilities of both quantitative and qualitative researchers, one might refer to this strategy as quantitative grounded theory.

A variety of programs are available that allow the researcher to derive structural equation models. Perhaps the most well known of these is the TETRAD program developed by Glymour, Schienes, Spirtes, and Kelly (1987) to automatically search for alternative models. Marcoulides and Ing (2012) reviewed a variety of automated search mechanisms based on data-mining techniques that, like TETRAD, are aimed at letting the data inform our development of a model.

Notes

1. It also helps to remember that in path diagrams, the hypothesized causal "flow" is traditionally from left to right (or top to bottom); that is, the independent (exogenous) variables or predictors are on the left (top), and the dependent (endogenous) variables or criteria are on the right (bottom).
2. Note that the use of a holdout sample is often recommended for this purpose. Set aside 25% of the original sample, then test and modify the model on the remaining 75%. When you have a model that fits the data on the original 75%, test the model on the remaining 25%. Although this procedure does not always result in replicated findings, it can help identify which paths are robust and which are not.

3

Assessing Model Fit

For many years, researchers obsessed about the assessment of model fit: New measures of model fit were developed, and there were many debates over how to assess the fit of a model to the data. Thankfully, this flurry of activity seems to have settled down. Although these issues continue to be debated (see, e.g., Fan & Sivo, 2007) and we can anticipate further developments, we do have some reasonable agreement on a set of indices and their interpretation (Hu & Bentler, 1999).

Mplus provides a reasonably small set of indices to test model fit, although there is a much broader range of indices in the literature. Before discussing these, it is instructive to consider exactly what we mean when we claim that a model "fits" the data.

At least two traditions in the assessment of model fit are apparent (Tanaka, 1993): the assessment of the *absolute* fit of a model and the assessment of the *comparative* fit of a model. The assessment of the comparative fit of a model may be further subdivided into the assessment of comparative fit and *parsimonious* fit. The assessment of absolute fit is concerned with the ability of a model to reproduce the actual covariance matrix. The assessment of comparative fit is concerned with comparing two or more competing models to assess which provides the better fit to the data.

The assessment of parsimonious fit is based on the recognition that one can always obtain a better fitting model by estimating more parameters. (At the extreme, one can always obtain a perfect fit to the data by estimating the just-identified model containing all possible parameters.) Thus, the assessment of parsimonious fit is based on the idea of a "cost-benefit" trade-off and asks, Is the cost (loss of a degree of freedom) worth the additional benefit (increased fit) of estimating more parameters? Although measures of comparative and absolute fit will always favor more complex models, measures of parsimonious fit provide a "fairer" basis for comparison by adjusting for the known effects of estimating more parameters.

In the remainder of this chapter, I present the most commonly used indices for assessing absolute, comparative, and parsimonious fit. Of necessity, the presentation is based on the formulas for calculating these indices; however, it should be remembered that structural equation modeling programs such as Mplus do the actual calculations for you. The researcher's task, therefore, is to understand what the fit indices are measuring and how they should be interpreted. The chapter concludes with some recommendations on assessing the fit of models.

Absolute Fit

Tests of absolute fit are concerned with the ability to reproduce the correlation or covariance matrix. As shown in the previous chapter, perhaps the most straightforward test of this ability is to work backward, that is, from the derived parameter estimates, calculate the implied covariance matrix and compare it, item by item, with the observed matrix. This was essentially the procedure used in early applications of path analysis (e.g., Wright, 1934). There are at least two major stumbling blocks to this procedure.

First, the computations are laborious when models are even moderately complex. Second, there are no hard and fast standards of how "close" the implied and observed covariance matrices must be to claim that a model fits the data. For example, if the actual correlation between two variables is .45 and the correlation implied by the model is .43, does the model fit the data or not? Early path analysts suggested that the reproduced correlation should be within ±.05 of the actual correlation (Blalock, 1964). Although this was essentially an arbitrary standard, we continue to see .05 as a cutoff for some fit indices.

Early in the history of structural equation modeling, researchers recognized that for some methods of estimation, a single test statistic (distributed as χ^2) was available to test the null hypothesis that

$$\Sigma = \Sigma(\Theta),$$

where Σ is the population covariance matrix and $\Sigma(\Theta)$ is the covariance matrix implied by the model (Bollen & Long, 1993). In the obverse of traditional hypothesis testing, a nonsignificant value of χ^2 implies that there is no significant discrepancy between the covariance matrix implied by the model and the population covariance matrix. Hence, a nonsignificant value of χ^2 indicates that the model "fits" the data in that the model can reproduce the population covariance matrix.

Figure 3.1

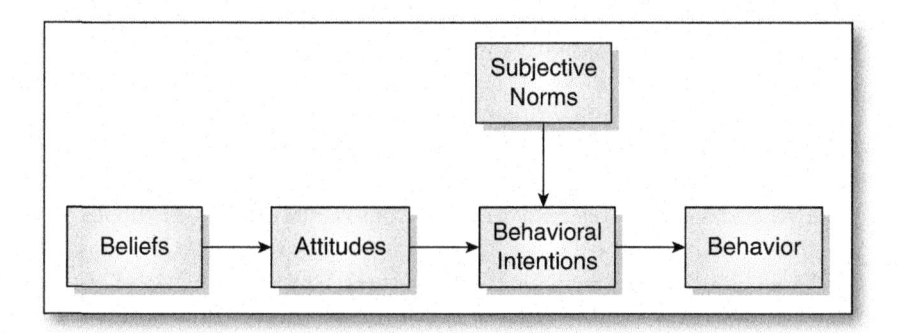

[Figure 3.1: Path diagram showing Beliefs → Attitudes → Behavioral Intentions → Behavior, with Subjective Norms → Behavioral Intentions]

The test is distributed with degrees of freedom equal to

$$1/2(q)(q+1) - k,$$

where q is the number of variables in the model, and k is the number of estimated parameters.

For example, Fishbein and Ajzen's (1975) model, introduced in Chapter 2 and repeated in Figure 3.1, is based on five variables and incorporates four paths:

1. Behavioral intentions predict behavior.
2. Attitudes predict behavioral intentions.
3. Subjective norms predict behavioral intentions.
4. Beliefs predict attitudes.

The model therefore has

$$df = 1/2(5)(6) - 4$$
$$df = 1/2(30) - 4$$
$$df = 15 - 4$$
$$df = 11.$$

Although the test is quite simple (indeed, Mplus calculates it for you), there are some problems with the χ^2 test in addition to the logical problem of being required to accept the null hypothesis. First, the approximation to the χ^2 distribution occurs only for large samples (e.g., $N \geq 200$). Second, just at the point at which the χ^2 distribution becomes a tenable assumption, the test has a great deal of power. Recall that the test is calculated as $N - 1 \times$ (the minimum of the fitting function); therefore, as N increases, the value of χ^2 must also increase. Thus, for a minimum fitting function of .5, the resulting χ^2 value would be 99.5 for $N = 200$, 149.5 for $N = 300$, and so on. This makes it highly unlikely that you will be able to obtain a nonsignificant test statistic with large sample sizes.

Mplus also reports the −2 log likelihood values for the model, which, in the case of maximum likelihood estimation, are distributed as χ^2. Two values are reported; one is labeled H_0 and is a measure of fit for the estimated model. The other, labeled H_1, pertains to the unconstrained model—essentially the same as a saturated model in which all parameters are estimated. There is not really an absolute interpretation of these values. Obviously, the closer the H_0 value is to the H_1 value, the better fitting the model (because by definition, the H_1 value will be the best fit to the data). A more common use for −2 log likelihood values is to compare competing models, with lower values associated with a better fit to the data.

Given the known problems of the χ^2 test as an assessment of model fit, numerous alternative fit indices have been proposed. Gerbing and Anderson (1992, p. 134) described the ideal properties of such indices to

1. indicate degree of fit along a continuum bounded by values such as 0 and 1, where 0 represents a lack of fit and 1 reflects perfect fit;

2. be independent of sample size; and

3. have known distributional characteristics to assist interpretation and allow the construction of a confidence interval.

With the possible exception of the root mean square error of approximation (RMSEA; Steiger, 1990), thus far, none of the fit indices commonly reported in the literature satisfy all three of these criteria; the requirement for known distributional characteristics is particularly lacking.

Mplus reports two indices of model fit based on the notion of a residual (i.e., the actual correlation minus the reproduced correlation). The first is the standardized root mean square residual (SRMR). This is the square root of the mean of the squared discrepancies between the implied and observed covariance matrices. The index is standardized to establish a metric for measure. Thus, the SRMR ranges from 0 to 1, with values less than .08 (Hu & Bentler, 1999) indicating a good fit to the data. Unfortunately, the index does not have a known distribution. This means that we are not able to speak with confidence about different SRMR values.

Most researchers, for example, would be tempted to say that a SRMR of .09 indicates a reasonably good fit to the data. They would base this conclusion on the observation that .09 is reasonably close to the cutoff value of .08. However, this conclusion would be unwarranted; because we do not know the distribution of the index, we do not know how "far" .09 is from .08.

As an aside, this tendency to suggest that model fit indices are "close" to accepted norms illustrates a pervasive problem in modeling. Researchers will invoke guidelines in the literature for establishing good fit (e.g., see Hu & Bentler, 1999) and then proceed to claim that their models are acceptable, even when their fit indices do not obtain the articulated standards. At some point, one wonders what the point is in model testing and whether any set of results would convince researchers to reject their models.

Mplus also reports the RMSEA, developed by Steiger (1990). Similar to the SRMR, the RMSEA is based on the analysis of residuals, with smaller values indicating a better fit to the data. Steiger suggested that values below .10 indicate a good fit to the data and values below 0.05 a very good fit to the data. In their review, Hu and Bentler (1999) suggested a cutoff of .06 for the RMSEA to indicate good fit to the data. Unlike all other fit indices discussed in this chapter, the RMSEA has the important advantage of going beyond point estimates to the provision of 90% confidence intervals for the point estimate. Moreover, Mplus also provides a test of the significance of the RMSEA by testing whether the value obtained is significantly different from 0.05 (the value Steiger suggested as indicating a very good fit to the data). This test is often referred to as a test of close fit and is sometimes labeled the PCLOSE test.

Although not reported by Mplus, two early indices of model fit were available in the LISREL program (Jöreskog & Sörbom, 1992) and are still widely referred to in the literature. The goodness-of-fit index (GFI) is based on a ratio of the sum of the squared discrepancies to the observed variances (for generalized least squares, the maximum likelihood version is somewhat more complicated). The GFI ranges from 0 to 1, with values exceeding .95 (Hu & Bentler, 1999) indicating a good fit to the data. It should be noted that this guideline is based on experience. Like many of the fit indices presented here, the GFI has no known sampling distribution. As a result, "rules" about when an index indicates a good fit to the data are highly arbitrary and should be treated with caution. Finally, the adjusted GFI (AGFI) adjusts the GFI for the degrees of freedom in the model. The AGFI also ranges from 0 to 1, with values above .9 indicating a good fit to the data. A discrepancy between the GFI and the AGFI typically indicates the inclusion of trivial (i.e., small) and often nonsignificant parameters.

With the exception of R^2 values, the indices discussed thus far assess whether a model as a whole provides an adequate fit to the data. More detailed information can be acquired from tests of specific parameters composing the model. James, Mulaik, and Brett (1982) described two types of statistical tests used in structural equation modeling, Condition 9 and Condition 10 tests. A Condition 10 test assesses the overidentifying restrictions placed on the model. The most common example of a Condition 10 test is the χ^2 likelihood test for goodness of fit. Using the term *test* loosely to include fit indices with unknown distributions, the fit indices discussed above would also qualify as Condition 10 tests.

In contrast, Condition 9 tests are tests of the specific parameters composing a model. Programs such as Mplus commonly report both the parameter and the standard error of estimate for that parameter. The ratio of the parameter to its standard error provides a statistical test of the parameter. Values of 2.00 or greater indicate that a parameter is significantly different from zero. A Condition 9 test, therefore, assesses whether parameters predicted to be nonzero in a structural equation model are in fact significantly different from zero.

Again, it is important to note that consideration of the individual parameters composing a model is important for assessing the accuracy of the model. The parameter tests are not, in and of themselves, tests of model fit. Two likely results in testing structural equation models are that (a) a proposed model fits the data even though some parameters are nonsignificant, and/or (b) a proposed model fits the data, but some of the specified parameters are significant and opposite in direction to that predicted. In either case, the researcher's theory is disconfirmed, even though the model may provide a good absolute fit to the data. The fit of the model has nothing to say about the validity of the individual predictions composing the model.

Comparative Fit

Perhaps because of the problems inherent in assessing the absolute fit of a model to the data, researchers increasingly have turned to the assessment of comparative fit. The question of comparative fit deals with whether the model under consideration is better than some competing model. For example, many of the indices discussed below are based on choosing a model as a "baseline" and comparing the fit of theoretically derived models with that of the baseline model.

In some sense, all tests of model fit are based on a comparison of models. The tests discussed previously implicitly compare a theoretical model against the just-identified model. Recall that the just-identified model consists of all possible recursive paths between the variables. As a result, the model has zero degrees of freedom (because the number of estimated paths is the same as the number of elements in the covariance matrix) and always provides a perfect fit to the data.

Indices of comparative fit are based on the opposite strategy. Rather than comparing against a model that provides a perfect fit to the data, indices of comparative fit typically choose as the baseline a model that is known a priori to provide a poor fit to the data. The most common baseline model is the "null," "baseline," or "independence" model (the terms *null* and *baseline* are used interchangeably; Mplus printouts refer to the baseline model, but much of the literature makes reference to the null model). The null model is a model that specifies no relationships between the variables composing the model. That is, if one were to draw the path model for the null model, it would have no paths connecting the variables (see Figure 3.2).

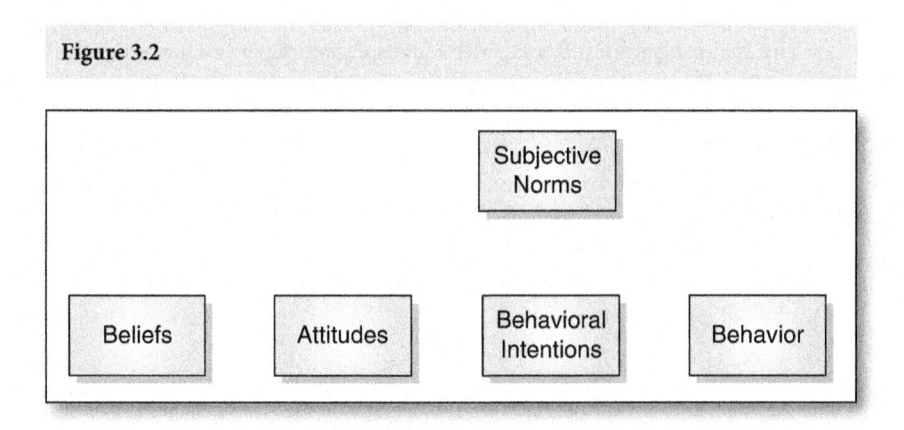

Figure 3.2

[Diagram showing five boxes labeled: Subjective Norms, Beliefs, Attitudes, Behavioral Intentions, Behavior — with no connecting paths.]

Mplus reports two indices of comparative fit: the comparative fit index (CFI) and the Tucker-Lewis index (TLI). Bentler (1990) based his CFI on the noncentral χ^2 distribution. The CFI also ranges between 0 and 1, with values exceeding .95 (Hu & Bentler, 1999) indicating a good fit to the data. The CFI is based on the noncentrality parameter, which can be estimated as $\chi^2 - df$. Thus, the CFI is given by

$$1 - [(\chi^2_{model} - df_{model})/(\chi^2_{indep} - df_{indep})].$$

The TLI or non-normed fit index is a measure of incremental fit that attempts to (a) capture the percentage improvement of a hypothesized model over the null model and (b) adjust this improvement for the number of parameters in the hypothesized model. Recognizing that one can always improve model fit by adding parameters, the TLI penalizes researchers for making models more complex. The TLI has a lower limit of 0. Although it can exceed 1 at the upper limit, values exceeding 1 are treated as if they were 1. Again, a value of .95 (Hu & Bentler, 1999) is a widely used cutoff for establishing good fit to the data. The TLI is calculated as

$$\frac{\chi^2/df(\text{Null Model}) - \chi^2/df(\text{Proposed Model})}{\chi^2/df(\text{Null Model}) - 1}.$$

There are many other indices of comparative or incremental fit reported in the literature, although they are not calculated by Mplus; however, the program does report the values needed to calculate these indices. For example, Bentler and Bonett (1980) suggested a normed fit index (NFI), defined as

$$(\chi^2_{indep} - \chi^2_{model})/\chi^2_{indep}.$$

The NFI ranges from 0 to 1, with values exceeding .95 indicating a good fit.[1] As Bentler and Bonett pointed out, the NFI indicates the percentage improvement in fit over the baseline independence model. Thus, an NFI of .90 means that a model is 90% better fitting than the null model. Although the NFI is widely used, it may underestimate the fit of a model in small samples and may not be sensitive to model misspecification (Hu & Bentler, 1999).

Bollen's (1989) incremental fit index (IFI) reintroduces the scaling factor, so that IFI values range between 0 and 1, with higher values indicating a better fit to the data. The IFI is given by

$$(\chi^2_{indep} - \chi^2_{model})/(\chi^2_{indep} - df_{model}).$$

Marsh, Balla, and MacDonald (1988) proposed a relative fit index (RFI), defined as

$$\frac{(\chi^2_{indep} - \chi^2_{model}) - [df_{indep} - (df_{model}/n)]}{\chi^2_{indep} - (df_{indep}/n)}.$$

Again, the RFI ranges between 0 and 1, with values approaching unity indicating a good fit to the data. The use of .95 as an indicator of a well-fitting model is also appropriate with this index.

Finally, Cudeck and Browne (1983) suggested the use of the cross-validation index as a measure of comparative fit. Cross-validation of models is well established in other areas of statistics (e.g., regression analysis; Browne & Cudeck, 1993; Cudeck & Browne, 1983). Traditionally, cross-validation required two samples: a calibration sample and a validation sample. The procedure relied on fitting a model to the calibration sample and then evaluating the discrepancy between the covariance matrix implied by the model to the covariance matrix of the validation sample. If the discrepancy was small, the model was judged to fit the data in that it cross-validated to other samples.

The obvious practical problem with this strategy is the requirement for two samples. Browne and Cudeck (1989) suggested a solution to the problem by estimating the expected value of the cross-validation index (ECVI) using only data from a single sample. Although the mathematics of the ECVI will not be presented here (the reader is referred to the source material cited above), the ECVI is thought to estimate the expected discrepancy (i.e., the difference between the implied and actual covariance matrices) over all possible calibration samples. The ECVI has a lower bound of zero but no upper bound. Smaller values indicate better fitting models.

Parsimonious Fit

Parsimonious fit indices are concerned primarily with the cost-benefit trade-off of fit and degrees of freedom. Mplus reports the information criteria as indices of parsimonious fit. The Akaike information criterion (AIC; Akaike, 1987) is a measure of parsimonious fit that considers both the fit of the model and the number of estimated parameters. The AIC is defined as

$$\chi^2_{\text{model}} - 2df_{\text{model}}.$$

For both indices, smaller values indicate a more parsimonious model. Neither index, however, is scaled to range between 0 and 1, and there are no conventions or guidelines to indicate what "small" means. Accordingly, this index is best used to choose between competing models.

As you will note, the AIC introduces a penalty of 2 for every degree of freedom in the model and thereby rewards parsimony. The Bayesian information criterion (BIC) effectively increases the penalty as the sample size increases and is calculated as

$$\chi^2 + \ln(N)[k(k+1)/2 - df].$$

Mplus also calculates the sample size–adjusted BIC (SABIC), which also penalizes parameters on the basis of sample size but does so less harshly than the BIC. As with the AIC, neither the BIC nor the SABIC has an absolute interpretation or a cutoff value. Rather, these indices are used to compare competing models, with a lower value indicating a better fitting model.

Although not reported by Mplus, several other parsimony indices can be calculated. For example, James et al. (1982) proposed the parsimonious NFI (PNFI), which adjusts the NFI for model parsimony. The PNFI is calculated as

$$(df_{\text{model}}/df_{\text{indep}}) \times \text{NFI}.$$

Similarly, the parsimonious GFI (PGFI) adjusts the GFI for the degrees of freedom in a model and is calculated as

$$1 - (P/N) \times \text{GFI},$$

where P is the number of estimated parameters in the model and N is the number of data points.

Both the PNFI and the PGFI range from 0 to 1, with higher values indicating a more parsimonious fit. Unlike the other fit indices we have discussed, there is no standard for how "high" either index should be to indicate parsimonious fit. Indeed, neither the PNFI nor the PGFI will likely reach the .95 cutoff used for other fit indices. Rather, these indices are best used to compare two competing theoretical models; that is, they would calculate an index of parsimonious fit for each model and choose the model with the highest level of parsimonious fit.

NESTED MODEL COMPARISONS

As should be apparent at this point, the assessment of model fit is not a straightforward task. Indeed, from the discussion thus far, it should be clear that there are at least three views of what "model fit" means:

1. the absolute fit of a model to the data,
2. the fit of a model to the data relative to other models, and
3. the degree of parsimonious fit of a model relative to other models.

Given the problems inherent in assessing model fit, it is commonly suggested that models of interest be tested against reasonable alternative models. If we cannot show that our model fits the data perfectly, we can at least demonstrate that our model fits better than some other reasonable model. Although this may sound suspiciously like the question of comparative fit, recall that indices of comparative fit are based on comparison with the independence model, which is purposely defined as a model that provides a poor fit to the data. In contrast, the procedures we are about to discuss are based on comparing two plausible models of the data.

Many such plausible and rival specifications exist. For example, consider the case of a confirmatory factor analysis model, shown in Figure 3.3. The model suggests that there are two common factors, which are correlated, causing six indicators. Plausible rival hypotheses might include a model suggesting two orthogonal common factors (Figure 3.4) or a unidimensional model (Figure 3.5).

In the case of path analyses, an alternative specification of Fishbein and Ajzen's (1975) model might include the hypothesis that subjective norms about a behavior influence both attitudes and behavioral intentions (see Figure 3.6). Support for this modification has been found in some tests of Fishbein and Ajzen–based models (e.g., Fullagar, McCoy, & Shull, 1992; Kelloway & Barling, 1993). Although we are always interested in whether the model(s) fit the data absolutely, we also may be interested in which of these competing specifications provides the best fit to the data.

If the alternative models are in hierarchical or nested relationships, these model comparisons may be made directly. A nested relationship exists between two models if one can obtain the model with the fewest number of free parameters by constraining some or all of the parameters in the model with the largest number of free parameters.

Chapter 3: Assessing Model Fit 31

Figure 3.3

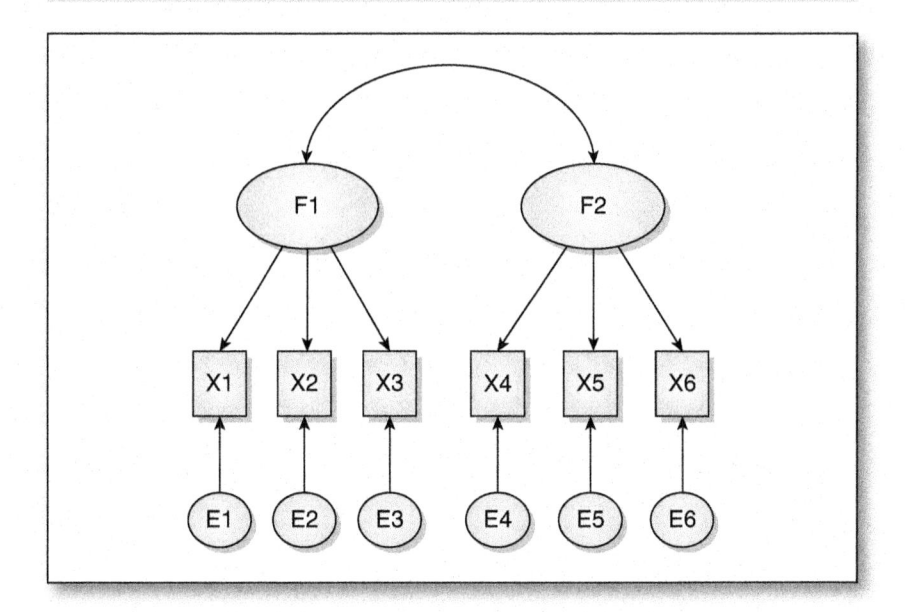

Figure 3.4

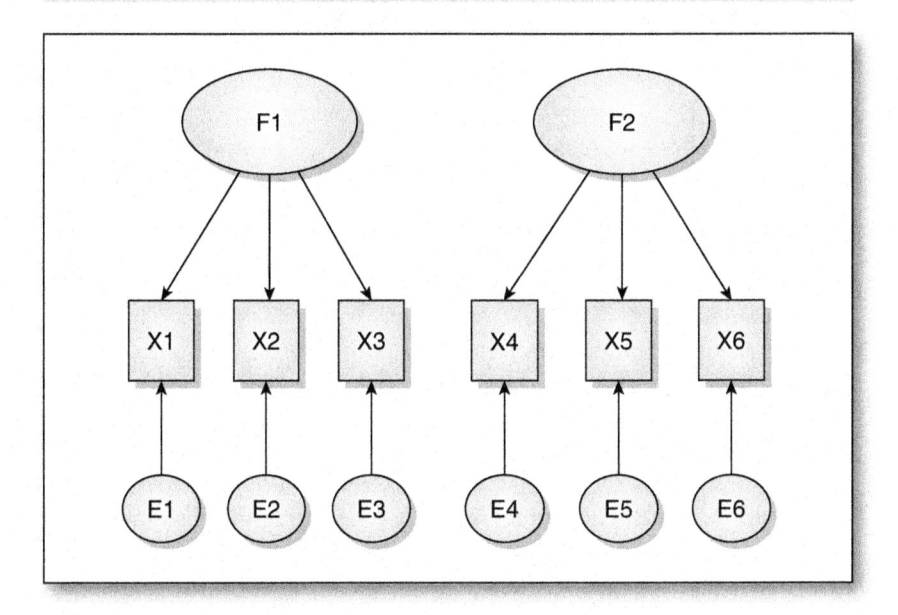

Figure 3.5

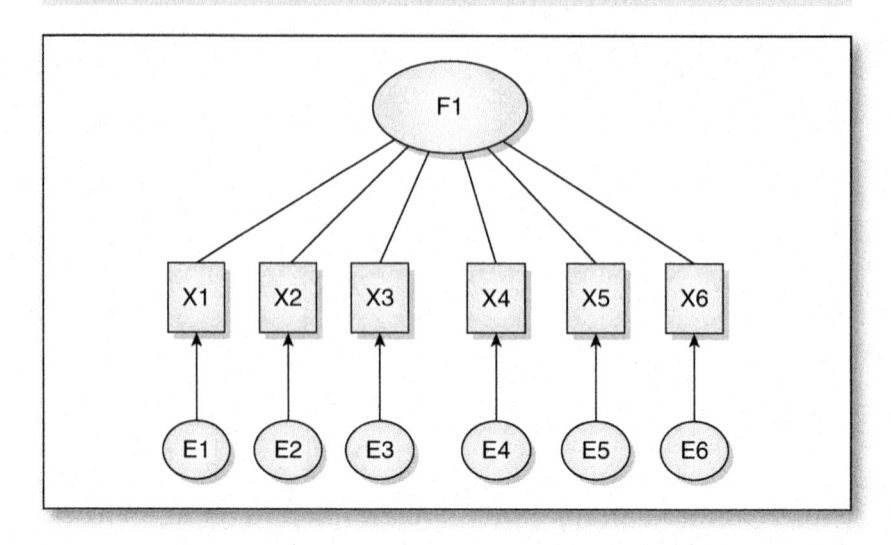

Figure 3.6

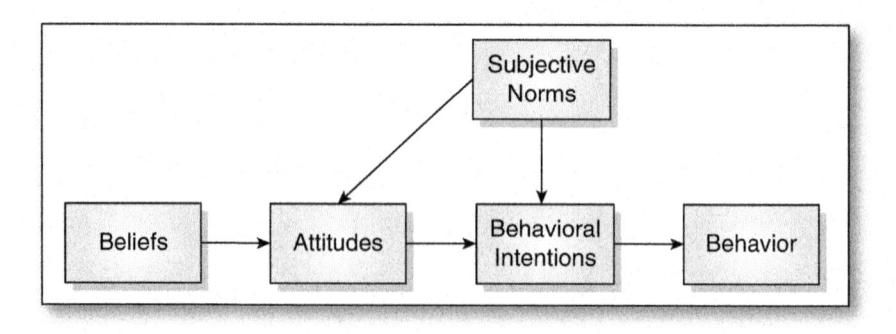

That is, the model with the fewest parameters is a subset of the model with more parameters.

For example, consider two factor models of an eight-item test. Model A suggests that four items load on each factor and that the two factors are correlated (oblique). Model B suggests that the same four items load on each factor but that the two factors are orthogonal. In this case, Model B is nested in Model A. By taking Model A and constraining the interfactor correlation to equal zero, one obtains Model B. The nesting sequence results from the observation that Model B is composed of all the same parameters as Model A, with the exception of the interfactor correlation (which is not estimated in Model B).

Similarly, for a path model example, consider the model shown in Figure 3.7. The model at the top suggests that A predicts both B and C directly. In contrast, the model at the bottom suggests that A predicts B, which in turn predicts C. Again, these models stand in a nested sequence. By deleting the direct prediction of C from A from the first model, we obtain the second model (ergo, the second model is nested within the first).

Figure 3.7

When two models stand in a nested sequence, the difference between the two may be directly tested with the chi-square difference test. The difference between the χ^2 values associated with each model is itself distributed as χ^2 with degrees of freedom equal to the difference in degrees of freedom for each model. For example, assume that the two-factor model with correlated factors generated $\chi^2(19) = 345.97$. Constraining the interfactor correlation between the two models to equal zero results in $\chi^2(20) = 347.58$. The $\chi^2_{\text{difference}}$ is

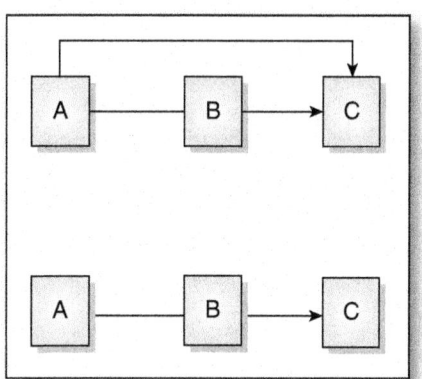

$$347.58 - 345.97 = 1.61,$$

which is distributed with

$$20 - 19 = 1 \text{ degree of freedom.}$$

Because the critical value for χ^2 with 1 degree of freedom is 3.84 and the obtained value is less than the critical value, we conclude that there is no significant difference between the two models. By inference, then, the model hypothesizing two oblique factors is overly complex. That is, the additional parameter (the interfactor correlation) did not result in a significant increase in fit.

In this simple example, the models differ in only one parameter, and the results of the chi-square difference test probably do not provide any information beyond the tests of individual parameters discussed at the beginning of this chapter. When models differ in more than one parameter, however, the chi-square difference test is a useful omnibus test of the additional parameters that can be followed up by the Condition 9 tests of specific parameters.

Before leaving the subject of nested model comparisons, it is important to note that a test is valid only when models stand in nested sequence. If the nesting sequence is not present, use of the chi-square difference test is inappropriate. The key test of whether Model A is nested in Model B is whether all the relationships constituting Model A exist in Model B. That is, if Model B simply adds relationships to Model A, the two models are nested. If there are other differences (e.g., Model B is obtained by deleting some parameters from Model A and adding some others), the models are not nested.

Although the test is not conclusive, it should be apparent that given two models in nested sequence, the model with the fewest parameters will always provide the worst fit to the data (i.e., be associated with the highest χ^2 value and the larger degrees of freedom). Moreover, the degrees of freedom for the chi-square difference test should always equal the number of additional paths contained in the more complex model.

MODEL RESPECIFICATION

As noted earlier, perhaps no aspect of structural equation modeling techniques is more controversial than the role of model respecification. Despite the controversy (see, e.g., Brannick, 1995; Kelloway, 1995; Williams, 1995), structural equation programs such as Mplus commonly provide the researcher with some guidelines for finding sources of model misspecification. That is, given that a proposed model does not fit the data, is there anything we can do to improve the fit of the model?

Two sources of information are particularly valuable. First, the tests of model parameters discussed at the beginning of this chapter provide some information about which parameters are contributing to the fit of the model and which parameters are not making such a contribution. Theory trimming (Pedhazur, 1982) is a common approach to model improvement. It essentially consists of deleting nonsignificant paths from the model to improve model fit.

Although these tests provide information about the estimated model parameters, Mplus also provides information about the nonestimated parameters. That is, the use of a theory-trimming approach asks, "What parameters can be deleted from the model?" One can also adopt a theory-building approach that asks, "What parameters should be added to the model?" For each parameter in a model that is set to zero, Mplus calculates the decrease in the model χ^2 that would be obtained from estimating that parameter. The amount of change in the model χ^2 is referred to as the modification index for that parameter.

Obviously, there is a trade-off between estimating more parameters (with the corresponding loss of degrees of freedom) and improving the fit of the model. Commonly, we would estimate any parameter that is associated with a modification index greater than 5.0; however, this rough guideline should be used with caution for several reasons.

First, recall that such specification searches are purely exploratory in nature. In contrast with the other parameters in the model, which are based on theory or previous research, parameters added on the basis of the modification indices (or, indeed, deleted on the basis of significance tests) may be reflecting sample-specific variance. The modifications made to the model following these procedures may not generalize to other samples.

Second, the process of theory trimming or theory building is analogous to the procedures of stepwise regression through either backward elimination (theory trimming) or forward entry (theory building). As such, both procedures are based on univariate procedures in which each parameter is considered in isolation. As a result, both theory trimming and theory building are based on a large number of statistical tests, with a corresponding inflation of Type I error rates. Moreover, the tests may be misleading in that adding a parameter to a model on the basis of the modification indices may change the value of parameters already in the model (i.e., making theoretically based parameters nonsignificant).

Third, even when the modification indices are greater than 5.0, the improvement in model fit obtained from freeing parameters may be trivial to the model as a whole. For example, if the overall χ^2 for the model is 349.23, it is questionable whether the improvement in fit (reduction of the χ^2 by 5.0) is worth the dangers of adding a parameter on the basis of the modification indices. Perhaps the final word on the issue of model modifications should go to Ullman (2006), who suggested that any such modifications should be (a) thoughtful, (b) few in number, and (c) replicated across samples whenever possible.

Toward a Strategy for Assessing Model Fit

As has been evident throughout this discussion, the assessment of model fit is a complex question. Numerous fit indices have been proposed, each with a slightly different conception of what it means to say that a model "fits the data." The literature is in agreement, however, on several fundamental points that provide the basis for a strategy of model testing.

First, the focus of assessing model fit almost invariably should be on comparing the fit of competing and theoretically plausible models. Simply stated, the available techniques for assessing model fit do a better job of contrasting models than they do of assessing one model in isolation. The researcher's task, then, is to generate plausible rival specifications and test them. Ideally, such rival specifications will consist of nested models allowing the use of direct methods of comparison such as the chi-square difference test.

Second, and in a similar vein, rather than relying on modification indices and parameter tests to guide the development of models, researchers should be prepared a priori to identify and test the sources of ambiguity in their models. I elaborate on this theme in subsequent chapters, in which examples of the major types of structural equation models are presented.

Third, given the varying definitions of model fit presented above, it is incumbent on researchers to use multiple measures of fit. As Loehlin (1987) noted, the use of multiple fit indices may place the researcher in the position of an individual with seven watches: If they all agree, then you know what time it is, but if they don't, you are no better off than if you had no watch. I suggest that the situation with regard to assessing model fit is not that serious. Understanding what each of the various fit indices means would suggest that, at a minimum, researchers would want to consider the issues of absolute fit, comparative fit, and parsimonious fit for each model tested. Fit indices therefore should be chosen so as to reflect each of these concerns (i.e., choosing one or two indices of each type of fit).

Finally, it is important for researchers to recognize that "model fit" does not equate to "truth" or "validity." The fit of a model is, at best, a necessary but not sufficient condition for the validity of the theory that generated the model predictions. Although the question of model fit is important, it is by no means the most important or only question we should ask about our data.

Note

1. Recall the previous discussion about the arbitrariness of such guidelines and the resultant need for cautious interpretation.

4

Using Mplus

Having considered the general approach to be used in structural equation modeling, it is now time to consider the specifics of using Mplus to estimate and evaluate such models. In Mplus there are two files; one contains the data and one contains the Mplus commands or instructions. The latter is created in the Mplus environment, and we will discuss the most common Mplus commands and their usage. Creation of the data file is a little more complex.

The Data File

It is probably fair to say that most social science researchers use a general statistical program such as SPSS or Stata to analyze their data. Indeed, one is probably better off using such a program to do data manipulation, compute scales, and so forth. Unfortunately, Mplus does not read data files created in these formats, and our first task is to create the data file for use in Mplus. Although for exposition purposes I sometimes create data files of summary statistics (e.g., means, standard deviations, and correlations), for reasons that will become apparent, it is probably better practice to create data files containing the actual data, and this is the practice followed throughout this book.

There is a certain amount of data preparation that is probably easier to do in a general statistics package than in Mplus. I would typically do my data cleaning and any scale computations in SPSS and then move the data to Mplus. I would also assign my missing-value codes in SPSS. Mplus handles missing data by implementing full information maximum likelihood (FIML) estimation, using all available information to estimate each model parameter. This is an appropriate strategy when data are missing at random (i.e., missing data may depend on other variables in the data set but do not depend on the variable itself) or missing completely at random (missing data do not depend on any variables in the data set; Little & Rubin, 2002). Graham (2009) suggested that either multiple imputation (also available in Mplus) or maximum likelihood (ML)–based methods such as FIML should be used as a matter of course in our analyses.

Going from a program such as SPSS to Mplus requires special attention to the issue of missing values. SPSS users are accustomed to leaving missing values blank in their data files, and SPSS will write out these blank spaces in the data file. However, this may alter the way in which Mplus reads a data file. It is generally a better practice to recode all missing values in SPSS to a marker value (e.g., 9 for single-digit variables that do not include 9 as a valid value) prior to writing out the data.

There are essentially two options in creating a data file: you can do it yourself, or you can use a program specifically designed to do data transfers. For example, to create a data file for Mplus from an SPSS data file, you would undertake the following steps:

Step 1: Open the SPSS data file.

Step 2: From the menus, select File, Save As.

Step 3: Use the dialog box to select a file name, a format, and the variables to be saved. (SPSS allows the choice of three formats Mplus can read: a csv [comma-separated values] file, a fixed ASCII data file, or a tab-delimited ASCII file. As noted below, the tab-delimited version appears to be the best bet for now.)

Although simple, this procedure is also fraught with peril. It is important, for example, to recall exactly which variables were written out and in which order. You will need this information to subsequently define the data in Mplus. SPSS generates an output file that documents this information, and it is a good idea to save or print that file for future reference. As previously mentioned, you must take some care to ensure that missing values are appropriately identified by Mplus as being missing. A recent discussion on the RMNET list server also suggested that this data export procedure in SPSS can write a hidden code at the beginning of the file; although this code would be ignored by most programs, Mplus may read it as a value, resulting in your data being offset by one character. Choosing tab-delimited ASCII as the save format seems to overcome this problem, but it is *always* recommended to verify that the data you are using in Mplus are being read in the way you intend. Comparing sample statistics (e.g., means and standard deviations) generated by Mplus with those generated by your other statistical software may provide a quick check on the accuracy of data translation.

Personally, this procedure has tripped me up often enough that I now prefer to use a data translation program. Stat/Transfer (http://www.stattransfer.com) is my tool of choice. It will read data in a number of formats (e.g., SPSS, Stata) and prepare an Mplus data file. As an added bonus, Stat/Transfer also writes the Mplus data definition statements for you (i.e., the start of an Mplus command file). Although verification remains important, I have found this method to be reliable and accurate. A freeware program called N2Mplus (http://www.daniel soper.com/n2mplus/) is also available to translate from SPSS and Microsoft Excel files to Mplus. Again, this program writes both a data file and the data definition statements for use in Mplus. Although its developer continues to make N2Mplus available, it is no longer being developed (or, presumably, supported). Users of programs that transfer data from one program to another should be aware that Mplus has limitations on variable names (i.e., names can be only eight characters long) that may be more stringent than used in the original program.

As a final note on data files, it is also good practice to ensure that data files are stored in the same directory as the Mplus command files. This saves you from typing long strings of file addresses and also ensures that all of the files for a project exist in the same place.

The Command File

The command (or inp) file is the set of Mplus commands that (a) define the data, (b) specify the model to be tested, and (c) specify the output the user would like to see. This is accomplished through a list of only 10 commands (most of which have many subcommands and specifications). In practice, only a subset of these commands is required to run different types of analysis. When you open Mplus, you are in a text-editing environment in which you can type in the commands, save them as an inp file, and run the analysis you want. There are several conventions in creating inp files.

All commands must end with a colon (:). If you have typed the command properly, when you add the colon, the text will turn blue. This provides some feedback that Mplus has recognized what you have typed as a valid command. Command lines in Mplus all end with a semicolon (;). You can always insert comments in your command files using an exclamation mark (!). Any text following an exclamation mark will be treated as a comment. To show that Mplus is reading this text as a comment, it will be displayed in green. In general, lines in the command file should not exceed 80 characters. Command lines can be split across multiple lines in the file. As a final convention, the words IS and ARE and the equal sign (=) are treated interchangeably.

SPECIFY THE DATA

The first four commands (TITLE, DATA, VARIABLE, and DEFINE) are used to define the data, that is, to tell Mplus where the data are and what variables are in the data set. The DATA and VARIABLE commands are the only two commands required in all Mplus files. For example,

```
TITLE:     This is a sample inp file ! This is a comment (use descriptive
           titles)
DATA:      FILE IS example.dat; ! The data are found in a file called
           example.dat
VARIABLE:  NAMES ARE X1-X6; ! There are six variables named X1, X2,
           ..., X6
```

It should go without saying that it is critically important that the names listed in the VARIABLE command are in exactly the same order in which they appear in the data file. Several subcommands are used in the VARIABLE command to define the data in more detail. For example, although the above command file reads in six variables, it is possible that I might want to use only four of these variables in the analysis. This can be accomplished with the USEVARIABLES subcommand. Thus,

```
VARIABLE:  NAMES ARE X1-X6;
           USEVARIABLES ARE X1-X4;
```

specifies that I want to use only the first four variables in the analysis. Although this seems like a minor point now, it will become apparent that model fit statistics are based on all of the variables named in the analysis. If you fail to specify only the variables you want to use, Mplus will generate wildly inaccurate fit statistics and warnings (because you are telling it to run a model in which there are some variables that are not predictors, outcomes, or correlates of other model variables).

The VARIABLE command can also be used to define the types of variables you are analyzing. For example,

```
VARIABLE:  NAMES ARE X1-X6 Y;
           USEVARIABLES ARE X1-X4 Y;
           CATEGORICAL IS Y;
```

says that there are seven variables (six X variables and one called Y), that in my analysis I want to use only the first four X variables and the Y variable, and, finally, that the Y variable is a categorical variable. As we shall see, if we subsequently specify a regression analysis using Y as the criterion, Mplus will recognize that Y is a categorical variable and automatically do a logistic or probit regression.

Missing value codes can also be defined in the VARIABLE command. For example,

```
VARIABLE:  NAMES ARE X1-X6 Y;
           USEVARIABLES ARE X1-X4 Y;
           CATEGORICAL IS Y;
           MISSING X1-Y (99);
```

adds a missing value code (99) to each of the variables.

The DEFINE command is used to create new variables from the existing variables. Although the format is simple (e.g., DEFINE: Bob = X1 + X2; creates a new variable, Bob, that is the sum of X1 and X2), its usage can be tricky in that you have to know how Mplus reads command files.

For the most part, we use the same format and order of commands for all command files (i.e., TITLE, DATA, VARIABLE, etc.). However, Mplus reads the entire file and then processes the instructions; to Mplus, the order of the commands does not matter, and all of the variables used in the analysis must be defined in the VARIABLE command. So if your command file says

```
VARIABLE:    NAMES ARE X1-X6;
DEFINE:      Bob = X1 + X2;
```

the file will run without error. However, if you refer to the variable Bob in any subsequent statement, you will get an error saying that Bob is an unknown variable. This is because Bob was not defined in the VARIABLE command. The correct version of the file would be

```
VARIABLE:    NAMES ARE X1-X6;
             USEVARIABLES ARE X1-X6 Bob;
DEFINE:      Bob = X1 + X2;
```

The variable Bob is now defined on the USEVARIABLES line, and this code will run without error, even if Bob is referenced later. Note that variables computed in this fashion should be listed last on the USEVARIABLES line (i.e., after all of the variables that are in the data file).

SPECIFY THE ANALYSIS

There are two commands that are used to specify the analysis we want to run in Mplus (ANALYSIS and MODEL), although for the most part, we will focus on the MODEL command. The ANALYSIS command is used to specify particular types of analyses (e.g., exploratory factor analysis, multilevel analysis), and we will see its use in subsequent chapters.

The real workhorse of the program is the MODEL command, which primarily uses three key words, BY, WITH, and ON, to specify a large variety of structural equation models. The general format of the model statements is "variable(s) keyword variable(s)." Thus, the statement

```
MODEL:    Y ON X1-X4;
```

specifies a regression equation with four predictors (X1 to X4) predicting Y. The statement

```
MODEL:    Y BY X1-X4;
```

defines a latent variable Y defined by four indicators (X1 to X4). The statement

```
MODEL:      X1 WITH X2;
```

will estimate a correlation between the variables X1 and X2.

In addition to these relationships, one can specify (a) the variance of a variable by referring to the variable name (i.e., X1 = 1 sets the variance of X1 to 1) and (b) the mean of a variable by referring to the variable in square brackets. Thus, [Y] refers to the mean of variable Y.

SPECIFY THE OUTPUT

Finally, one can control numerous aspects of the output through the OUTPUT command. Although there are numerous options, we will concern ourselves primarily with three aspects of the output. The SAMPSTAT command is used to request the sample statistics for all model variables. The STANDARDIZED command requests the standardized solution. Finally, the MODINDICES command requests the modification indices. To request all three of these options (which I almost always do), the statement would be

```
OUTPUT:     SAMPSTAT STANDARDIZED MODINDICES (ALL);
```

Putting It All Together: Some Basic Analyses

REGRESSION ANALYSIS

Although we do not often think of it this way, a standard multiple regression analysis can be thought of as a form of structural equation model. In light of our preceding discussion, regression models are fully saturated models. There are no degrees of freedom, because one is estimating all possible parameters. Of course, this means that questions of model fit are not germane in a regression context, because all regression models provide a perfect fit to the data. However, regression provides a useful context in which to illustrate some of the features of Mplus. The program below reads six variables from the file Chapter4b.dat. The variables are respondents' sex, age, perceptions of transformational leadership (TLead), and perceptions of passive leadership (PLead), the number of workplace injuries experienced by respondents, and their scores on the General Health Questionnaire (GHQ)(Banks et al., 1980).

```
TITLE:      Example of regression
DATA:       FILE IS Chapter4b.dat;
VARIABLE:   NAMES ARE Sex Age TLead PLead Injuries GHQ;
            USEVARIABLES = Sex-Injuries;
MODEL:      Injuries ON TLead PLead Sex Age;
OUTPUT:     SAMPSTAT STANDARDIZED MODINDICES (ALL);
```

The USEVARIABLES line tells Mplus that all of the variables except for GHQ are to be used in the analysis. The MODEL command specifies a regression using Injuries as the dependent variable and Sex, Age, and both leadership scales (TLead and PLead) as predictors. I have requested the sample statistics, the standardized solutions, and the modification indices for these analyses.

Running this file results in the following output. First, the program repeats the command file and gives some details on the data that were read from the data file:

```
Mplus VERSION 7 (Mac)
MUTHEN & MUTHEN

INPUT INSTRUCTIONS

TITLE:      Example of regression
DATA:       FILE IS Chapter4b.dat;
VARIABLE:   NAMES ARE Sex Age TLead PLead Injuries GHQ;
            USEVARIABLES = Sex-Injuries;
MODEL:      Injuries on TLead PLead Sex Age;
OUTPUT:     SAMPSTAT STANDARDIZED MODINDICES (ALL);
```

Note: The program first repeats the command file.

```
INPUT READING TERMINATED NORMALLY
```

Note: This is a good sign.

```
Example of regression

SUMMARY OF ANALYSIS

Number of groups                                  1
Number of observations                          152
Number of dependent variables                     1
Number of independent variables                   4
Number of continuous latent variables             0

Observed dependent variables
  Continuous
  INJURIES

Observed independent variables
   SEX      AGE      TLEAD     PLEAD
```

Note: In this section, Mplus tells you how it read the data according to your instructions. It found 152 cases or observations in the data file and understands that each case has one continuous dependent variable (Injuries) and four predictors. One group is the default.

```
Estimator                                        ML
Information matrix                         OBSERVED
Maximum number of iterations                   1000
Convergence criterion                     0.500D-04
Maximum number of steepest descent iterations    20
```

44 USING MPLUS FOR STRUCTURAL EQUATION MODELING

Note: Here Mplus provides some technical details on the analysis (e.g., the number of iterations). Of most import, Mplus is using ML estimation (the default).

```
Input data file(s)
Chapter4b.dat
Input data format FREE

SAMPLE STATISTICS
          Means
                INJURIES     SEX       AGE      TLEAD     PLEAD
                --------   -------   -------   -------   -------
                  3.588     1.493    18.855     1.735     4.520

          Covariances
                INJURIES     SEX       AGE      TLEAD     PLEAD
                --------   -------   -------   -------   -------
INJURIES          2.683
SEX              -0.071     0.250
AGE               0.319     0.210     9.492
TLEAD             0.157     0.035     0.030     0.479
PLEAD             0.052     0.036    -0.054    -0.219     2.125

          Correlations
                INJURIES     SEX       AGE      TLEAD     PLEAD
                --------   -------   -------   -------   -------
INJURIES          1.000
SEX              -0.086     1.000
AGE               0.063     0.136     1.000
TLEAD             0.138     0.101     0.014     1.000
PLEAD             0.022     0.050    -0.012    -0.217     1.000

THE MODEL ESTIMATION TERMINATED NORMALLY
```

Note: This is the output you get from the SAMPSTAT specification on the OUTPUT line. For each variable, Mplus reports the mean. It then reports the covariance matrix and the correlation matrix. Note that the variance of each variable is found on the diagonal of the covariance matrix. Thus, the variance for Injuries is 2.683.

```
MODEL FIT INFORMATION

Number of Free Parameters                                        6
Loglikelihood
         H0 Value                                         -287.664
         H1 Value                                         -287.664
Information Criteria
         Akaike (AIC)                                      587.327
         Bayesian (BIC)                                    605.471
         Sample-Size Adjusted BIC                          586.481
            (n* = (n + 2) / 24)
```

```
Chi-Square Test of Model Fit
        Value                                              0.000
        Degrees of Freedom                                     0
        P-Value                                             0.0000
RMSEA (Root Mean Square Error Of Approximation)
        Estimate                                           0.000
        90 Percent C.I.                              0.000  0.000
        Probability RMSEA <= .05                           0.000
CFI/TLI
        CFI                                                1.000
        TLI                                                1.000
Chi-Square Test of Model Fit for the Baseline Model
        Value                                              6.023
        Degrees of Freedom                                     4
        P-Value                                            0.1975
SRMR (Standardized Root Mean Square Residual)
        Value                                              0.000
```

Note: This is the standard set of fit statistics reported by Mplus. As previously mentioned, a regression model is saturated or just identified and fits the data perfectly. The χ^2 statistic for the baseline model is the value associated with null (independence model).

```
MODEL RESULTS

                                                        Two-Tailed
                    Estimate     S.E.    Est./S.E.      P-Value
 INJURIES  ON
    TLEAD             0.385     0.194      1.984         0.047
    PLEAD             0.072     0.092      0.781         0.435
    SEX              -0.382     0.265     -1.440         0.150
    AGE               0.041     0.043      0.966         0.334
 Intercepts
    INJURIES          2.389     1.021      2.340         0.019
 Residual Variances
    INJURIES          2.578     0.296      8.718         0.000
```

Note: These are the unstandardized regression weight results. For each predictor, Mplus reports the *B* weight (estimate), the standard error (S.E.) of *B*, the test statistic (Est./S.E., analogous to a *t* test) and the *p* value for the test. In this case, TLead is a significant ($B = 0.385$, $p < .05$) predictor of Injuries.

```
STDYX Standardization
                                                        Two-Tailed
                    Estimate     S.E.    Est./S.E.      P-Value
 INJURIES  ON
    TLEAD             0.163     0.081      2.009         0.045
    PLEAD             0.064     0.082      0.782         0.434
    SEX              -0.117     0.080     -1.450         0.147
    AGE               0.078     0.080      0.969         0.332
```

Intercepts
  INJURIES   1.458   0.639   2.281   0.023
Residual Variances
  INJURIES   0.961   0.031   31.275   0.000

STDY Standardization

                                                Two-Tailed
                 Estimate   S.E.   Est./S.E.   P-Value
INJURIES ON
  TLEAD   0.235   0.116   2.022   0.043
  PLEAD   0.044   0.056   0.783   0.434
  SEX   -0.233   0.160   -1.455   0.146
  AGE   0.025   0.026   0.971   0.332
Intercepts
  INJURIES   1.458   0.639   2.281   0.023
Residual Variances
  INJURIES   0.961   0.031   31.275   0.000

STD Standardization

                                                Two-Tailed
                 Estimate   S.E.   Est./S.E.   P-Value
INJURIES ON
  TLEAD   0.385   0.194   1.984   0.047
  PLEAD   0.072   0.092   0.781   0.435
  SEX   -0.382   0.265   -1.440   0.150
  AGE   0.041   0.043   0.966   0.334
Intercepts
  INJURIES   2.389   1.021   2.340   0.019
Residual Variances
  INJURIES   2.578   0.296   8.718   0.000

Note: Mplus reports three different versions of the standardized solution (see the following discussion).

R-SQUARE
  Observed   Two-Tailed
  Variable   Estimate   S.E.   Est./S.E.   P-Value
  INJURIES   0.039   0.031   1.264   0.206

Note: As part of the standardized solution for the model, Mplus reports the R^2 value for each dependent variable. In this case, our model explains 3.9% (*ns*) of the variance in Injuries.

QUALITY OF NUMERICAL RESULTS

Condition Number for the Information Matrix   0.584E-04
(ratio of smallest to largest eigenvalue)

THE STANDARDIZED SOLUTION IN MPLUS

As shown in the printout, when you ask for the standardized solution in Mplus, you actually get three versions: STDYX standardization, STDY standardization, and STD standardization. STDYX standardizes the variables according to the variances of both the latent and the observed variables. STD uses only the variances of the latent variables, and STDY uses the variances of the observed variables. Because each of these has a different sampling distribution, you may find that these values differ from one another. What you might not expect is that the significance tests may differ. For example, the p value for TLead varies (albeit slightly) across the three solutions ($p < .045$, $p < .043$, and $p < .047$, respectively); moreover, the tests for the standardized solution may not agree with the tests for the unstandardized solution! Which value to report is a source of frequent confusion and depends on the characteristics of the data. However, in models with continuous observed and continuous latent variables (i.e., the vast majority of applications of structural equation modeling), the STDYX solution is comparable with the standardized coefficients or "completely standardized solution" reported in other structural equation modeling programs.

LOGISTIC REGRESSION

Logistic regression is used when one has an ordinal or categorical outcome variable. To specify such a model in Mplus, we need to make two changes to the regression commands we have previously considered. First, we need to indicate to Mplus that the dependent variable is categorical in nature. Second, we need to specify the ML estimator on the analysis command. Specifying the ML estimator will result in a logistic regression and will produce the output expected from that analysis (e.g., the odds ratios). If we do not change the method of analysis, Mplus will use the WLSMV estimator, which is a probit regression. The choice between probit and logistic regression is a matter of personal choice, although the latter may be more familiar in the social sciences. The command syntax and output for the logistic regression are shown below.

```
Mplus VERSION 7 (Mac)
MUTHEN & MUTHEN

INPUT INSTRUCTIONS
  TITLE:    Example of logistic regression
  DATA:     FILE IS CH4C.dat;
  VARIABLE: NAMES ARE Gender Age Stress Injuries;
            CATEGORICAL IS Injuries;
```

```
ANALYSIS: ESTIMATOR = ML;
MODEL:    Injuries ON Gender Age Stress;
OUTPUT:   STANDARDIZED;
```

Note: This is the command file for a logistic regression. The primary changes from a normal multiple regression are to declare the dependent variable (Injuries) as categorical and to change the default estimator from WLSMV (probit regression) to ML (logistic regression).

```
INPUT READING TERMINATED NORMALLY

Example of logistic regression

SUMMARY OF ANALYSIS
Number of groups                                                 1
Number of observations                                         312
Number of dependent variables                                    1
Number of independent variables                                  3
Number of continuous latent variables                            0


Observed dependent variables
  Binary and ordered categorical (ordinal)
    INJURIES

Observed independent variables
  GENDER      AGE       STRESS


Estimator                                                       ML
Information matrix                                        OBSERVED
Optimization Specifications for the Quasi-Newton Algorithm for
Continuous Outcomes
  Maximum number of iterations                                 100
  Convergence criterion                                  0.100D-05
Optimization Specifications for the EM Algorithm
  Maximum number of iterations                                 500
  Convergence criteria
    Loglikelihood change                                 0.100D-02
    Relative loglikelihood change                        0.100D-05
    Derivative                                           0.100D-02
Optimization Specifications for the M step of the EM Algorithm for
Categorical Latent variables
  Number of M step iterations                                    1
  M step convergence criterion                           0.100D-02
  Basis for M step termination                           ITERATION
Optimization Specifications for the M step of the EM Algorithm for
Censored, Binary or Ordered Categorical (Ordinal), Unordered
Categorical (Nominal) and Count Outcomes
```

Chapter 4: Using Mplus   49

```
    Number of M step iterations                                  1
    M step convergence criterion                          0.100D-02
    Basis for M step termination                          ITERATION
    Maximum value for logit thresholds                           15
    Minimum value for logit thresholds                          -15
    Minimum expected cell size for chi-square             0.100D-01
Optimization algorithm                                          EMA
Integration Specifications
    Type                                                   STANDARD
    Number of integration points                                 15
    Dimensions of numerical integration                           0
    Adaptive quadrature                                          ON
Link                                                          LOGIT
Cholesky                                                        OFF

Input data file(s)
CH4C.dat
Input data format FREE


UNIVARIATE PROPORTIONS AND COUNTS FOR CATEGORICAL VARIABLES


INJURIES
      Category 1      0.705       220.000
      Category 2      0.295        92.000
```

Note: This is the frequency distribution for the Injuries variable; 220 respondents experienced no injuries, and 92 reported at least one workplace injury.

```
THE MODEL ESTIMATION TERMINATED NORMALLY

MODEL FIT INFORMATION

Number of Free Parameters                        4
Loglikelihood
        H0 Value                           -186.185
Information Criteria
        Akaike (AIC)                        380.370
        Bayesian (BIC)                      395.342
        Sample-Size Adjusted BIC            382.656
           (n* = (n + 2) / 24)
```

Note: For logistic regression, a reduced set of fit indices is reported. Although these are useful to compare competing models, there is no absolute interpretation (and because this is a regression model, it is saturated and fits the data exactly).

MODEL RESULTS

	Estimate	S.E.	Est./S.E.	Two-Tailed P-Value
INJURIES ON				
GENDER	0.333	0.319	1.043	0.297
AGE	0.030	0.031	0.964	0.335
STRESS	0.299	0.131	2.290	0.022
Thresholds				
INJURIES$1	2.661	1.063	2.504	0.012

Note: As in regression, these are the unstandardized weights (estimates), the standard errors, the test statistic, and the associated *p* value.

LOGISTIC REGRESSION ODDS RATIO RESULTS

INJURIES ON
   GENDER   1.395
   AGE   1.030
   STRESS   1.349

Note: Odds ratios are commonly reported with logistic regression. In the current example, an increase of 1 standard deviation in the variable Stress results in one being 1.35 times more likely to experience a workplace injury.

STANDARDIZED MODEL RESULTS

STDYX Standardization

	Estimate	S.E.	Est./S.E.	Two-Tailed P-Value
INJURIES ON				
GENDER	0.077	0.073	1.048	0.295
AGE	0.066	0.068	0.968	0.333
STRESS	0.151	0.065	2.333	0.020
Thresholds				
INJURIES$1	1.448	0.567	2.555	0.011

STDY Standardization

	Estimate	S.E.	Est./S.E.	Two-Tailed P-Value
INJURIES ON				
GENDER	0.181	0.173	1.049	0.294
AGE	0.016	0.017	0.968	0.333
STRESS	0.163	0.069	2.343	0.019
Thresholds				
INJURIES$1	1.448	0.567	2.555	0.011

STD Standardization

```
                                                         Two-Tailed
                     Estimate       S.E.     Est./S.E.    P-Value
INJURIES ON
   GENDER             0.333        0.319       1.043       0.297
   AGE                0.030        0.031       0.964       0.335
   STRESS             0.299        0.131       2.290       0.022
Thresholds
   INJURIES$1         2.661        1.063       2.504       0.012

R-SQUARE
   Observed                                              Two-Tailed
   Variable          Estimate       S.E.     Est./S.E.    P-Value
   INJURIES           0.027        0.021       1.252       0.211


QUALITY OF NUMERICAL RESULTS

Condition Number for the Information Matrix    0.264E-04
(ratio of smallest to largest eigenvalue)
```

Through a similar procedure, one can obtain different regressions for different types of data. For example, if the outcome variable is declared as a count variable (i.e., "COUNT IS Injuries") in the VARIABLE command, Mplus will perform a Poisson regression. In the same way, using the declaration "COUNT IS Injuries (i)" results in a zero-inflated Poisson regression. The point is that Mplus will perform the appropriate analysis depending on how you specify the dependent variable. This flexibility extends beyond regression: One can use categorical or count variables in the other analyses discussed in this book. As mentioned in the introductory chapter, it is this ability to combine analyses that gives Mplus its power to deal with almost any analytic problem.

5

Confirmatory Factor Analysis

In this chapter, we consider the operationalization of a measurement model through confirmatory factor analysis. As will become apparent, applications of confirmatory factor analysis are particularly appropriate when there is a debate about the dimensionality or factor structure of a scale or measure. In this chapter, we consider the dimensionality of a measure of union commitment.

O'Keefe, Kelloway, and Francis (2012) introduced OCEAN.20, a short (20-item) measure designed to measure the "Big 5" personality traits (openness to experience, conscientiousness, extraversion, agreeableness, and neuroticism). In this chapter, we will conduct a confirmatory factor analysis of the scale on the basis of data drawn from 299 young workers. In doing so, we will draw on the five-stage process outlined earlier:

1. model specification,
2. identification,
3. estimation,
4. testing fit, and
5. respecification.

Model Specification

The first step in operationalizing the model is to clarify exactly what relationships the model proposes. Figure 5.1 presents the proposed model. Note that each of the five factors is indicated by four items. Note also that each observed variable is also caused by a second latent variable representing the residual (or unique factors for factor analysts). Finally, each of the five factors is allowed to correlate with the other latent variables (i.e., the factors are oblique).

Figure 5.1

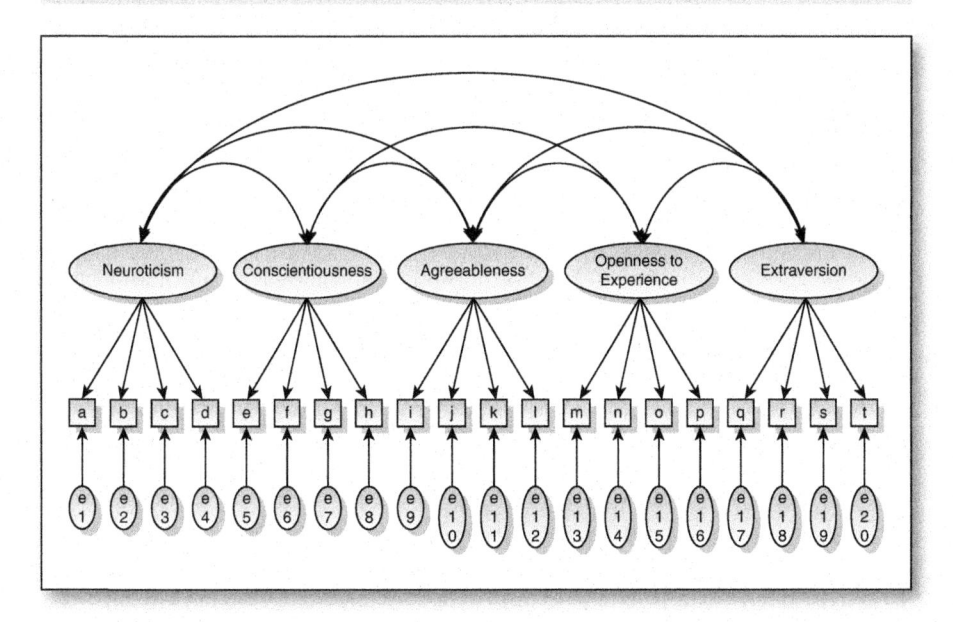

Given our focus on comparing models, it is appropriate to develop rival models to contrast with the proposed five-factor solutions. As noted earlier, ideally these rival models will stand in nested sequence with the model of interest to allow the use of direct comparisons with the chi-square difference test. The best source of such rival specifications is the literature.

Figure 5.2

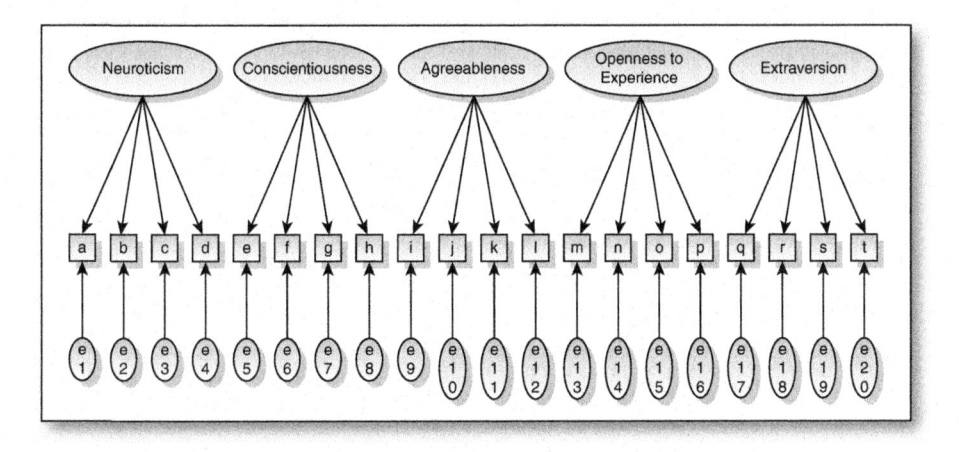

54 USING MPLUS FOR STRUCTURAL EQUATION MODELING

If the literature does not provide a reasonable alternative to the factor structure you hypothesize, alternative structures may be obtained by constraining one or more parameters in the original model. In general, for any model that contains a number of correlated factors, nested models may be obtained by estimating (a) a model containing orthogonal factors (i.e., constraining all interfactor correlations to equal 0; see Figure 5.2) and/or (b) a unidimensional model (i.e., constraining all interfactor correlations to equal 1.0; see Figure 5.3).

Figure 5.3

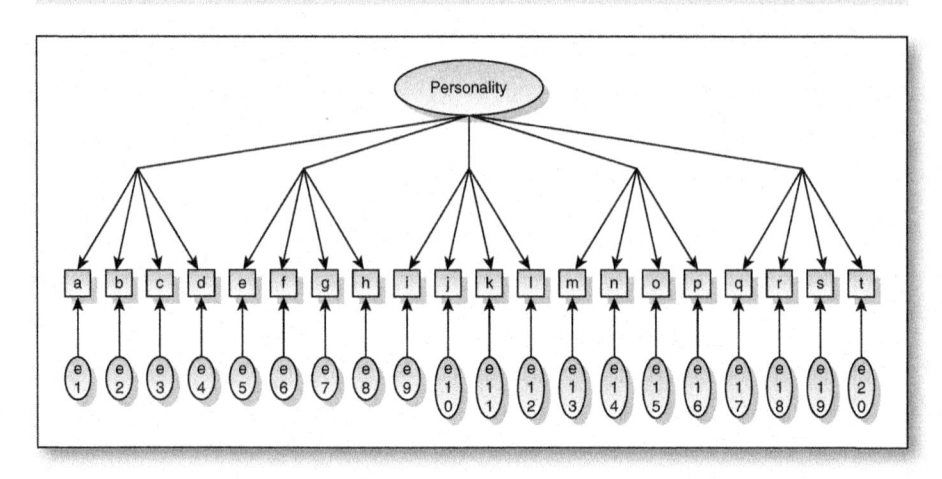

FROM PICTURES TO MPLUS

The model thought to explain the observed correlations between the union commitment items implies a set of structural equations. In the Mplus environment, you do not have to worry about the exact form of the equations. Rather, in the MODEL statement, we will use the keyword BY to define the five latent variables. The specification for the five-factor model is shown below.

```
TITLE:     Example of a confirmatory factor analysis
DATA:      FILE IS Chapter5.dat;
VARIABLE:  NAMES ARE Ocean1-Ocean20;
MODEL:     Intra BY Ocean1 Ocean5 Ocean7 Ocean19;
           Consc BY Ocean2 Ocean4 Ocean9 Ocean14;
           Agree BY Ocean3 Ocean6 Ocean11 Ocean17;
           Neur BY Ocean10 Ocean12 Ocean16 Ocean18;
           Open BY Ocean8 Ocean13 Ocean15 Ocean20;
OUTPUT:    STANDARDIZED MODINDICES (ALL);
```

IN THE BACKGROUND

There are several things going on in the background—processes Mplus is performing automatically—that we should be aware of. First, by default, Mplus is allowing all of the latent variables to be correlated. If we do not want that to happen (i.e., if we want to test an orthogonal factor model), we need to declare these correlations to be zero. In the MODEL command, we can do so with the following statements:

```
Intra WITH Consc @ 0;
Intra WITH Agree @ 0;
Intra WITH Neur @ 0;
```

and so on.

Second, latent variables are by definition unobserved and as such have no scale of measurement. As we shall see in the output, Mplus will set the first parameter on each latent variable (e.g., "INTRA BY Ocean1," "CONSC BY Ocean2," "AGREEE BY Ocean3," "NEUR BY Ocean10," and "OPEN BY Ocean8") to equal 1.0. In effect, this says that the latent variable is measured on the same scale as the observed variable. As we will see in the output file, these parameters are not estimated; they are simply declared to equal 1.0. If for some reason you want the latent variables to be defined by the second (or any other) indicator variable, you would need to use statements in the MODEL command that (a) free the default existing parameter and then (b) assign a new fixed parameter. Thus,

```
Intra BY Ocean1 *;
Intra BY Ocean4 @ 1;
```

A second way to set the measurement scale for a latent variable is to fix the variance of the latent variable to 1.0; in effect, this declares the latent variable to be in standard score form (i.e., with a mean of 0 and a variance of 1). To use this form of specification, your MODEL statements would have to free the existing parameter specification and then impose a constraint on the latent variable's variance. Recall that simply naming a variable is read as a reference to the variance of the variable; thus,

```
Intra BY Ocean1 *;
Intra @ 1.0;
```

Whether one chooses to go with the default, to fix another parameter, or to fix the variance of the latent variable, the important thing is that all latent variables need to have defined scales of measurement. Without some sort of procedure to define this aspect of the latent variables, it is not possible to estimate a solution.

Identification

For confirmatory factor analyses, issues of model identification typically are dealt with by default. That is, in most applications of confirmatory factor analysis, the latent variables or factors are hypothesized to "cause" the observed variables. In such applications, the model is recursive in that the causal flow is expected to be from the latent variables to the observed variables. Bollen (1989) summarized the issue of model identification in confirmatory factor analyses by citing three rules for model identification. As previously discussed, the "t rule" suggests that the number of estimated parameters be less than the number of nonredundant elements in the covariance matrix. Bollen also indicated that confirmatory factor analysis models are identified if (a) there are at least three indicators (observed variables) for each latent variable (factor) or (b) there are at least two indicators for each latent variable and the factors are allowed to correlate (i.e., an oblique solution). Both the two-indicator and three-indicator rules assume that the unique factor loadings (i.e., error terms) are uncorrelated.

Although the three-indicator rule is perhaps the most commonly cited, the empirical evidence supports the use of two indicators for each latent variable when the sample size is large. Specifically, in their Monte Carlo study, Anderson and Gerbing (1984) found that with small samples (e.g., $n < 100$), the use of only two indicators for each latent variable led to both convergence failures and improper solutions for confirmatory factor analyses. Using three indicators for each latent variable and sample sizes above 200 almost eliminated both convergence failures and the occurrence of improper solutions.

Although this formulation of the measurement model (i.e., based on the common factor model) is the most common in the literature, it is not the only specification possible. Bollen and Lennox (1991) distinguished between the use of "effect" indicators (those that are caused by latent variables) and "causal" indicators (those that cause latent variables). Current discussions of this issue often use the terms *reflective* and *formative* to denote the same distinction (MacKenzie, Podsakoff, & Jarvis, 2005; Podsakoff, Shen, & Podsakoff, 2006). The key difference between a reflective and a formative indicator is the direction of causality. As Williams, Vandenberg, and Edwards (2009) noted, this distinction is one that has attracted increasing attention in the organizational literatures.

Many constructs we study have been defined using reflective indicators but may be better thought of as comprising formative indicators. For example, research on workplace violence has commonly treated specific incidents (e.g., "was punched," "was kicked," "was pushed") as indicators of a construct "violence." However, there is no necessary relation between the indicators—being punched does not mean that you were also kicked—and workplace violence may be thought of as a formative indicator.

Figure 5.4

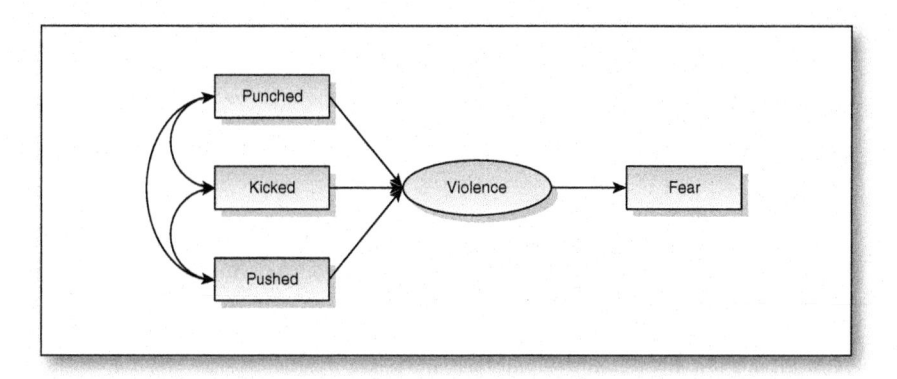

[Diagram: Punched, Kicked, Pushed → Violence → Fear]

Operationalizing a formative indicator in Mplus requires us to "trick" the program to some extent. In the following example, the model being estimated is shown in Figure 5.4. As shown, the model suggests that there are three indicators that "cause" the latent variable. The latent variable, in turn, predicts an observed outcome variable. This type of model is often called a MIMIC (multiple indicators, multiple causes) model. The way to operationalize a formative indicator is to treat the factor-outcome relationship as a factor loading that is freely estimated and to treat the factor as an outcome of the three indicators. Note that in this example, the variance of the latent variable Factor is declared to be 0; this is required for the model to be identified. Similarly, the Factor-by-Indicator1 relationship is fixed at 1.0 to give the latent variable a scale of measurement.

```
MODEL:  Factor BY outcome *;
        Factor @ 0;
        Factor ON Indicator1 @ 1 Indicator2 Indicator3;
```

Estimation

Coming back to our five-factor model, the following is a sample of the type of output you will obtain from Mplus:

```
Mplus VERSION 7 (Mac)
MUTHEN & MUTHEN

INPUT INSTRUCTIONS
```

58   USING MPLUS FOR STRUCTURAL EQUATION MODELING

```
TITLE:     Example of a confirmatory factor analysis
DATA:      FILE IS Chapter5.dat;
VARIABLE:  NAMES ARE Ocean1-Ocean20;
MODEL:     Intra BY Ocean1 Ocean5 Ocean7 Ocean19;
           Consc BY Ocean2 Ocean4 Ocean9 Ocean14;
           Agree BY Ocean3 Ocean6 Ocean11 Ocean17;
           Neur BY Ocean10 Ocean12 Ocean16 Ocean18;
           Open BY Ocean8 Ocean13 Ocean15 Ocean20;
OUTPUT:    STANDARDIZED MODINDICES (ALL);

INPUT READING TERMINATED NORMALLY
```

Note: Mplus repeats the input file and confirms that it was read without error or warnings.

```
Example of a confirmatory factor analysis

SUMMARY OF ANALYSIS

Number of groups                                             1
Number of observations                                     299
Number of dependent variables                               20
Number of independent variables                              0
Number of continuous latent variables                        5

Observed dependent variables
  Continuous
    OCEAN1     OCEAN2     OCEAN3     OCEAN4     OCEAN5     OCEAN6
    OCEAN7     OCEAN8     OCEAN9     OCEAN10    OCEAN11    OCEAN12
    OCEAN13    OCEAN14    OCEAN15    OCEAN16    OCEAN17    OCEAN18
    OCEAN19    OCEAN20

Continuous latent variables
    INTRA      CONSC      AGREE      NEUR       OPEN
```

Note: Mplus next indicates what data were read from the file. It has read 299 observations, each with 20 observed dependent variables. Five latent variables will be estimated. Note that because the observed variables are caused by the latent variables, they are deemed to be dependent variables.

```
Estimator                                                   ML
Information matrix                                    OBSERVED
Maximum number of iterations                              1000
Convergence criterion                                 0.500D-04
Maximum number of steepest descent iterations               20

Input data file(s)
Chapter5.dat
Input data format FREE

THE MODEL ESTIMATION TERMINATED NORMALLY
```

Note: Details on the analysis are provided here; the maximum likelihood (ML) estimator is used by default.

```
MODEL FIT INFORMATION

Number of Free Parameters                                    70
Loglikelihood
        H0 Value                                      -9703.864
        H1 Value                                      -9498.636
Information Criteria
        Akaike (AIC)                                  19547.729
        Bayesian (BIC)                                19806.760
        Sample-Size Adjusted BIC                      19584.763
            (n* = (n + 2) / 24)
Chi-Square Test of Model Fit
        Value                                           410.456
        Degrees of Freedom                                  160
        P-Value                                          0.0000
RMSEA (Root Mean Square Error Of Approximation)
        Estimate                                          0.072
        90 Percent C.I.                           0.064   0.081
        Probability RMSEA <= .05                          0.000
CFI/TLI
        CFI                                               0.921
        TLI                                               0.906
Chi-Square Test of Model Fit for the Baseline Model
        Value                                          3343.759
        Degrees of Freedom                                  190
        P-Value                                          0.0000
SRMR (Standardized Root Mean Square Residual)
        Value                                             0.061
```

Note: The fit indices suggest a reasonable but not outstanding fit to the data. The comparative fit index (CFI) and Tucker-Lewis index (TLI) do not achieve the recommended cutoffs of .95. The RMSEA is less than .08, as is the SRMR.

```
MODEL RESULTS

                                                      Two-Tailed
                  Estimate      S.E.   Est./S.E.       P-Value
   INTRA  BY
     OCEAN1         1.000      0.000     999.000       999.000
     OCEAN5         0.717      0.054      13.330         0.000
     OCEAN7         1.049      0.049      21.274         0.000
     OCEAN19        0.961      0.054      17.653         0.000
   CONSC  BY
     OCEAN2         1.000      0.000     999.000       999.000
     OCEAN4         0.957      0.052      18.244         0.000
     OCEAN9         0.980      0.059      16.561         0.000
     OCEAN14        0.956      0.073      13.135         0.000
```

AGREE BY				
OCEAN3	1.000	0.000	999.000	999.000
OCEAN6	1.059	0.084	12.591	0.000
OCEAN11	1.144	0.100	11.483	0.000
OCEAN17	1.112	0.092	12.029	0.000
NEUR BY				
OCEAN10	1.000	0.000	999.000	999.000
OCEAN12	1.156	0.092	12.537	0.000
OCEAN16	1.070	0.090	11.892	0.000
OCEAN18	0.881	0.087	10.084	0.000
OPEN BY				
OCEAN8	1.000	0.000	999.000	999.000
OCEAN13	1.345	0.132	10.156	0.000
OCEAN15	1.008	0.108	9.328	0.000
OCEAN20	1.241	0.124	9.988	0.000
CONSC WITH				
INTRA	0.451	0.120	3.757	0.000
AGREE WITH				
INTRA	0.072	0.083	0.866	0.386
CONSC	0.484	0.076	6.369	0.000
NEUR WITH				
INTRA	0.797	0.153	5.206	0.000
CONSC	0.158	0.102	1.544	0.123
AGREE	0.273	0.078	3.504	0.000
OPEN WITH				
INTRA	0.062	0.125	0.494	0.621
CONSC	0.184	0.094	1.953	0.051
AGREE	0.083	0.066	1.246	0.213
NEUR	-0.060	0.109	-0.549	0.583
Intercepts				
OCEAN1	3.599	0.103	34.876	0.000
OCEAN2	5.271	0.078	67.381	0.000
OCEAN3	5.726	0.067	85.227	0.000
OCEAN4	5.482	0.074	74.450	0.000
OCEAN5	3.475	0.097	36.009	0.000
OCEAN6	5.910	0.061	97.483	0.000
OCEAN7	4.167	0.106	39.449	0.000
OCEAN8	4.251	0.110	38.672	0.000
OCEAN9	5.258	0.078	67.203	0.000
OCEAN10	4.358	0.105	41.314	0.000
OCEAN11	5.726	0.069	83.387	0.000
OCEAN12	4.398	0.109	40.359	0.000
OCEAN13	3.973	0.111	35.661	0.000
OCEAN14	4.973	0.090	55.120	0.000
OCEAN15	4.388	0.110	39.979	0.000
OCEAN16	4.355	0.105	41.624	0.000
OCEAN17	5.806	0.061	94.601	0.000
OCEAN18	4.348	0.102	42.771	0.000
OCEAN19	3.943	0.106	37.061	0.000
OCEAN20	3.013	0.108	27.780	0.000
Variances				
INTRA	2.464	0.262	9.391	0.000
CONSC	1.317	0.150	8.773	0.000

Chapter 5: Confirmatory Factor Analysis 61

AGREE	0.645	0.101	6.385	0.000
NEUR	1.739	0.259	6.713	0.000
OPEN	1.440	0.262	5.503	0.000
Residual Variances				
OCEAN1	0.719	0.089	8.050	0.000
OCEAN2	0.513	0.060	8.485	0.000
OCEAN3	0.705	0.068	10.317	0.000
OCEAN4	0.416	0.052	8.037	0.000
OCEAN5	1.519	0.137	11.109	0.000
OCEAN6	0.375	0.044	8.494	0.000
OCEAN7	0.626	0.089	7.050	0.000
OCEAN8	2.172	0.211	10.316	0.000
OCEAN9	0.566	0.065	8.752	0.000
OCEAN10	1.588	0.164	9.702	0.000
OCEAN11	0.565	0.060	9.426	0.000
OCEAN12	1.228	0.157	7.800	0.000
OCEAN13	1.107	0.169	6.529	0.000
OCEAN14	1.229	0.115	10.647	0.000
OCEAN15	2.139	0.210	10.202	0.000
OCEAN16	1.280	0.149	8.566	0.000
OCEAN17	0.328	0.043	7.659	0.000
OCEAN18	1.740	0.168	10.371	0.000
OCEAN19	1.110	0.115	9.633	0.000
OCEAN20	1.300	0.161	8.092	0.000

Note: This is the unstandardized solution, so that the estimates can exceed 1. As shown, each observed variable is significantly associated with its hypothesized factor. Note that the first item on each factor is fixed at 1.000. Mplus uses 999.000 to indicate that a value was not calculated (e.g., test statistics, p values).

STANDARDIZED MODEL RESULTS

STDYX Standardization

	Estimate	S.E.	Est./S.E.	Two-Tailed P-Value
INTRA BY				
OCEAN1	0.880	0.018	49.569	0.000
OCEAN5	0.674	0.035	19.257	0.000
OCEAN7	0.901	0.016	55.563	0.000
OCEAN19	0.820	0.023	35.836	0.000
CONSC BY				
OCEAN2	0.848	0.021	39.581	0.000
OCEAN4	0.862	0.020	42.296	0.000
OCEAN9	0.831	0.023	35.734	0.000
OCEAN14	0.703	0.034	20.943	0.000
AGREE BY				
OCEAN3	0.691	0.036	19.194	0.000
OCEAN6	0.812	0.027	30.531	0.000
OCEAN11	0.774	0.029	26.629	0.000
OCEAN17	0.842	0.024	34.512	0.000

NEUR BY				
OCEAN10	0.723	0.035	20.946	0.000
OCEAN12	0.809	0.029	27.813	0.000
OCEAN16	0.780	0.031	25.344	0.000
OCEAN18	0.661	0.039	16.873	0.000
OPEN BY				
OCEAN8	0.631	0.043	14.788	0.000
OCEAN13	0.838	0.029	29.112	0.000
OCEAN15	0.637	0.043	14.965	0.000
OCEAN20	0.794	0.030	26.158	0.000
CONSC WITH				
INTRA	0.251	0.060	4.143	0.000
AGREE WITH				
INTRA	0.057	0.065	0.874	0.382
CONSC	0.525	0.050	10.504	0.000
NEUR WITH				
INTRA	0.385	0.058	6.612	0.000
CONSC	0.104	0.066	1.578	0.115
AGREE	0.257	0.064	4.010	0.000
OPEN WITH				
INTRA	0.033	0.066	0.496	0.620
CONSC	0.134	0.066	2.024	0.043
AGREE	0.086	0.068	1.272	0.204
NEUR	-0.038	0.069	-0.549	0.583
Intercepts				
OCEAN1	2.017	0.101	20.023	0.000
OCEAN2	3.897	0.170	22.987	0.000
OCEAN3	4.929	0.210	23.506	0.000
OCEAN4	4.306	0.185	23.233	0.000
OCEAN5	2.082	0.103	20.230	0.000
OCEAN6	5.638	0.238	23.719	0.000
OCEAN7	2.281	0.110	20.785	0.000
OCEAN8	2.236	0.108	20.668	0.000
OCEAN9	3.886	0.169	22.980	0.000
OCEAN10	2.389	0.114	21.044	0.000
OCEAN11	4.822	0.206	23.466	0.000
OCEAN12	2.334	0.112	20.914	0.000
OCEAN13	2.062	0.102	20.168	0.000
OCEAN14	3.188	0.143	22.353	0.000
OCEAN15	2.312	0.111	20.861	0.000
OCEAN16	2.407	0.114	21.085	0.000
OCEAN17	5.471	0.231	23.676	0.000
OCEAN18	2.473	0.117	21.229	0.000
OCEAN19	2.143	0.105	20.411	0.000
OCEAN20	1.607	0.088	18.355	0.000
Variances				
INTRA	1.000	0.000	999.000	999.000
CONSC	1.000	0.000	999.000	999.000
AGREE	1.000	0.000	999.000	999.000
NEUR	1.000	0.000	999.000	999.000
OPEN	1.000	0.000	999.000	999.000

Residual Variances

OCEAN1	0.226	0.031	7.236	0.000
OCEAN2	0.280	0.036	7.709	0.000
OCEAN3	0.522	0.050	10.483	0.000
OCEAN4	0.257	0.035	7.306	0.000
OCEAN5	0.545	0.047	11.550	0.000
OCEAN6	0.341	0.043	7.910	0.000
OCEAN7	0.188	0.029	6.415	0.000
OCEAN8	0.601	0.054	11.151	0.000
OCEAN9	0.309	0.039	8.005	0.000
OCEAN10	0.477	0.050	9.567	0.000
OCEAN11	0.401	0.045	8.916	0.000
OCEAN12	0.346	0.047	7.352	0.000
OCEAN13	0.298	0.048	6.183	0.000
OCEAN14	0.505	0.047	10.688	0.000
OCEAN15	0.594	0.054	10.943	0.000
OCEAN16	0.391	0.048	8.142	0.000
OCEAN17	0.292	0.041	7.100	0.000
OCEAN18	0.563	0.052	10.877	0.000
OCEAN19	0.328	0.038	8.744	0.000
OCEAN20	0.370	0.048	7.666	0.000

STDY Standardization

	Estimate	S.E.	Est./S.E.	Two-Tailed P-Value
INTRA BY				
OCEAN1	0.880	0.018	49.569	0.000
OCEAN5	0.674	0.035	19.257	0.000
OCEAN7	0.901	0.016	55.563	0.000
OCEAN19	0.820	0.023	35.836	0.000
CONSC BY				
OCEAN2	0.848	0.021	39.581	0.000
OCEAN4	0.862	0.020	42.296	0.000
OCEAN9	0.831	0.023	35.734	0.000
OCEAN14	0.703	0.034	20.943	0.000
AGREE BY				
OCEAN3	0.691	0.036	19.194	0.000
OCEAN6	0.812	0.027	30.531	0.000
OCEAN11	0.774	0.029	26.629	0.000
OCEAN17	0.842	0.024	34.512	0.000
NEUR BY				
OCEAN10	0.723	0.035	20.946	0.000
OCEAN12	0.809	0.029	27.813	0.000
OCEAN16	0.780	0.031	25.344	0.000
OCEAN18	0.661	0.039	16.873	0.000
OPEN BY				
OCEAN8	0.631	0.043	14.788	0.000
OCEAN13	0.838	0.029	29.112	0.000
OCEAN15	0.637	0.043	14.965	0.000
OCEAN20	0.794	0.030	26.158	0.000

```
CONSC    WITH
   INTRA              0.251      0.060       4.143      0.000
AGREE    WITH
   INTRA              0.057      0.065       0.874      0.382
   CONSC              0.525      0.050      10.504      0.000
NEUR WITH
   INTRA              0.385      0.058       6.612      0.000
   CONSC              0.104      0.066       1.578      0.115
   AGREE              0.257      0.064       4.010      0.000
OPEN WITH
   INTRA              0.033      0.066       0.496      0.620
   CONSC              0.134      0.066       2.024      0.043
   AGREE              0.086      0.068       1.272      0.204
   NEUR              -0.038      0.069      -0.549      0.583
Intercepts
   OCEAN1             2.017      0.101      20.023      0.000
   OCEAN2             3.897      0.170      22.987      0.000
   OCEAN3             4.929      0.210      23.506      0.000
   OCEAN4             4.306      0.185      23.233      0.000
   OCEAN5             2.082      0.103      20.230      0.000
   OCEAN6             5.638      0.238      23.719      0.000
   OCEAN7             2.281      0.110      20.785      0.000
   OCEAN8             2.236      0.108      20.668      0.000
   OCEAN9             3.886      0.169      22.980      0.000
   OCEAN10            2.389      0.114      21.044      0.000
   OCEAN11            4.822      0.206      23.466      0.000
   OCEAN12            2.334      0.112      20.914      0.000
   OCEAN13            2.062      0.102      20.168      0.000
   OCEAN14            3.188      0.143      22.353      0.000
   OCEAN15            2.312      0.111      20.861      0.000
   OCEAN16            2.407      0.114      21.085      0.000
   OCEAN17            5.471      0.231      23.676      0.000
   OCEAN18            2.473      0.117      21.229      0.000
   OCEAN19            2.143      0.105      20.411      0.000
   OCEAN20            1.607      0.088      18.355      0.000
Variances
   INTRA              1.000      0.000     999.000    999.000
   CONSC              1.000      0.000     999.000    999.000
   AGREE              1.000      0.000     999.000    999.000
   NEUR               1.000      0.000     999.000    999.000
   OPEN               1.000      0.000     999.000    999.000
Residual Variances
   OCEAN1             0.226      0.031       7.236      0.000
   OCEAN2             0.280      0.036       7.709      0.000
   OCEAN3             0.522      0.050      10.483      0.000
   OCEAN4             0.257      0.035       7.306      0.000
   OCEAN5             0.545      0.047      11.550      0.000
   OCEAN6             0.341      0.043       7.910      0.000
   OCEAN7             0.188      0.029       6.415      0.000
   OCEAN8             0.601      0.054      11.151      0.000
   OCEAN9             0.309      0.039       8.005      0.000
   OCEAN10            0.477      0.050       9.567      0.000
   OCEAN11            0.401      0.045       8.916      0.000
```

	Estimate	S.E.	Est./S.E.	P-Value
OCEAN12	0.346	0.047	7.352	0.000
OCEAN13	0.298	0.048	6.183	0.000
OCEAN14	0.505	0.047	10.688	0.000
OCEAN15	0.594	0.054	10.943	0.000
OCEAN16	0.391	0.048	8.142	0.000
OCEAN17	0.292	0.041	7.100	0.000
OCEAN18	0.563	0.052	10.877	0.000
OCEAN19	0.328	0.038	8.744	0.000
OCEAN20	0.370	0.048	7.666	0.000

STD Standardization

	Estimate	S.E.	Est./S.E.	Two-Tailed P-Value
INTRA BY				
OCEAN1	1.570	0.084	18.781	0.000
OCEAN5	1.125	0.089	12.707	0.000
OCEAN7	1.646	0.084	19.523	0.000
OCEAN19	1.508	0.090	16.789	0.000
CONSC BY				
OCEAN2	1.147	0.065	17.546	0.000
OCEAN4	1.098	0.061	17.990	0.000
OCEAN9	1.124	0.066	16.927	0.000
OCEAN14	1.098	0.082	13.314	0.000
AGREE BY				
OCEAN3	0.803	0.063	12.769	0.000
OCEAN6	0.851	0.053	16.041	0.000
OCEAN11	0.919	0.061	15.035	0.000
OCEAN17	0.893	0.053	16.935	0.000
NEUR BY				
OCEAN10	1.319	0.098	13.425	0.000
OCEAN12	1.524	0.098	15.576	0.000
OCEAN16	1.411	0.095	14.845	0.000
OCEAN18	1.162	0.098	11.894	0.000
OPEN BY				
OCEAN8	1.200	0.109	11.006	0.000
OCEAN13	1.614	0.100	16.118	0.000
OCEAN15	1.209	0.109	11.095	0.000
OCEAN20	1.489	0.098	15.128	0.000
CONSC WITH				
INTRA	0.251	0.060	4.143	0.000
AGREE WITH				
INTRA	0.057	0.065	0.874	0.382
CONSC	0.525	0.050	10.504	0.000
NEUR WITH				
INTRA	0.385	0.058	6.612	0.000
CONSC	0.104	0.066	1.578	0.115
AGREE	0.257	0.064	4.010	0.000
OPEN WITH				
INTRA	0.033	0.066	0.496	0.620
CONSC	0.134	0.066	2.024	0.043
AGREE	0.086	0.068	1.272	0.204
NEUR	-0.038	0.069	-0.549	0.583

66 USING MPLUS FOR STRUCTURAL EQUATION MODELING

```
Intercepts
    OCEAN1         3.599      0.103      34.876      0.000
    OCEAN2         5.271      0.078      67.381      0.000
    OCEAN3         5.726      0.067      85.227      0.000
    OCEAN4         5.482      0.074      74.450      0.000
    OCEAN5         3.475      0.097      36.009      0.000
    OCEAN6         5.910      0.061      97.483      0.000
    OCEAN7         4.167      0.106      39.449      0.000
    OCEAN8         4.251      0.110      38.672      0.000
    OCEAN9         5.258      0.078      67.203      0.000
    OCEAN10        4.358      0.105      41.314      0.000
    OCEAN11        5.726      0.069      83.387      0.000
    OCEAN12        4.398      0.109      40.359      0.000
    OCEAN13        3.973      0.111      35.661      0.000
    OCEAN14        4.973      0.090      55.120      0.000
    OCEAN15        4.388      0.110      39.979      0.000
    OCEAN16        4.355      0.105      41.624      0.000
    OCEAN17        5.806      0.061      94.601      0.000
    OCEAN18        4.348      0.102      42.771      0.000
    OCEAN19        3.943      0.106      37.061      0.000
    OCEAN20        3.013      0.108      27.780      0.000
Variances
    INTRA          1.000      0.000     999.000    999.000
    CONSC          1.000      0.000     999.000    999.000
    AGREE          1.000      0.000     999.000    999.000
    NEUR           1.000      0.000     999.000    999.000
    OPEN           1.000      0.000     999.000    999.000
Residual Variances
    OCEAN1         0.719      0.089       8.050      0.000
    OCEAN2         0.513      0.060       8.485      0.000
    OCEAN3         0.705      0.068      10.317      0.000
    OCEAN4         0.416      0.052       8.037      0.000
    OCEAN5         1.519      0.137      11.109      0.000
    OCEAN6         0.375      0.044       8.494      0.000
    OCEAN7         0.626      0.089       7.050      0.000
    OCEAN8         2.172      0.211      10.316      0.000
    OCEAN9         0.566      0.065       8.752      0.000
    OCEAN10        1.588      0.164       9.702      0.000
    OCEAN11        0.565      0.060       9.426      0.000
    OCEAN12        1.228      0.157       7.800      0.000
    OCEAN13        1.107      0.169       6.529      0.000
    OCEAN14        1.229      0.115      10.647      0.000
    OCEAN15        2.139      0.210      10.202      0.000
    OCEAN16        1.280      0.149       8.566      0.000
    OCEAN17        0.328      0.043       7.659      0.000
    OCEAN18        1.740      0.168      10.371      0.000
    OCEAN19        1.110      0.115       9.633      0.000
    OCEAN20        1.300      0.161       8.092      0.000

R-SQUARE
    Observed                                        Two-Tailed
    Variable      Estimate      S.E.   Est./S.E.    P-Value
    OCEAN1         0.774      0.031      24.785      0.000
```

OCEAN2	0.720	0.036	19.790	0.000
OCEAN3	0.478	0.050	9.597	0.000
OCEAN4	0.743	0.035	21.148	0.000
OCEAN5	0.455	0.047	9.628	0.000
OCEAN6	0.659	0.043	15.266	0.000
OCEAN7	0.812	0.029	27.782	0.000
OCEAN8	0.399	0.054	7.394	0.000
OCEAN9	0.691	0.039	17.867	0.000
OCEAN10	0.523	0.050	10.473	0.000
OCEAN11	0.599	0.045	13.314	0.000
OCEAN12	0.654	0.047	13.906	0.000
OCEAN13	0.702	0.048	14.556	0.000
OCEAN14	0.495	0.047	10.472	0.000
OCEAN15	0.406	0.054	7.483	0.000
OCEAN16	0.609	0.048	12.672	0.000
OCEAN17	0.708	0.041	17.256	0.000
OCEAN18	0.437	0.052	8.437	0.000
OCEAN19	0.672	0.038	17.918	0.000
OCEAN20	0.630	0.048	13.079	0.000

Note: Recall that Mplus reports three versions of the standardized solution. In reporting the solution, I would rely on the STDYX (i.e., completely standardized) solution. The R^2 values reported above are the communalities of the solution (i.e., the percentages of item variance explained by the hypothesized model).

```
QUALITY OF NUMERICAL RESULTS

Condition Number for the Information Matrix      0.132E-02
(ratio of smallest to largest eigenvalue)

MODEL MODIFICATION INDICES

Minimum M.I. value for printing the modification index    10.000

                         M.I.     E.P.C.   Std E.P.C.   StdYX E.P.C.
ON/BY Statements

OCEAN3   ON INTRA    /
INTRA    BY OCEAN3      12.203    0.122      0.191         0.164
OCEAN14  ON OPEN     /
OPEN     BY OCEAN14     21.321    0.288      0.346         0.222
OCEAN19  ON NEUR     /
NEUR     BY OCEAN19     11.024    0.206      0.272         0.148
OCEAN20  ON AGREE    /
AGREE    BY OCEAN20     12.752   -0.381     -0.306        -0.163
```

ON Statements

INTRA	ON	OCEAN1	10.380	0.905	0.577	1.029
INTRA	ON	OCEAN18	10.921	0.237	0.151	0.266
AGREE	ON	OCEAN18	11.860	0.121	0.151	0.265
NEUR	ON	OCEAN1	10.392	-0.356	-0.270	-0.482
NEUR	ON	OCEAN12	12.013	0.636	0.483	0.910
NEUR	ON	OCEAN18	20.018	-0.584	-0.443	-0.779
NEUR	ON	OCEAN19	11.728	0.277	0.210	0.386
OPEN	ON	OCEAN14	21.932	0.336	0.280	0.437
OCEAN1	ON	OCEAN7	13.456	0.726	0.726	0.743
OCEAN1	ON	OCEAN12	10.696	-0.110	-0.110	-0.116
OCEAN1	ON	OCEAN19	12.185	-0.328	-0.328	-0.339
OCEAN3	ON	OCEAN1	10.169	0.093	0.093	0.143
OCEAN3	ON	OCEAN5	12.799	0.111	0.111	0.160
OCEAN3	ON	OCEAN6	15.052	0.436	0.436	0.394
OCEAN3	ON	OCEAN17	15.883	-0.523	-0.523	-0.478
OCEAN3	ON	OCEAN18	31.330	0.168	0.168	0.254
OCEAN4	ON	OCEAN6	17.062	0.203	0.203	0.167
OCEAN5	ON	OCEAN7	17.402	-0.579	-0.579	-0.634
OCEAN5	ON	OCEAN20	11.957	0.137	0.137	0.154
OCEAN6	ON	OCEAN3	15.052	0.232	0.232	0.257
OCEAN7	ON	OCEAN1	13.456	0.632	0.632	0.617
OCEAN7	ON	OCEAN5	17.403	-0.239	-0.239	-0.218
OCEAN8	ON	OCEAN15	31.184	0.392	0.392	0.391
OCEAN9	ON	OCEAN14	23.205	0.252	0.252	0.291
OCEAN11	ON	OCEAN17	17.588	0.596	0.596	0.533
OCEAN12	ON	OCEAN1	10.139	-0.155	-0.155	-0.147
OCEAN13	ON	OCEAN20	33.882	1.092	1.092	1.063
OCEAN14	ON	OCEAN9	23.205	0.547	0.547	0.474
OCEAN14	ON	OCEAN13	20.362	0.160	0.160	0.198
OCEAN14	ON	OCEAN20	19.070	0.159	0.159	0.191
OCEAN15	ON	OCEAN8	31.182	0.386	0.386	0.386
OCEAN17	ON	OCEAN3	15.882	-0.244	-0.244	-0.267
OCEAN17	ON	OCEAN11	17.589	0.346	0.346	0.387
OCEAN18	ON	OCEAN3	31.595	0.405	0.405	0.267
OCEAN18	ON	OCEAN19	17.639	0.201	0.201	0.210
OCEAN19	ON	OCEAN1	12.185	-0.507	-0.507	-0.492
OCEAN19	ON	OCEAN18	21.352	0.184	0.184	0.176
OCEAN20	ON	OCEAN13	33.885	1.282	1.282	1.317
OCEAN20	ON	OCEAN17	12.657	-0.266	-0.266	-0.151

WITH Statements

OCEAN1	WITH	INTRA	10.381	0.651	0.415	0.489
OCEAN1	WITH	NEUR	10.393	-0.256	-0.194	-0.229
OCEAN6	WITH	OCEAN3	15.052	0.164	0.164	0.318
OCEAN6	WITH	OCEAN4	19.582	0.138	0.138	0.349
OCEAN7	WITH	OCEAN1	13.457	0.454	0.454	0.677
OCEAN7	WITH	OCEAN5	17.403	-0.363	-0.363	-0.372
OCEAN12	WITH	NEUR	12.019	0.782	0.593	0.535

```
OCEAN14 WITH OPEN      21.932    0.413    0.344    0.310
OCEAN14 WITH OCEAN9    23.206    0.310    0.310    0.371
OCEAN15 WITH OCEAN8    31.182    0.838    0.838    0.389
OCEAN17 WITH OCEAN3    15.883   -0.172   -0.172   -0.357
OCEAN17 WITH OCEAN11   17.588    0.196    0.196    0.454
OCEAN18 WITH INTRA     10.920    0.413    0.263    0.199
OCEAN18 WITH AGREE     11.859    0.211    0.263    0.199
OCEAN18 WITH NEUR      20.014   -1.016   -0.771   -0.584
OCEAN18 WITH OCEAN3    30.489    0.400    0.400    0.361
OCEAN19 WITH NEUR      11.727    0.307    0.233    0.221
OCEAN19 WITH OCEAN1    12.185   -0.365   -0.365   -0.408
OCEAN19 WITH OCEAN18   13.882    0.351    0.351    0.252
OCEAN20 WITH OCEAN13   33.885    1.419    1.419    1.183
```

Note: The modification indices indicate the amount that the χ^2 value will decrease if a given parameter were to be freed. For example, freeing the residual correlation between Ocean19 and Ocean18 (Ocean19 WITH Ocean18) would decrease the model χ^2 value by 13.882. Mplus also reports the expected parameter change, the STD expected parameter change, and the STDYX expected parameter change. Thus, if we were to free this residual correlation, the unstandardized estimate for the parameter would be .251, and the standardardized parameter would be .252.

Assessment of Fit

Given the models described earlier, assessing the fit of the five-factor model is based on (a) whether the model fits better than rival specifications and (b) whether the model provides a good absolute fit to the data. The fit indices for all the models described earlier are presented in Table 5.1.

As shown, the fit indices all converge, suggesting the superiority of the model hypothesizing five oblique factors. Comparison with the other models shows that the five-factor (oblique) model provides a better fit to the data than does a model hypothesizing five orthogonal factors, $\chi^2_{difference}(10) = 145.66$, $p < .01$, or one factor, $\chi^2_{difference}(10) = 1,987.57$, $p < .01$.

As is often the case in confirmatory factor analysis (Kelloway, 1995, 1996), although the five-factor model provides a better fit to the data than do rival specifications, the model itself does not provide a great fit to the data. Although inspection of the preceding printout suggests that all the estimated parameters in the hypothesized three-factor model are significant, the χ^2 value associated with the model is also significant. The other fit indices approach but do not obtain the criteria for indicating a good fit to the data.

Table 5.1 Fit Indices for the Three Models

Model	χ^2	df	CFI	TLI	RMSEA	SRMR
One factor	2,398.03	170	.29	.21	.21	.20
Five factors (orthogonal)	556.12	170	.88	.86	.09	.15
Five factors (oblique)	410.46	160	.92	.91	.07	.06

Thus, the most that can be concluded from these results is that the hypothesized five-factor model provides a better fit than do plausible rival specifications, a rather unsatisfying conclusion.

Model Modification

Faced with results such as these, researchers may well be tempted to engage in a post hoc specification search to improve the fit of the model. Given that all the estimated parameters are significant, theory trimming (i.e., deleting nonsignificant paths) does not seem to be a viable option. Theory building (i.e., adding parameters on the basis of the empirical results) remains an option.

Inspection of the Mplus-produced modification indices suggests several likely additional parameters (i.e., modification indices greater than 5.0). Although the modification index suggests that a substantial improvement in fit could be obtained from making these modifications, the reader is reminded of the dangers associated with post hoc model modifications. In this case, I would not typically make the change, (a) because of the dangers of empirically generated modifications, (b) because there is no theoretical justification for the change, and (c) because no single change is likely to alter the conclusions obtained from the original analysis (i.e., it would not change the fit indices sufficiently to change the overall conclusion).

There are two other options potentially available to researchers faced with ill-fitting confirmatory factor analyses. One is the somewhat controversial application of item-parceling techniques, and the other is the relatively new notion of exploratory structural equation modeling (Asparouhov & Muthén, 2009; Marsh et al., 2009).

ITEM PARCELING

In operationalizing an item-level confirmatory factor analysis, researchers can choose between a strategy of total disaggregation (Williams et al., 2009), in which items are used as the indicators of latent variables, or a strategy of partial disaggregation, in which items are combined into sets, and these sets are then used as indicators of the latent variable. Partial disaggregation can have several advantages. First, it can reduce the number of parameters in the model, and simpler models are more likely to fit the data. Second, combinations of items are more likely to be reliable and normally distributed than are individual items, again leading to better fitting models. On the other hand, combining items can also lead to disguising sources of misspecification (e.g., the effect of "bad" items) in a model. If item parcels are to be formed, the question arises of how best to construct these parcels. The answer appears to depend on whether the underlying scale is unidimensional or multidimensional (Williams & O'Boyle, 2008).

For unidimensional scales, the factorial algorithm (Rogers & Schmitt, 2004) is based on standardized loadings from a unidimensional exploratory factor analysis. In this approach, the researcher would attempt to balance the factor loadings within each item parcel (e.g., having one strong loading, one weak loading, and one moderate loading in each parcel). This approach seems to obtain better results in terms of overall model fit (Rogers & Schmitt, 2004).

For multidimensional scales, the researcher can opt for either an internal-consistency approach (Little, Cunningham, Shahar, & Widaman, 2002), in which scales are formed from the items constituting each dimension, or a domain-representativeness approach, in which parcels are formed from items representing each of the dimensions. Williams and O'Boyle (2008) advocated this approach, as it results in indicators that can serve as stand-alone representatives of the latent construct.

In the current case, the small number of items constituting each of the five personality factors in OCEAN.20 does not really permit the construction of item parcels. At best, one could form two parcels of two items each within each factor, which may create problems with identification. Another, and newer, approach may be to consider an exploratory structural equation model.

EXPLORATORY STRUCTURAL EQUATION MODELS

As is evident in our preceding discussion, the confirmatory factor analysis model, in which items are forced to load on one and only one factor, is extremely restrictive. If an item loads substantially on its intended factor and moderately on another factor, the confirmatory model (which does not account for the moderate cross-loading) will not fit the data. Exploratory structural equation modeling combines features of both exploratory and confirmatory factor analysis in that researchers can explore (without constraining items to one factor) the underlying factor structure. Parameter tests and goodness-of-fit tests are still available as in confirmatory factor analysis (see Asparouhov & Muthén, 2009; Marsh et al., 2009). O'Keefe et al. (2012) originally used exploratory structural equation modeling techniques in their development of OCEAN.20.

Normally, one would be advised against performing exploratory and confirmatory analyses on the same sample. An outdated, and erroneous, practice was to run exploratory factor analysis on a set of data to derive the factor structure and then to "confirm" that model using confirmatory techniques. Aside from the observation that the confirmatory analysis rarely confirms the exploratory model, there is an inherent problem in generating and confirming a model on the same set of data. However, I would suggest that one can make more of a case for running exploratory analysis following confirmatory analysis, especially when one labels the analysis as exploratory.

In the case of an exploratory structural equation model, one is essentially performing a nested model comparison. The original model specifying only 20 factor loading parameters is being compared against a model that estimates 100 factor loadings (i.e., each of 20 variables loading on each of five factors). In this sense, the nested comparison can be thought of as an omnibus test of the 80 omitted factor loading parameters in the original model.

The source code used to generate an exploratory structural equation model looks very much like our original confirmatory factor analysis code, with some important changes. In the MODEL statement, we can still specify that there are five factors, but it would not make sense to name these factors, because at this point we do not know what the factors are. The five factors are indicated by 20 items, with "(*1)" indicating to Mplus that this is an exploratory structural equation model and that indicators can load across the five factors.

```
TITLE:      Example of an exploratory structural equation analysis
DATA:       FILE IS Chapter5.dat;
VARIABLE:   NAMES ARE Ocean1-Ocean20;
MODEL:      F1-F5 BY Ocean1-Ocean20(*1);
OUTPUT:     STANDARDIZED MODINDICES (ALL);
```

Running this analysis results in a substantially better fitting model. Although the items principally load on the five factors as intended, there are also minor (but statistically significant) cross-loadings on other factors. Ignoring these cross-loadings results in an ill-fitting confirmatory factor analysis; incorporating them into the current exploratory model results in a substantially better fitting model but does not alter the interpretation of the scale as we originally intended (O'Keefe et al., 2012). Thus, Factor 1 is principally defined by the items constituting the conscientiousness dimension of OCEAN.20.

Chapter 5: Confirmatory Factor Analysis   73

Factor 2 is defined by the extraversion items, Factor 3 by the agreeableness items, Factor 4 by the neuroticism items, and Factor 5 by the openness items.

```
Mplus VERSION 7 (Mac)
MUTHEN & MUTHEN

INPUT INSTRUCTIONS

TITLE:     Example of an exploratory structural equation model
DATA:      FILE IS Chapter5.dat;
VARIABLE:  NAMES ARE Ocean1-Ocean20;
MODEL:     F1-F5 by ocean1-ocean20(*1);
OUTPUT:    STANDARDIZED MODINDICES (ALL);

INPUT READING TERMINATED NORMALLY

Example of an exploratory structural equation model

SUMMARY OF ANALYSIS

Number of groups                                                 1
Number of observations                                         299
Number of dependent variables                                   20
Number of independent variables                                  0
Number of continuous latent variables                            5

Observed dependent variables
  Continuous
    OCEAN1    OCEAN2    OCEAN3    OCEAN4    OCEAN5    OCEAN6
    OCEAN7    OCEAN8    OCEAN9    OCEAN10   OCEAN11   OCEAN12
    OCEAN13   OCEAN14   OCEAN15   OCEAN16   OCEAN17   OCEAN18
    OCEAN19   OCEAN20

Continuous latent variables
  EFA factors
    *1:     F1      F2      F3      F4      F5

Estimator                                                       ML
Rotation                                                    GEOMIN
Row standardization                                    CORRELATION
Type of rotation                                           OBLIQUE
Epsilon value                                               Varies
Information matrix                                        OBSERVED
Maximum number of iterations                                  1000
Convergence criterion                                    0.500D-04
Maximum number of steepest descent iterations                   20
Optimization Specifications for the Exploratory Factor Analysis
Rotation Algorithm
  Number of random starts                                       30
  Maximum number of iterations                               10000
  Derivative convergence criterion                       0.100D-04
```

74 USING MPLUS FOR STRUCTURAL EQUATION MODELING

```
Input data file(s)
Chapter5.dat
Input data format FREE

THE MODEL ESTIMATION TERMINATED NORMALLY

MODEL FIT INFORMATION

Number of Free Parameters                                   130
Loglikelihood
        H0 Value                                      -9614.019
        H1 Value                                      -9498.636
Information Criteria
        Akaike (AIC)                                  19488.037
        Bayesian (BIC)                                19969.095
        Sample-Size Adjusted BIC                      19556.814
            (n* = (n + 2) / 24)
Chi-Square Test of Model Fit
        Value                                           230.765
        Degrees of Freedom                                  100
        P-Value                                          0.0000
RMSEA (Root Mean Square Error Of Approximation)
        Estimate                                          0.066
        90 Percent C.I.                             0.055 0.077
        Probability RMSEA <= .05                          0.010
CFI/TLI
        CFI                                               0.959
        TLI                                               0.921
Chi-Square Test of Model Fit for the Baseline Model
        Value                                          3343.759
        Degrees of Freedom                                  190
        P-Value                                          0.0000
SRMR (Standardized Root Mean Square Residual)
        Value                                             0.024
```

Note: The model provides a substantially better fit to the data. The CFI exceeds .95, the SRMR is .02, and the RMSEA is .066. Although not a perfect fit, the exploratory model substantially improves on the original five-factor model.

```
MODEL RESULTS

                                                        Two-Tailed
                   Estimate       S.E.      Est./S.E.    P-Value
    F1 BY
        OCEAN1      -0.024       0.053       -0.452       0.652
        OCEAN2       1.057       0.076       13.933       0.000
        OCEAN3       0.071       0.061        1.166       0.243
        OCEAN4       1.037       0.073       14.210       0.000
        OCEAN5      -0.008       0.066       -0.127       0.899
        OCEAN6       0.009       0.040        0.231       0.817
```

OCEAN7	0.108	0.071	1.528	0.127
OCEAN8	-0.019	0.093	-0.199	0.842
OCEAN9	**1.143**	**0.068**	**16.726**	**0.000**
OCEAN10	0.149	0.098	1.521	0.128
OCEAN11	-0.014	0.047	-0.288	0.774
OCEAN12	0.105	0.055	1.896	0.058
OCEAN13	0.027	0.063	0.432	0.666
OCEAN14	**1.123**	**0.090**	**12.457**	**0.000**
OCEAN15	0.174	0.111	1.571	0.116
OCEAN16	-0.143	0.085	-1.683	0.092
OCEAN17	0.031	0.041	0.751	0.453
OCEAN18	-0.142	0.087	-1.638	0.101
OCEAN19	0.057	0.071	0.795	0.427
OCEAN20	-0.093	0.074	-1.261	0.207

F2 BY

OCEAN1	**1.648**	**0.089**	**18.456**	**0.000**
OCEAN2	0.092	0.050	1.833	0.067
OCEAN3	0.125	0.060	2.072	0.038
OCEAN4	-0.063	0.043	-1.466	0.143
OCEAN5	**1.062**	**0.095**	**11.212**	**0.000**
OCEAN6	0.031	0.030	1.031	0.302
OCEAN7	**1.603**	**0.087**	**18.419**	**0.000**
OCEAN8	0.026	0.079	0.334	0.739
OCEAN9	-0.016	0.039	-0.405	0.686
OCEAN10	0.023	0.054	0.420	0.674
OCEAN11	-0.082	0.051	-1.599	0.110
OCEAN12	-0.149	0.085	-1.762	0.078
OCEAN13	-0.065	0.062	-1.058	0.290
OCEAN14	0.065	0.059	1.109	0.267
OCEAN15	-0.166	0.098	-1.699	0.089
OCEAN16	0.108	0.079	1.356	0.175
OCEAN17	-0.039	0.034	-1.156	0.248
OCEAN18	0.320	0.105	3.044	0.002
OCEAN19	**1.403**	**0.097**	**14.540**	**0.000**
OCEAN20	0.149	0.079	1.895	0.058

F3 BY

OCEAN1	0.077	0.056	1.361	0.173
OCEAN2	0.153	0.074	2.062	0.039
OCEAN3	**0.757**	**0.072**	**10.445**	**0.000**
OCEAN4	0.154	0.073	2.105	0.035
OCEAN5	-0.202	0.093	-2.166	0.030
OCEAN6	**0.866**	**0.060**	**14.330**	**0.000**
OCEAN7	0.045	0.055	0.824	0.410
OCEAN8	0.114	0.104	1.092	0.275
OCEAN9	-0.016	0.029	-0.553	0.580
OCEAN10	0.020	0.075	0.269	0.788
OCEAN11	**0.906**	**0.069**	**13.099**	**0.000**
OCEAN12	-0.091	0.073	-1.247	0.212
OCEAN13	0.054	0.057	0.952	0.341
OCEAN14	-0.119	0.072	-1.641	0.101
OCEAN15	0.134	0.107	1.255	0.210
OCEAN16	0.061	0.072	0.840	0.401
OCEAN17	**0.877**	**0.059**	**14.779**	**0.000**

OCEAN18	0.348	0.107	3.249	0.001
OCEAN19	-0.032	0.060	-0.537	0.591
OCEAN20	-0.105	0.075	-1.400	0.161
F4 BY				
OCEAN1	-0.136	0.066	-2.071	0.038
OCEAN2	-0.044	0.046	-0.966	0.334
OCEAN3	0.082	0.059	1.407	0.159
OCEAN4	0.006	0.039	0.153	0.878
OCEAN5	0.234	0.096	2.445	0.014
OCEAN6	-0.036	0.036	-1.007	0.314
OCEAN7	-0.007	0.032	-0.217	0.828
OCEAN8	0.062	0.088	0.699	0.485
OCEAN9	-0.010	0.046	-0.210	0.834
OCEAN10	**1.280**	**0.102**	**12.501**	**0.000**
OCEAN11	0.061	0.049	1.235	0.217
OCEAN12	**1.635**	**0.108**	**15.136**	**0.000**
OCEAN13	-0.069	0.063	-1.105	0.269
OCEAN14	0.043	0.059	0.730	0.466
OCEAN15	0.128	0.094	1.363	0.173
OCEAN16	**1.362**	**0.103**	**13.188**	**0.000**
OCEAN17	-0.022	0.033	-0.671	0.502
OCEAN18	**0.973**	**0.107**	**9.068**	**0.000**
OCEAN19	0.250	0.092	2.718	0.007
OCEAN20	-0.170	0.086	-1.975	0.048
F5 BY				
OCEAN1	-0.033	0.042	-0.776	0.438
OCEAN2	-0.086	0.043	-2.028	0.043
OCEAN3	0.048	0.046	1.048	0.295
OCEAN4	-0.044	0.027	-1.623	0.105
OCEAN5	0.233	0.079	2.938	0.003
OCEAN6	-0.051	0.036	-1.397	0.163
OCEAN7	-0.051	0.048	-1.075	0.282
OCEAN8	**1.183**	**0.108**	**10.939**	**0.000**
OCEAN9	0.092	0.048	1.924	0.054
OCEAN10	-0.005	0.071	-0.075	0.940
OCEAN11	0.027	0.039	0.704	0.482
OCEAN12	-0.015	0.055	-0.274	0.784
OCEAN13	**1.604**	**0.099**	**16.277**	**0.000**
OCEAN14	0.339	0.077	4.388	0.000
OCEAN15	**1.187**	**0.106**	**11.149**	**0.000**
OCEAN16	0.022	0.063	0.349	0.727
OCEAN17	0.037	0.033	1.100	0.271
OCEAN18	-0.043	0.068	-0.633	0.527
OCEAN19	0.011	0.053	0.216	0.829
OCEAN20	**1.525**	**0.097**	**15.747**	**0.000**

Note: The items that should load together on each factor are in boldface type. As shown, each of the items loads strongly on the hypothesized factor. Having said that, there are also smaller, albeit significant, cross-loadings. Thus, Ocean14 loads significantly ($B = 0.339$, $p < .001$) on Factor 5, although it also loads on its hypothesized factor (Factor 1).

It is these smaller, yet significant, cross-loadings that led to the original five-factor model's lack of fit to the data.

```
F2   WITH
     F1                   0.219      0.059       3.699      0.000
F3   WITH
     F1                   0.451      0.055       8.205      0.000
     F2                   0.027      0.059       0.458      0.647
F4   WITH
     F1                   0.072      0.062       1.167      0.243
     F2                   0.338      0.056       6.014      0.000
     F3                   0.216      0.059       3.644      0.000
F5   WITH
     F1                   0.102      0.061       1.683      0.092
     F2                   0.043      0.061       0.695      0.487
     F3                   0.060      0.060       1.004      0.315
     F4                  -0.006      0.063      -0.094      0.925
Intercepts
     OCEAN1               3.599      0.103      34.876      0.000
     OCEAN2               5.271      0.078      67.381      0.000
     OCEAN3               5.726      0.067      85.227      0.000
     OCEAN4               5.482      0.074      74.450      0.000
     OCEAN5               3.475      0.097      36.009      0.000
     OCEAN6               5.910      0.061      97.483      0.000
     OCEAN7               4.167      0.106      39.449      0.000
     OCEAN8               4.251      0.110      38.672      0.000
     OCEAN9               5.258      0.078      67.203      0.000
     OCEAN10              4.358      0.105      41.314      0.000
     OCEAN11              5.726      0.069      83.387      0.000
     OCEAN12              4.398      0.109      40.359      0.000
     OCEAN13              3.973      0.111      35.661      0.000
     OCEAN14              4.973      0.090      55.120      0.000
     OCEAN15              4.388      0.110      39.979      0.000
     OCEAN16              4.355      0.105      41.624      0.000
     OCEAN17              5.806      0.061      94.601      0.000
     OCEAN18              4.348      0.102      42.771      0.000
     OCEAN19              3.943      0.106      37.061      0.000
     OCEAN20              3.013      0.108      27.780      0.000
Variances
     F1                   1.000      0.000     999.000    999.000
     F2                   1.000      0.000     999.000    999.000
     F3                   1.000      0.000     999.000    999.000
     F4                   1.000      0.000     999.000    999.000
     F5                   1.000      0.000     999.000    999.000
Residual Variances
     OCEAN1               0.615      0.092       6.677      0.000
     OCEAN2               0.515      0.059       8.759      0.000
     OCEAN3               0.649      0.064      10.165      0.000
     OCEAN4               0.410      0.052       7.931      0.000
     OCEAN5               1.358      0.124      10.983      0.000
     OCEAN6               0.355      0.047       7.636      0.000
     OCEAN7               0.683      0.090       7.625      0.000
```

78 USING MPLUS FOR STRUCTURAL EQUATION MODELING

OCEAN8	2.179	0.206	10.562	0.000
OCEAN9	0.518	0.065	7.970	0.000
OCEAN10	1.603	0.162	9.919	0.000
OCEAN11	0.569	0.062	9.141	0.000
OCEAN12	1.055	0.168	6.284	0.000
OCEAN13	1.114	0.158	7.064	0.000
OCEAN14	1.046	0.105	10.010	0.000
OCEAN15	2.054	0.197	10.414	0.000
OCEAN16	1.288	0.150	8.604	0.000
OCEAN17	0.335	0.045	7.385	0.000
OCEAN18	1.621	0.152	10.675	0.000
OCEAN19	1.081	0.111	9.746	0.000
OCEAN20	1.155	0.152	7.594	0.000

STANDARDIZED MODEL RESULTS

STDYX Standardization

	Estimate	S.E.	Est./S.E.	Two-Tailed P-Value
F1 BY				
OCEAN1	-0.013	0.030	-0.451	0.652
OCEAN2	0.781	0.040	19.477	0.000
OCEAN3	0.062	0.053	1.168	0.243
OCEAN4	0.814	0.041	19.818	0.000
OCEAN5	-0.005	0.039	-0.127	0.899
OCEAN6	0.009	0.038	0.231	0.817
OCEAN7	0.059	0.039	1.530	0.126
OCEAN8	-0.010	0.049	-0.199	0.842
OCEAN9	0.845	0.027	31.481	0.000
OCEAN10	0.082	0.054	1.525	0.127
OCEAN11	-0.011	0.040	-0.288	0.774
OCEAN12	0.056	0.029	1.899	0.058
OCEAN13	0.014	0.033	0.432	0.666
OCEAN14	0.720	0.043	16.812	0.000
OCEAN15	0.092	0.058	1.575	0.115
OCEAN16	-0.079	0.047	-1.684	0.092
OCEAN17	0.029	0.038	0.751	0.452
OCEAN18	-0.081	0.049	-1.640	0.101
OCEAN19	0.031	0.039	0.796	0.426
OCEAN20	-0.050	0.039	-1.262	0.207
F2 BY				
OCEAN1	0.923	0.023	39.375	0.000
OCEAN2	0.068	0.037	1.835	0.066
OCEAN3	0.108	0.052	2.079	0.038
OCEAN4	-0.049	0.034	-1.465	0.143
OCEAN5	0.637	0.044	14.496	0.000
OCEAN6	0.030	0.029	1.031	0.303
OCEAN7	0.877	0.022	40.182	0.000
OCEAN8	0.014	0.042	0.334	0.739
OCEAN9	-0.012	0.029	-0.405	0.686
OCEAN10	0.013	0.030	0.420	0.674
OCEAN11	-0.069	0.043	-1.601	0.109
OCEAN12	-0.079	0.045	-1.763	0.078

OCEAN13	-0.034	0.032	-1.058	0.290
OCEAN14	0.042	0.037	1.110	0.267
OCEAN15	-0.088	0.051	-1.703	0.088
OCEAN16	0.060	0.044	1.358	0.174
OCEAN17	-0.037	0.032	-1.157	0.247
OCEAN18	0.182	0.059	3.078	0.002
OCEAN19	0.763	0.034	22.140	0.000
OCEAN20	0.079	0.042	1.896	0.058

F3 BY

OCEAN1	0.043	0.032	1.362	0.173
OCEAN2	0.113	0.055	2.069	0.039
OCEAN3	0.651	0.050	12.937	0.000
OCEAN4	0.121	0.057	2.113	0.035
OCEAN5	-0.121	0.056	-2.173	0.030
OCEAN6	0.826	0.038	21.521	0.000
OCEAN7	0.025	0.030	0.825	0.410
OCEAN8	0.060	0.055	1.094	0.274
OCEAN9	-0.012	0.022	-0.553	0.580
OCEAN10	0.011	0.041	0.269	0.788
OCEAN11	0.763	0.041	18.744	0.000
OCEAN12	-0.048	0.039	-1.248	0.212
OCEAN13	0.028	0.029	0.953	0.341
OCEAN14	-0.076	0.046	-1.642	0.101
OCEAN15	0.070	0.056	1.257	0.209
OCEAN16	0.033	0.040	0.840	0.401
OCEAN17	0.826	0.036	22.643	0.000
OCEAN18	0.198	0.060	3.287	0.001
OCEAN19	-0.018	0.033	-0.537	0.591
OCEAN20	-0.056	0.040	-1.401	0.161

F4 BY

OCEAN1	-0.076	0.037	-2.072	0.038
OCEAN2	-0.033	0.034	-0.966	0.334
OCEAN3	0.071	0.050	1.410	0.159
OCEAN4	0.005	0.031	0.153	0.878
OCEAN5	0.140	0.057	2.459	0.014
OCEAN6	-0.034	0.034	-1.007	0.314
OCEAN7	-0.004	0.017	-0.217	0.828
OCEAN8	0.032	0.046	0.699	0.485
OCEAN9	-0.007	0.034	-0.210	0.834
OCEAN10	0.702	0.039	17.841	0.000
OCEAN11	0.051	0.042	1.236	0.216
OCEAN12	0.868	0.036	23.938	0.000
OCEAN13	-0.036	0.033	-1.107	0.268
OCEAN14	0.028	0.038	0.730	0.466
OCEAN15	0.068	0.049	1.365	0.172
OCEAN16	0.753	0.040	19.017	0.000
OCEAN17	-0.021	0.031	-0.671	0.502
OCEAN18	0.553	0.052	10.622	0.000
OCEAN19	0.136	0.050	2.730	0.006
OCEAN20	-0.090	0.046	-1.981	0.048

F5 BY

OCEAN1	-0.018	0.024	-0.776	0.438
OCEAN2	-0.064	0.031	-2.033	0.042

	OCEAN3	0.041	0.039	1.049	0.294
	OCEAN4	-0.034	0.021	-1.627	0.104
	OCEAN5	0.139	0.047	2.959	0.003
	OCEAN6	-0.048	0.035	-1.396	0.163
	OCEAN7	-0.028	0.026	-1.076	0.282
	OCEAN8	0.623	0.043	14.613	0.000
	OCEAN9	0.068	0.035	1.922	0.055
	OCEAN10	-0.003	0.039	-0.075	0.940
	OCEAN11	0.023	0.033	0.704	0.481
	OCEAN12	-0.008	0.029	-0.274	0.784
	OCEAN13	0.832	0.028	30.006	0.000
	OCEAN14	0.217	0.049	4.454	0.000
	OCEAN15	0.626	0.042	14.848	0.000
	OCEAN16	0.012	0.035	0.349	0.727
	OCEAN17	0.035	0.031	1.101	0.271
	OCEAN18	-0.024	0.039	-0.633	0.527
	OCEAN19	0.006	0.029	0.216	0.829
	OCEAN20	0.813	0.030	27.532	0.000
F2 WITH					
	F1	0.219	0.059	3.699	0.000
F3 WITH					
	F1	0.451	0.055	8.205	0.000
	F2	0.027	0.059	0.458	0.647
F4 WITH					
	F1	0.072	0.062	1.167	0.243
	F2	0.338	0.056	6.014	0.000
	F3	0.216	0.059	3.644	0.000
F5 WITH					
	F1	0.102	0.061	1.683	0.092
	F2	0.043	0.061	0.695	0.487
	F3	0.060	0.060	1.004	0.315
	F4	-0.006	0.063	-0.094	0.925
Intercepts					
	OCEAN1	2.017	0.101	20.023	0.000
	OCEAN2	3.897	0.170	22.987	0.000
	OCEAN3	4.929	0.210	23.506	0.000
	OCEAN4	4.306	0.185	23.233	0.000
	OCEAN5	2.082	0.103	20.230	0.000
	OCEAN6	5.638	0.238	23.719	0.000
	OCEAN7	2.281	0.110	20.785	0.000
	OCEAN8	2.236	0.108	20.668	0.000
	OCEAN9	3.886	0.169	22.980	0.000
	OCEAN10	2.389	0.114	21.044	0.000
	OCEAN11	4.822	0.206	23.466	0.000
	OCEAN12	2.334	0.112	20.914	0.000
	OCEAN13	2.062	0.102	20.168	0.000
	OCEAN14	3.188	0.143	22.353	0.000
	OCEAN15	2.312	0.111	20.861	0.000
	OCEAN16	2.407	0.114	21.085	0.000
	OCEAN17	5.471	0.231	23.676	0.000
	OCEAN18	2.474	0.117	21.229	0.000
	OCEAN19	2.143	0.105	20.411	0.000
	OCEAN20	1.607	0.088	18.355	0.000

Variances				
F1	1.000	0.000	999.000	999.000
F2	1.000	0.000	999.000	999.000
F3	1.000	0.000	999.000	999.000
F4	1.000	0.000	999.000	999.000
F5	1.000	0.000	999.000	999.000
Residual Variances				
OCEAN1	0.193	0.031	6.139	0.000
OCEAN2	0.282	0.036	7.917	0.000
OCEAN3	0.481	0.048	10.033	0.000
OCEAN4	0.253	0.035	7.216	0.000
OCEAN5	0.488	0.045	10.875	0.000
OCEAN6	0.323	0.045	7.158	0.000
OCEAN7	0.205	0.030	6.877	0.000
OCEAN8	0.603	0.053	11.484	0.000
OCEAN9	0.283	0.039	7.324	0.000
OCEAN10	0.482	0.049	9.803	0.000
OCEAN11	0.404	0.046	8.685	0.000
OCEAN12	0.297	0.050	5.972	0.000
OCEAN13	0.300	0.045	6.635	0.000
OCEAN14	0.430	0.045	9.570	0.000
OCEAN15	0.570	0.052	10.988	0.000
OCEAN16	0.394	0.048	8.184	0.000
OCEAN17	0.297	0.043	6.893	0.000
OCEAN18	0.525	0.048	10.881	0.000
OCEAN19	0.319	0.036	8.789	0.000
OCEAN20	0.328	0.046	7.135	0.000

STDY Standardization

	Estimate	S.E.	Est./S.E.	Two-Tailed P-Value
F1 BY				
OCEAN1	-0.013	0.030	-0.451	0.652
OCEAN2	0.781	0.040	19.477	0.000
OCEAN3	0.062	0.053	1.168	0.243
OCEAN4	0.814	0.041	19.818	0.000
OCEAN5	-0.005	0.039	-0.127	0.899
OCEAN6	0.009	0.038	0.231	0.817
OCEAN7	0.059	0.039	1.530	0.126
OCEAN8	-0.010	0.049	-0.199	0.842
OCEAN9	0.845	0.027	31.481	0.000
OCEAN10	0.082	0.054	1.525	0.127
OCEAN11	-0.011	0.040	-0.288	0.774
OCEAN12	0.056	0.029	1.899	0.058
OCEAN13	0.014	0.033	0.432	0.666
OCEAN14	0.720	0.043	16.812	0.000
OCEAN15	0.092	0.058	1.575	0.115
OCEAN16	-0.079	0.047	-1.684	0.092
OCEAN17	0.029	0.038	0.751	0.452
OCEAN18	-0.081	0.049	-1.640	0.101
OCEAN19	0.031	0.039	0.796	0.426
OCEAN20	-0.050	0.039	-1.262	0.207

F2 BY					
	OCEAN1	0.923	0.023	39.375	0.000
	OCEAN2	0.068	0.037	1.835	0.066
	OCEAN3	0.108	0.052	2.079	0.038
	OCEAN4	-0.049	0.034	-1.465	0.143
	OCEAN5	0.637	0.044	14.496	0.000
	OCEAN6	0.030	0.029	1.031	0.303
	OCEAN7	0.877	0.022	40.182	0.000
	OCEAN8	0.014	0.042	0.334	0.739
	OCEAN9	-0.012	0.029	-0.405	0.686
	OCEAN10	0.013	0.030	0.420	0.674
	OCEAN11	-0.069	0.043	-1.601	0.109
	OCEAN12	-0.079	0.045	-1.763	0.078
	OCEAN13	-0.034	0.032	-1.058	0.290
	OCEAN14	0.042	0.037	1.110	0.267
	OCEAN15	-0.088	0.051	-1.703	0.088
	OCEAN16	0.060	0.044	1.358	0.174
	OCEAN17	-0.037	0.032	-1.157	0.247
	OCEAN18	0.182	0.059	3.078	0.002
	OCEAN19	0.763	0.034	22.140	0.000
	OCEAN20	0.079	0.042	1.896	0.058
F3 BY					
	OCEAN1	0.043	0.032	1.362	0.173
	OCEAN2	0.113	0.055	2.069	0.039
	OCEAN3	0.651	0.050	12.937	0.000
	OCEAN4	0.121	0.057	2.113	0.035
	OCEAN5	-0.121	0.056	-2.173	0.030
	OCEAN6	0.826	0.038	21.521	0.000
	OCEAN7	0.025	0.030	0.825	0.410
	OCEAN8	0.060	0.055	1.094	0.274
	OCEAN9	-0.012	0.022	-0.553	0.580
	OCEAN10	0.011	0.041	0.269	0.788
	OCEAN11	0.763	0.041	18.744	0.000
	OCEAN12	-0.048	0.039	-1.248	0.212
	OCEAN13	0.028	0.029	0.953	0.341
	OCEAN14	-0.076	0.046	-1.642	0.101
	OCEAN15	0.070	0.056	1.257	0.209
	OCEAN16	0.033	0.040	0.840	0.401
	OCEAN17	0.826	0.036	22.643	0.000
	OCEAN18	0.198	0.060	3.287	0.001
	OCEAN19	-0.018	0.033	-0.537	0.591
	OCEAN20	-0.056	0.040	-1.401	0.161
F4 BY					
	OCEAN1	-0.076	0.037	-2.072	0.038
	OCEAN2	-0.033	0.034	-0.966	0.334
	OCEAN3	0.071	0.050	1.410	0.159
	OCEAN4	0.005	0.031	0.153	0.878
	OCEAN5	0.140	0.057	2.459	0.014
	OCEAN6	-0.034	0.034	-1.007	0.314
	OCEAN7	-0.004	0.017	-0.217	0.828
	OCEAN8	0.032	0.046	0.699	0.485
	OCEAN9	-0.007	0.034	-0.210	0.834
	OCEAN10	0.702	0.039	17.841	0.000

OCEAN11	0.051	0.042	1.236	0.216
OCEAN12	0.868	0.036	23.938	0.000
OCEAN13	-0.036	0.033	-1.107	0.268
OCEAN14	0.028	0.038	0.730	0.466
OCEAN15	0.068	0.049	1.365	0.172
OCEAN16	0.753	0.040	19.017	0.000
OCEAN17	-0.021	0.031	-0.671	0.502
OCEAN18	0.553	0.052	10.622	0.000
OCEAN19	0.136	0.050	2.730	0.006
OCEAN20	-0.090	0.046	-1.981	0.048
F5 BY				
OCEAN1	-0.018	0.024	-0.776	0.438
OCEAN2	-0.064	0.031	-2.033	0.042
OCEAN3	0.041	0.039	1.049	0.294
OCEAN4	-0.034	0.021	-1.627	0.104
OCEAN5	0.139	0.047	2.959	0.003
OCEAN6	-0.048	0.035	-1.396	0.163
OCEAN7	-0.028	0.026	-1.076	0.282
OCEAN8	0.623	0.043	14.613	0.000
OCEAN9	0.068	0.035	1.922	0.055
OCEAN10	-0.003	0.039	-0.075	0.940
OCEAN11	0.023	0.033	0.704	0.481
OCEAN12	-0.008	0.029	-0.274	0.784
OCEAN13	0.832	0.028	30.006	0.000
OCEAN14	0.217	0.049	4.454	0.000
OCEAN15	0.626	0.042	14.848	0.000
OCEAN16	0.012	0.035	0.349	0.727
OCEAN17	0.035	0.031	1.101	0.271
OCEAN18	-0.024	0.039	-0.633	0.527
OCEAN19	0.006	0.029	0.216	0.829
OCEAN20	0.813	0.030	27.532	0.000
F2 WITH				
F1	0.219	0.059	3.699	0.000
F3 WITH				
F1	0.451	0.055	8.205	0.000
F2	0.027	0.059	0.458	0.647
F4 WITH				
F1	0.072	0.062	1.167	0.243
F2	0.338	0.056	6.014	0.000
F3	0.216	0.059	3.644	0.000
F5 WITH				
F1	0.102	0.061	1.683	0.092
F2	0.043	0.061	0.695	0.487
F3	0.060	0.060	1.004	0.315
F4	-0.006	0.063	-0.094	0.925
Intercepts				
OCEAN1	2.017	0.101	20.023	0.000
OCEAN2	3.897	0.170	22.987	0.000
OCEAN3	4.929	0.210	23.506	0.000
OCEAN4	4.306	0.185	23.233	0.000
OCEAN5	2.082	0.103	20.230	0.000
OCEAN6	5.638	0.238	23.719	0.000
OCEAN7	2.281	0.110	20.785	0.000

OCEAN8	2.236	0.108	20.668	0.000
OCEAN9	3.886	0.169	22.980	0.000
OCEAN10	2.389	0.114	21.044	0.000
OCEAN11	4.822	0.206	23.466	0.000
OCEAN12	2.334	0.112	20.914	0.000
OCEAN13	2.062	0.102	20.168	0.000
OCEAN14	3.188	0.143	22.353	0.000
OCEAN15	2.312	0.111	20.861	0.000
OCEAN16	2.407	0.114	21.085	0.000
OCEAN17	5.471	0.231	23.676	0.000
OCEAN18	2.474	0.117	21.229	0.000
OCEAN19	2.143	0.105	20.411	0.000
OCEAN20	1.607	0.088	18.355	0.000

Variances

F1	1.000	0.000	999.000	999.000
F2	1.000	0.000	999.000	999.000
F3	1.000	0.000	999.000	999.000
F4	1.000	0.000	999.000	999.000
F5	1.000	0.000	999.000	999.000

Residual Variances

OCEAN1	0.193	0.031	6.139	0.000
OCEAN2	0.282	0.036	7.917	0.000
OCEAN3	0.481	0.048	10.033	0.000
OCEAN4	0.253	0.035	7.216	0.000
OCEAN5	0.488	0.045	10.875	0.000
OCEAN6	0.323	0.045	7.158	0.000
OCEAN7	0.205	0.030	6.877	0.000
OCEAN8	0.603	0.053	11.484	0.000
OCEAN9	0.283	0.039	7.324	0.000
OCEAN10	0.482	0.049	9.803	0.000
OCEAN11	0.404	0.046	8.685	0.000
OCEAN12	0.297	0.050	5.972	0.000
OCEAN13	0.300	0.045	6.635	0.000
OCEAN14	0.430	0.045	9.570	0.000
OCEAN15	0.570	0.052	10.988	0.000
OCEAN16	0.394	0.048	8.184	0.000
OCEAN17	0.297	0.043	6.893	0.000
OCEAN18	0.525	0.048	10.881	0.000
OCEAN19	0.319	0.036	8.789	0.000
OCEAN20	0.328	0.046	7.135	0.000

STD Standardization

	Estimate	S.E.	Est./S.E.	Two-Tailed P-Value
F1 BY				
OCEAN1	-0.024	0.053	-0.452	0.652
OCEAN2	1.057	0.076	13.933	0.000
OCEAN3	0.071	0.061	1.166	0.243
OCEAN4	1.037	0.073	14.210	0.000
OCEAN5	-0.008	0.066	-0.127	0.899
OCEAN6	0.009	0.040	0.231	0.817
OCEAN7	0.108	0.071	1.528	0.127
OCEAN8	-0.019	0.093	-0.199	0.842

OCEAN9	1.143	0.068	16.726	0.000
OCEAN10	0.149	0.098	1.521	0.128
OCEAN11	-0.014	0.047	-0.288	0.774
OCEAN12	0.105	0.055	1.896	0.058
OCEAN13	0.027	0.063	0.432	0.666
OCEAN14	1.123	0.090	12.457	0.000
OCEAN15	0.174	0.111	1.571	0.116
OCEAN16	-0.143	0.085	-1.683	0.092
OCEAN17	0.031	0.041	0.751	0.453
OCEAN18	-0.142	0.087	-1.638	0.101
OCEAN19	0.057	0.071	0.795	0.427
OCEAN20	-0.093	0.074	-1.261	0.207

F2 BY

OCEAN1	1.648	0.089	18.456	0.000
OCEAN2	0.092	0.050	1.833	0.067
OCEAN3	0.125	0.060	2.072	0.038
OCEAN4	-0.063	0.043	-1.466	0.143
OCEAN5	1.062	0.095	11.212	0.000
OCEAN6	0.031	0.030	1.031	0.302
OCEAN7	1.603	0.087	18.419	0.000
OCEAN8	0.026	0.079	0.334	0.739
OCEAN9	-0.016	0.039	-0.405	0.686
OCEAN10	0.023	0.054	0.420	0.674
OCEAN11	-0.082	0.051	-1.599	0.110
OCEAN12	-0.149	0.085	-1.762	0.078
OCEAN13	-0.065	0.062	-1.058	0.290
OCEAN14	0.065	0.059	1.109	0.267
OCEAN15	-0.166	0.098	-1.699	0.089
OCEAN16	0.108	0.079	1.356	0.175
OCEAN17	-0.039	0.034	-1.156	0.248
OCEAN18	0.320	0.105	3.044	0.002
OCEAN19	1.403	0.097	14.540	0.000
OCEAN20	0.149	0.079	1.895	0.058

F3 BY

OCEAN1	0.077	0.056	1.361	0.173
OCEAN2	0.153	0.074	2.062	0.039
OCEAN3	0.757	0.072	10.445	0.000
OCEAN4	0.154	0.073	2.105	0.035
OCEAN5	-0.202	0.093	-2.166	0.030
OCEAN6	0.866	0.060	14.330	0.000
OCEAN7	0.045	0.055	0.824	0.410
OCEAN8	0.114	0.104	1.092	0.275
OCEAN9	-0.016	0.029	-0.553	0.580
OCEAN10	0.020	0.075	0.269	0.788
OCEAN11	0.906	0.069	13.099	0.000
OCEAN12	-0.091	0.073	-1.247	0.212
OCEAN13	0.054	0.057	0.952	0.341
OCEAN14	-0.119	0.072	-1.641	0.101
OCEAN15	0.134	0.107	1.255	0.210
OCEAN16	0.061	0.072	0.840	0.401
OCEAN17	0.877	0.059	14.779	0.000
OCEAN18	0.348	0.107	3.249	0.001
OCEAN19	-0.032	0.060	-0.537	0.591
OCEAN20	-0.105	0.075	-1.400	0.161

F4 BY					
	OCEAN1	-0.136	0.066	-2.071	0.038
	OCEAN2	-0.044	0.046	-0.966	0.334
	OCEAN3	0.082	0.059	1.407	0.159
	OCEAN4	0.006	0.039	0.153	0.878
	OCEAN5	0.234	0.096	2.445	0.014
	OCEAN6	-0.036	0.036	-1.007	0.314
	OCEAN7	-0.007	0.032	-0.217	0.828
	OCEAN8	0.062	0.088	0.699	0.485
	OCEAN9	-0.010	0.046	-0.210	0.834
	OCEAN10	1.280	0.102	12.501	0.000
	OCEAN11	0.061	0.049	1.235	0.217
	OCEAN12	1.635	0.108	15.136	0.000
	OCEAN13	-0.069	0.063	-1.105	0.269
	OCEAN14	0.043	0.059	0.730	0.466
	OCEAN15	0.128	0.094	1.363	0.173
	OCEAN16	1.362	0.103	13.188	0.000
	OCEAN17	-0.022	0.033	-0.671	0.502
	OCEAN18	0.973	0.107	9.068	0.000
	OCEAN19	0.250	0.092	2.718	0.007
	OCEAN20	-0.170	0.086	-1.975	0.048
F5 BY					
	OCEAN1	-0.033	0.042	-0.776	0.438
	OCEAN2	-0.086	0.043	-2.028	0.043
	OCEAN3	0.048	0.046	1.048	0.295
	OCEAN4	-0.044	0.027	-1.623	0.105
	OCEAN5	0.233	0.079	2.938	0.003
	OCEAN6	-0.051	0.036	-1.397	0.163
	OCEAN7	-0.051	0.048	-1.075	0.282
	OCEAN8	1.183	0.108	10.939	0.000
	OCEAN9	0.092	0.048	1.924	0.054
	OCEAN10	-0.005	0.071	-0.075	0.940
	OCEAN11	0.027	0.039	0.704	0.482
	OCEAN12	-0.015	0.055	-0.274	0.784
	OCEAN13	1.604	0.099	16.277	0.000
	OCEAN14	0.339	0.077	4.388	0.000
	OCEAN15	1.187	0.106	11.149	0.000
	OCEAN16	0.022	0.063	0.349	0.727
	OCEAN17	0.037	0.033	1.100	0.271
	OCEAN18	-0.043	0.068	-0.633	0.527
	OCEAN19	0.011	0.053	0.216	0.829
	OCEAN20	1.525	0.097	15.747	0.000
F2 WITH					
	F1	0.219	0.059	3.699	0.000
F3 WITH					
	F1	0.451	0.055	8.205	0.000
	F2	0.027	0.059	0.458	0.647
F4 WITH					
	F1	0.072	0.062	1.167	0.243
	F2	0.338	0.056	6.014	0.000
	F3	0.216	0.059	3.644	0.000

```
F5      WITH
   F1              0.102     0.061      1.683      0.092
   F2              0.043     0.061      0.695      0.487
   F3              0.060     0.060      1.004      0.315
   F4             -0.006     0.063     -0.094      0.925
Intercepts
   OCEAN1          3.599     0.103     34.876      0.000
   OCEAN2          5.271     0.078     67.381      0.000
   OCEAN3          5.726     0.067     85.227      0.000
   OCEAN4          5.482     0.074     74.450      0.000
   OCEAN5          3.475     0.097     36.009      0.000
   OCEAN6          5.910     0.061     97.483      0.000
   OCEAN7          4.167     0.106     39.449      0.000
   OCEAN8          4.251     0.110     38.672      0.000
   OCEAN9          5.258     0.078     67.203      0.000
   OCEAN10         4.358     0.105     41.314      0.000
   OCEAN11         5.726     0.069     83.387      0.000
   OCEAN12         4.398     0.109     40.359      0.000
   OCEAN13         3.973     0.111     35.661      0.000
   OCEAN14         4.973     0.090     55.120      0.000
   OCEAN15         4.388     0.110     39.979      0.000
   OCEAN16         4.355     0.105     41.624      0.000
   OCEAN17         5.806     0.061     94.601      0.000
   OCEAN18         4.348     0.102     42.771      0.000
   OCEAN19         3.943     0.106     37.061      0.000
   OCEAN20         3.013     0.108     27.780      0.000
Variances
   F1              1.000     0.000    999.000    999.000
   F2              1.000     0.000    999.000    999.000
   F3              1.000     0.000    999.000    999.000
   F4              1.000     0.000    999.000    999.000
   F5              1.000     0.000    999.000    999.000
Residual Variances
   OCEAN1          0.615     0.092      6.677      0.000
   OCEAN2          0.515     0.059      8.759      0.000
   OCEAN3          0.649     0.064     10.165      0.000
   OCEAN4          0.410     0.052      7.931      0.000
   OCEAN5          1.358     0.124     10.983      0.000
   OCEAN6          0.355     0.047      7.636      0.000
   OCEAN7          0.683     0.090      7.625      0.000
   OCEAN8          2.179     0.206     10.562      0.000
   OCEAN9          0.518     0.065      7.970      0.000
   OCEAN10         1.603     0.162      9.919      0.000
   OCEAN11         0.569     0.062      9.141      0.000
   OCEAN12         1.055     0.168      6.284      0.000
   OCEAN13         1.114     0.158      7.064      0.000
   OCEAN14         1.046     0.105     10.010      0.000
   OCEAN15         2.054     0.197     10.414      0.000
   OCEAN16         1.288     0.150      8.604      0.000
   OCEAN17         0.335     0.045      7.385      0.000
   OCEAN18         1.621     0.152     10.675      0.000
```

OCEAN19	1.081	0.111	9.746	0.000
OCEAN20	1.155	0.152	7.594	0.000

R-SQUARE

Observed Variable	Estimate	S.E.	Est./S.E.	Two-Tailed P-Value
OCEAN1	0.807	0.031	25.631	0.000
OCEAN2	0.718	0.036	20.188	0.000
OCEAN3	0.519	0.048	10.834	0.000
OCEAN4	0.747	0.035	21.318	0.000
OCEAN5	0.512	0.045	11.423	0.000
OCEAN6	0.677	0.045	14.993	0.000
OCEAN7	0.795	0.030	26.711	0.000
OCEAN8	0.397	0.053	7.552	0.000
OCEAN9	0.717	0.039	18.541	0.000
OCEAN10	0.518	0.049	10.537	0.000
OCEAN11	0.596	0.046	12.837	0.000
OCEAN12	0.703	0.050	14.135	0.000
OCEAN13	0.700	0.045	15.472	0.000
OCEAN14	0.570	0.045	12.696	0.000
OCEAN15	0.430	0.052	8.282	0.000
OCEAN16	0.606	0.048	12.602	0.000
OCEAN17	0.703	0.043	16.296	0.000
OCEAN18	0.475	0.048	9.858	0.000
OCEAN19	0.681	0.036	18.727	0.000
OCEAN20	0.672	0.046	14.606	0.000

QUALITY OF NUMERICAL RESULTS

Condition Number for the Information Matrix   0.532E-02
(ratio of smallest to largest eigenvalue)

MODEL MODIFICATION INDICES

Minimum M.I. value for printing the modification index   10.000

	M.I.	E.P.C.	Std E.P.C.	StdYX E.P.C.

ON Statements

		M.I.	E.P.C.	Std E.P.C.	StdYX E.P.C.
OCEAN1	ON OCEAN19	17.942	-0.410	-0.410	-0.423
OCEAN2	ON OCEAN4	13.251	0.486	0.486	0.458
OCEAN3	ON OCEAN6	12.721	0.417	0.417	0.376
OCEAN3	ON OCEAN17	16.562	-0.506	-0.506	-0.462
OCEAN3	ON OCEAN18	25.387	0.212	0.212	0.320
OCEAN4	ON OCEAN2	13.248	0.387	0.387	0.411
OCEAN4	ON OCEAN6	15.974	0.361	0.361	0.297
OCEAN5	ON OCEAN7	11.846	-0.413	-0.413	-0.452
OCEAN6	ON OCEAN3	12.723	0.228	0.228	0.253
OCEAN6	ON OCEAN4	15.979	0.312	0.312	0.379
OCEAN7	ON OCEAN5	11.846	-0.208	-0.208	-0.190
OCEAN8	ON OCEAN15	30.069	0.385	0.385	0.385

```
OCEAN9   ON   OCEAN14    12.656    0.224     0.224     0.258
OCEAN11  ON   OCEAN17    24.501    0.716     0.716     0.640
OCEAN13  ON   OCEAN20    19.633    0.820     0.820     0.798
OCEAN14  ON   OCEAN9     12.656    0.451     0.451     0.391
OCEAN15  ON   OCEAN8     30.068    0.363     0.363     0.363
OCEAN17  ON   OCEAN3     16.559   -0.261    -0.261    -0.286
OCEAN17  ON   OCEAN11    24.499    0.421     0.421     0.471
OCEAN18  ON   OCEAN3     25.386    0.528     0.528     0.349
OCEAN18  ON   OCEAN19    10.022    0.265     0.265     0.277
OCEAN19  ON   OCEAN1     17.943   -0.720    -0.720    -0.699
OCEAN19  ON   OCEAN18    10.021    0.176     0.176     0.169
OCEAN20  ON   OCEAN13    19.633    0.850     0.850     0.873

WITH Statements

OCEAN4   WITH OCEAN2     13.249    0.199     0.199     0.434
OCEAN6   WITH OCEAN3     12.723    0.148     0.148     0.308
OCEAN6   WITH OCEAN4     15.977    0.128     0.128     0.336
OCEAN7   WITH OCEAN5     11.846   -0.282    -0.282    -0.293
OCEAN14  WITH OCEAN9     12.657    0.234     0.234     0.318
OCEAN15  WITH OCEAN8     30.070    0.791     0.791     0.374
OCEAN17  WITH OCEAN3     16.560   -0.169    -0.169    -0.364
OCEAN17  WITH OCEAN11    24.499    0.240     0.240     0.549
OCEAN18  WITH OCEAN3     25.386    0.343     0.343     0.334
OCEAN19  WITH OCEAN1     17.942   -0.443    -0.443    -0.543
OCEAN19  WITH OCEAN18    10.021    0.286     0.286     0.216
OCEAN20  WITH OCEAN13    19.633    0.947     0.947     0.835
```

Sample Results Section

We conclude this example of confirmatory factor analysis with the presentation of a sample results section. A useful guide to reporting the results of structural equation modeling was provided by Raykov, Tomer, and Nesselroade (1991). They suggested that all reports of structural equation modeling analyses include, as a minimum set of reporting standards:

1. a graphic presentation of the structural equation model using conventional symbols (see, e.g., Bentler, 1990; Jöreskog & Sörbom, 1992);

2. parameters for the structural equation run, including the type of matrix analyzed, the treatment of missing values and outliers, the number of groups to be analyzed (if appropriate), and the method of parameter estimation;

3. an assessment of model fit, such as Condition 10 tests (James, Mulaik, & Brett, 1982) (as previously noted, researchers are well advised to report multiple fit indices and should report indices that reflect different conceptions of model fit);

4. an examination of the obtained solution, including the Condition 9 tests (James et al., 1982) referred to earlier, the coefficient of determination, the R^2 values

associated with each equation in the model, and examination of direct and indirect effects (when appropriate);

5. nested model comparisons; and

6. model modifications and alternate models—when the model is modified on the basis of empirical results, a minimum standard of reporting would include the change in overall fit associated with modification as well as the change in specific parameters as a result of model modification (as noted earlier, such modifications should be treated as exploratory until cross-validated on an independent sample).

RESULTS

All model tests were based on the covariance matrix and used ML estimation as implemented in Mplus 7.2 (Muthén & Muthén, 1998-2013).

Fit indices for the initial three models are presented in Table 5.1 (page 70). As shown, the indices converge, suggesting the superiority of the model hypothesizing five oblique factors. In particular, the five-factor model provides a better fit to the data than does a model hypothesizing five orthogonal factors, $\chi^2_{difference}(10) = 145.66$, $p < .01$, or one factor, $\chi^2_{difference}(10) = 1,987.57$, $p < .01$.

Standardized parameter estimates for the model are presented in Table 5.2. As shown, model parameters were all significant ($p < .01$) and explained substantial amounts of item variance ($R^2 = .37$ to .74). Table 5.3 presents the disattenuated correlations between the factors.

EXPLORATORY ANALYSIS

Although the five-factor model provided the best fit to the data of the models considered, it did not provide an absolute good fit to the data. Therefore, an exploratory structural equation model was also estimated in which the items were allowed to load across the five factors. This resulted in a better fitting model, $\chi^2_{difference}(60) = 179.99$, $p < .001$, that provided an absolutely good fit to the data, $\chi^2(100) = 230.77$, $p < .001$, CFI = .96, TLI = .92, RMSEA = .07, SRMR = .02. All items loaded significantly ($p < 01$) and substantially on their hypothesized factors, although some items also cross-loaded on the other factors (see Table 5.4). Table 5.5 presents the disattenuated correlations between the factors.

Table 5.2 Standardized Parameter Estimates for the Five-Factor Model

Item	Openness	Conscientiousness	Extraversion	Agreeableness	Neuroticism	h^2
1			.88			.77
2		.85				.72
3				.69		.48
4		.86				.74
5			.67			.46
6				.81		.66
7			.90			.81
8	.63					.40
9		.83				.69
10					.72	.52
11				.77		.60
12					.81	.65
13	.84					.70
14		.70				.50
15	.64					.41
16					.78	.61
17				.84		.71
18					.66	.44
19			.82			.67
20	.79					.63

Note: For all values, $p < .001$.

Table 5.3 Interfactor Correlations

	1	2	3	4	5
Openness	1.00				
Conscientiousness	.13*	1.00			
Extraversion	.03	.25**	1.00		
Agreeableness	.09	.53**	.06	1.00	
Neuroticism	−.04	.10	.39**	.26**	1.00

*$p < .05$. **$p < .01$.

Table 5.4 Standardized Parameter Estimates for the Five-Factor Model From the Exploratory Structural Equation Model

Item	Conscientiousness	Extraversion	Agreeableness	Neuroticism	Openness	h^2
1	−.01	**.92****	.04	−.08*	−.02	.81**
2	**.78****	.07	.11*	−.03	−.06	.72**
3	.06	.11*	**.65****	.07	.04	.52**
4	**.81****	−.05	.12*	.01	−.03	.75**
5	−.01	**.64****	−.12*	.14**	.14**	.51**
6	.01	.03	**.83****	−.03	−.05	.68**
7	.06	**.88****	.03	.00	−.03	.80**
8	−.01	.01	.06	.03	**.62****	.40**
9	**.85****	−.01	−.01	−.01	.07	.72**
10	.08	.01	.01	**.70****	−.00	.52**
11	−.01	−.07	**.76****	.05	.02	.60**
12	.06	−.08	−.05	**.87****	−.01	.70**
13	.01	−.03	.03	−.04	**.83****	.70**
14	**.72****	.04	−.08	.03	.22**	.57**

Item	Conscientiousness	Extraversion	Agreeableness	Neuroticism	Openness	h^2
15	.09	−.09	.07	.07	**.63****	.43**
16	−.08	.06	.03	**.75****	.01	.61**
17	.03	−.04	**.83****	−.02	.04	.70**
18	−.08	.18**	.20**	**.55****	−.02	.48**
19	.03	**.76****	−.02	.14**	.01	.68**
20	−.05	.08	−.06	−.09	**.82**	.67**

Note: Hypothesized factor loadings are in boldface type.
*p < .05. **p < .01.

Table 5.5 Interfactor Correlations

	1	2	3	4	5
Conscientiousness	1.00				
Extraversion	.22**	1.00			
Agreeableness	.45**	.03	1.00		
Neuroticism	.07	.34**	.22**	1.00	
Openness	.10	.04	.06	.01	1.00

**p < .01.

6

Observed Variable Path Analysis

Path analysis with observed variables is the "oldest" variety of structural equation modeling. In contrast to the assessment of a measurement model as presented in the previous chapter, the goal of path analysis is to test a "structural" model, that is, a model comprising theoretically based statements of relationships among constructs. For an example of path analysis, I will test a model of how leadership in organizations can affect the occurrence of aggression. The data are drawn from a random survey of 588 employees. After reviewing the development and analysis of the model, we will then use these data to illustrate (a) the process of testing indirect or mediated relationships and (b) testing equality constraints using Mplus and (c) the use of Mplus to conduct multisample analysis.

Model Specification

The models I tested are depicted in Figure 6.1. In the study, I measured both transformational leadership (Bass & Avolio, 1994) and abusive supervision (Tepper, 2007). I thought that employees who experienced positive leadership (e.g., rated their leaders highly on transformational leadership and low on abusive supervision) would also express enhanced affective commitment to the organization (Allen & Meyer, 1990). Reasoning that employees who are affectively committed to the organization may be more motivated to comply with organizational policies and that most organizations had policies against employees behaving aggressively, I hypothesized that affective commitment would result in less enacted aggression on the part of employees.

As an alternative to this model, I will test a second model that adds a path from abusive supervision directly to enacted aggression (i.e., the dashed line in Figure 6.1). Substantively, this path recognizes that supervisors might model

Figure 6.1

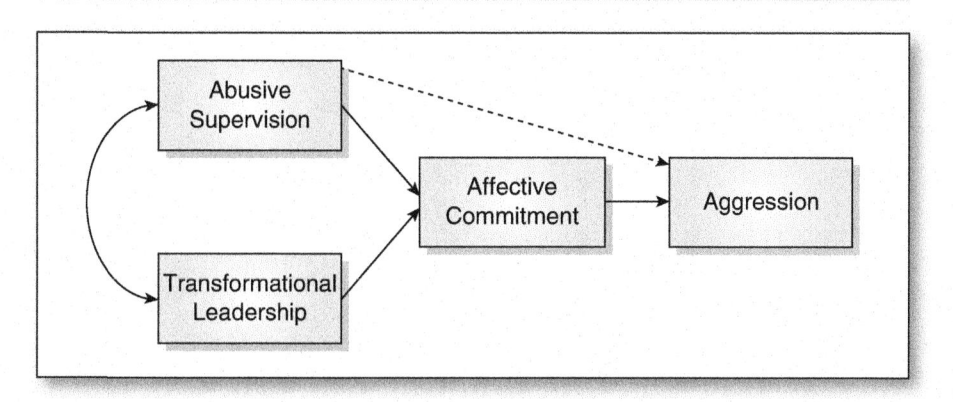

[Figure showing path diagram: Abusive Supervision and Transformational Leaderships (correlated exogenous variables) both have arrows to Affective Commitment, which has an arrow to Aggression. A dashed arrow also goes from Abusive Supervision to Aggression.]

(Bandura, 1977) aggressive behavior for employees and that employees may engage in aggressive acts as a form of retaliation against supervisors.

The model, therefore, contains two exogenous variables (abusive supervision and transformational leadership) that are allowed to correlate freely. There are two endogenous variables (i.e., affective commitment and enacted aggression). Because this is an observed variable path analysis, we are treating the scale scores as the variables and, essentially, conducting a series of regression equations. The measurement model is ignored. Note that one of the assumptions of observed variable path analysis is that all variables are measured without error. Although this assumption is untenable in the social sciences, it typically is satisfied by the requirement that all variables manifest high levels of reliability (often defined as α values > .70; Pedhazur, 1982). This assumption was met in the current example, with all α values exceeding .80.

FROM PICTURES TO MPLUS

The Mplus code that tests the proposed model is presented below. As can be seen, there is a regression equation (i.e., using the keyword ON), corresponding to the arrows depicted in Figure 6.1. Note also that the data file contains some additional variables (i.e., ID, Gender, GHQ) that are not used in the model. The USEVARIABLES statement is used to select only the variables contained in the model; failure to do this would result in misleading and inaccurate results.

```
TITLE:     Example of observed variable path analysis
DATA:      FILE IS apws.dat;
VARIABLE:  NAMES ARE ID Gender TFL Abuse GHQ Affcom Enagg;
           USEVARIABLES ARE TFL Abuse Affcom Enagg;
```

```
MODEL:      Enagg ON Affcom;
            Affcom ON Abuse TFL;
OUTPUT:     STANDARDIZED MODINDICES (ALL);
```

ALTERNATIVE MODELS

The code for the alternative model is presented below. As shown, the only substantive change to the code is to add abuse as a predictor of enacted aggression.

```
TITLE:      Example of observed variable path analysis
DATA:       FILE IS apws.dat;
VARIABLE:   NAMES ARE ID Gender TFL Abuse GHQ Affcom Enagg;
            USEVARIABLES ARE TFL Abuse Affcom Enagg;
MODEL:      Enagg ON Affcom Abuse;
            Affcom ON Abuse TFL;
OUTPUT:     STANDARDIZED MODINDICES (ALL);
```

Although in this case I had an a priori rationale for the additional path, in general, alternative models can be generated by considering (a) omitted parameters and (b) indirect effects in structural equation models. I have previously noted (Kelloway, 1996) that most researchers build models from the "bottom up," offering a theoretical or empirical rationale for the inclusion of certain parameters in their models. In contrast to this procedure, I also have suggested (Kelloway, 1995) that there is some advantage in developing models from the top down, that is, providing justification for the omission of parameters from the model. The rationale for this suggestion is that tests of model fit are, in essence, tests of omitted parameters. That is, because the just-identified or saturated model always provides a perfect fit to the data, testing an overidentified model for fit is, in essence, testing whether the overidentifying restrictions (e.g., omitted paths) are necessary. Thus, although researchers should continue to justify the inclusion of specific parameters in their models, I suggest that there is considerable merit in paying equal attention to the parameters omitted from the model. When researchers have no particular justification for the inclusion or omission of a particular parameter, an opportunity is created to formulate and test competing models.

In particular, researchers need to consider the implications of indirect relationships posited in their models. The indirect relationship of X on Z (through Y) can be diagrammed as $X \rightarrow Y \rightarrow Z$. There are at least two interpretations of such relationships. First, Y may be viewed as a mediator of the $X \rightarrow Z$ relationship such that the effects of X on Z are completely mediated by Y. The rationale and sequence for mediator tests as presented by Baron and Kenny (1986) require that X and Z be significantly related. In many applications of structural models containing indirect relationships, however, there is no significant relationship between X and Z, and the indirect relationship may be more appropriately thought of as simply an indirect relationship

(Williams, Vandenberg, & Edwards, 2009). Considering the interpretation of indirect relationships a priori would assist in the identification of alternative models for analyses (Kelloway, 1995) and assist researchers in formulating more precise hypotheses in their models.

For each mediated or indirect relationship in a model, there are two plausible rival specifications: a partially mediated model and a nonmediated model. First, the mediated model suggests that abusive and transformational leadership causes affective commitment, which in turn causes enacted aggression. Second, the partially mediated model suggests that abusive leadership causes both affective commitment and enacted aggression directly. In the partially mediated model, affective commitment is also hypothesized as a cause of enacted aggression. Finally, the nonmediated model suggests that abusive supervision causes both commitment and enacted aggression but that there is no direct relationship between affective commitment and enacted aggression. In terms of the nesting sequence for these three models, both the fully mediated and nonmediated models are nested within the partially mediated model.

Identification

Bollen (1989) cited four rules for the identification of structural models: the t rule (see Chapter 5), the null B rule, the recursive rule, and rank-and-order conditions.[1] The null B rule states that a model is identified if there are no predictive relationships between the endogenous variables. The null B rule is a sufficient condition for model identification, and its most common example is the estimation of a multiple regression equation. Note that the null B rule is a sufficient but not necessary condition for the identification of a structural model.

The recursive rule states that recursive models, incorporating only one-way causal flow, are identified. Again, recursion is a sufficient but not necessary condition for identification. Although we will not deal with nonrecursive models, it is possible to estimate identified models allowing for bidirectional causality. Given our focus on recursive models, the models described earlier are, by definition, identified.

Estimation

FIT AND MODEL MODIFICATION

Running the first set of code presented above resulted in the following output:

```
Mplus VERSION 7 (Mac)
MUTHEN & MUTHEN
```

98 USING MPLUS FOR STRUCTURAL EQUATION MODELING

```
INPUT INSTRUCTIONS

TITLE:      Example of observed variable path analysis
DATA:       FILE IS apws.dat;
VARIABLE:   NAMES ARE ID Gender TFL Abuse GHQ Affcom Enagg;
            USEVARIABLES ARE TFL Abuse Affcom Enagg;
MODEL:      Enagg ON Affcom;
            Affcom ON Abuse TFL;
OUTPUT:     STANDARDIZED MODINDICES (AL);
```

Note: Mplus repeats the command file.

```
INPUT READING TERMINATED NORMALLY

Example of observed variable path analysis

SUMMARY OF ANALYSIS

Number of groups                                           1
Number of observations                                   588
Number of dependent variables                              2
Number of independent variables                            2
Number of continuous latent variables                      0

Observed dependent variables
  Continuous
    AFFCOM      ENAGG

Observed independent variables
    TFL         ABUSE
```

Note: The program read two endogenous or dependent (Affcom and Enagg) and two exogenous or independent (TFL and Abuse) variables from a file containing 588 cases.

```
Estimator                                                 ML
Information matrix                                  OBSERVED
Maximum number of iterations                            1000
Convergence criterion                              0.500D-04
Maximum number of steepest descent iterations             20

Input data file(s)
  apws.dat

Input data format FREE

THE MODEL ESTIMATION TERMINATED NORMALLY

MODEL FIT INFORMATION
```

```
Number of Free Parameters                                         7

Loglikelihood
        H0 Value                                          -838.628
        H1 Value                                          -812.061

Information Criteria
        Akaike (AIC)                                      1691.256
        Bayesian (BIC)                                    1721.893
        Sample-Size Adjusted BIC                          1699.671
           (n* = (n + 2) / 24)

Chi-Square Test of Model Fit
        Value                                               53.135
        Degrees of Freedom                                       2
        P-Value                                             0.0000

RMSEA (Root Mean Square Error Of Approximation)
        Estimate                                             0.209
        90 Percent C.I.                              0.162   0.259
        Probability RMSEA <= .05                             0.000

CFI/TLI
        CFI                                                  0.840
        TLI                                                  0.599

Chi-Square Test of Model Fit for the Baseline Model
        Value                                              324.176
        Degrees of Freedom                                       5
        P-Value                                             0.0000

SRMR (Standardized Root Mean Square Residual)
        Value                                    0.077
```

Note: The model provides a poor fit to the data according to all of the fit indices.

```
MODEL RESULTS

                                                        Two-Tailed
                    Estimate       S.E.    Est./S.E.     P-Value

ENAGG  ON
    AFFCOM            -0.035      0.007       -5.374       0.000

AFFCOM ON
    ABUSE             -0.248      0.082       -3.033       0.002
    TFL                0.791      0.060       13.129       0.000

Intercepts
    AFFCOM             2.305      0.283        8.137       0.000
    ENAGG              1.298      0.031       41.868       0.000
```

```
Residual Variances
    AFFCOM         1.255      0.073     17.146     0.000
    ENAGG          0.047      0.003     17.146     0.000
```

Note: Although the model does not fit, all of the estimated parameters are significant (Enagg on Affcom, Affcom on Abuse, and Affcom on TFL).

```
STANDARDIZED MODEL RESULTS

STDYX Standardization

                                                    Two-Tailed
                   Estimate      S.E.    Est./S.E.   P-Value

ENAGG  ON
    AFFCOM         -0.216      0.039     -5.504     0.000

AFFCOM ON
    ABUSE          -0.118      0.039     -3.044     0.002
    TFL             0.512      0.035     14.596     0.000

Intercepts
    AFFCOM          1.674      0.225      7.423     0.000
    ENAGG           5.822      0.186     31.273     0.000

Residual Variances
    AFFCOM          0.662      0.032     20.844     0.000
    ENAGG           0.953      0.017     56.039     0.000

STDY Standardization

                                                    Two-Tailed
                   Estimate      S.E.    Est./S.E.   P-Value

ENAGG  ON
    AFFCOM         -0.216      0.039     -5.504     0.000

AFFCOM ON
    ABUSE          -0.180      0.059     -3.053     0.002
    TFL             0.574      0.038     15.073     0.000

Intercepts
    AFFCOM          1.674      0.225      7.423     0.000
    ENAGG           5.822      0.186     31.273     0.000

Residual Variances
    AFFCOM          0.662      0.032     20.844     0.000
    ENAGG           0.953      0.017     56.039     0.000

STD Standardization

                                                    Two-Tailed
                   Estimate      S.E.    Est./S.E.   P-Value

ENAGG  ON
    AFFCOM         -0.035      0.007     -5.374     0.000
```

```
AFFCOM ON
    ABUSE            -0.248       0.082       -3.033       0.002
    TFL               0.791       0.060       13.129       0.000

Intercepts
    AFFCOM            2.305       0.283        8.137       0.000
    ENAGG             1.298       0.031       41.868       0.000

Residual Variances
    AFFCOM            1.255       0.073       17.146       0.000
    ENAGG             0.047       0.003       17.146       0.000

R-SQUARE

          Observed                                       Two-Tailed
          Variable      Estimate      S.E.    Est./S.E.   P-Value

          AFFCOM         0.338       0.032      10.659      0.000
          ENAGG          0.047       0.017       2.752      0.006
```

QUALITY OF NUMERICAL RESULTS

Condition Number for the Information Matrix   0.506E-04
(ratio of smallest to largest eigenvalue)

MODEL MODIFICATION INDICES

Minimum M.I. value for printing the modification index   10.000

```
                       M.I.      E.P.C.    Std E.P.C.   StdYX E.P.C.
ON Statements

AFFCOM   ON ENAGG     23.688      1.776       1.776        0.287
ENAGG    ON TFL       13.277     -0.045      -0.045       -0.179
ENAGG    ON ABUSE     49.820      0.104       0.104        0.307

WITH Statements

ENAGG  WITH AFFCOM    23.688      0.084       0.084        0.345
ABUSE  WITH ENAGG     34.222      0.030       0.030        0.208
```

Note: The modification indices make several suggestions. Some of these have no a priori rationale (e.g., allowing a residual correlation between Enagg and Affcom). Others are more reasonable. In particular, the indices suggest the viability of predicting Enagg directly from abuse, which corresponds to our alternative model. The index suggests that this will result in a decrease of 49.82 in the χ^2 value.

102   USING MPLUS FOR STRUCTURAL EQUATION MODELING

Although all of the parameters comprising the model are significant, the model does not provide an overall fit to the data. Accordingly, I tested the alternative model, which hypothesizes that the effect of abusive supervision on enacted aggression is partially mediated by affective commitment. The output is shown below.

```
Mplus VERSION 7 (Mac)
MUTHEN & MUTHEN

INPUT INSTRUCTIONS

TITLE:     Example of observed variable path analysis
DATA:      FILE IS apws.dat;
VARIABLE:  NAMES ARE ID Gender TFL Abuse GHQ Affcom Enagg;
           USEVARIABLES ARE TFL Abuse Affcom Enagg;
MODEL:     Enagg ON Affcom Abuse;
           Affcom ON Abuse TFL;
OUTPUT:    STANDARDIZED MODINDICES (ALL);

INPUT READING TERMINATED NORMALLY
```

Note: Mplus repeats the command file.

```
Example of observed variable path analysis

SUMMARY OF ANALYSIS

Number of groups                                                 1
Number of observations                                         588
Number of dependent variables                                    2
Number of independent variables                                  2
Number of continuous latent variables                            0

Observed dependent variables
  Continuous
    AFFCOM      ENAGG

Observed independent variables
    TFL         ABUSE
```

Note: Two endogenous (Affcom and Enagg) and two exogenous (TFL and Abuse) variables were read from a file with 588 cases.

```
Estimator                                                       ML
Information matrix                                        OBSERVED
Maximum number of iterations                                  1000
Convergence criterion                                    0.500D-04
Maximum number of steepest descent iterations                   20
```

Input data file(s)
apws.dat

Input data format FREE

Note: Details of the estimation: the maximum likelihood estimator is the default.

THE MODEL ESTIMATION TERMINATED NORMALLY

MODEL FIT INFORMATION

Number of Free Parameters   8

Loglikelihood
        H0 Value   -812.599
        H1 Value   -812.061

Information Criteria
        Akaike (AIC)   1641.198
        Bayesian (BIC)   1676.212
        Sample-Size Adjusted BIC   1650.815
          (n* = (n + 2) / 24)

Chi-Square Test of Model Fit
        Value   1.077
        Degrees of Freedom   1
        P-Value   0.2994

RMSEA (Root Mean Square Error Of Approximation)
        Estimate   0.011
        90 Percent C.I.   0.000   0.111
        Probability RMSEA <= .05   0.582

CFI/TLI
        CFI   1.000
        TLI   0.999

Chi-Square Test of Model Fit for the Baseline Model
        Value   324.176
        Degrees of Freedom   5
        P-Value   0.0000

SRMR (Standardized Root Mean Square Residual)
        Value   0.008

Note: The revised model provides an excellent fit to the data. The χ^2 value is nonsignificant, the RMSEA is close to zero, and the test of close fit is nonsignificant. Both the confirmatory fit index (CFI) and the Tucker-Lewis index (TLI) exceed .95, and the SRMR is very close to zero.

```
MODEL RESULTS

                                                    Two-Tailed
                    Estimate       S.E.   Est./S.E.   P-Value

ENAGG ON
    AFFCOM          -0.016        0.007    -2.392     0.017
    ABUSE            0.104        0.014     7.377     0.000

AFFCOM ON
    ABUSE           -0.248        0.082    -3.033     0.002
    TFL              0.791        0.060    13.129     0.000

Intercepts
    AFFCOM           2.305        0.283     8.136     0.000
    ENAGG            1.059        0.044    24.158     0.000

Residual Variances
    AFFCOM           1.255        0.073    17.146     0.000
    ENAGG            0.043        0.003    17.146     0.000
```

Note: These are the unstandardized results. All model parameters are significant ($p < .05$).

```
STANDARDIZED MODEL RESULTS

STDYX Standardization

                                                    Two-Tailed
                    Estimate       S.E.   Est./S.E.   P-Value

ENAGG ON
    AFFCOM          -0.100        0.041    -2.402     0.016
    ABUSE            0.307        0.040     7.691     0.000

AFFCOM ON
    ABUSE           -0.118        0.039    -3.044     0.002
    TFL              0.512        0.035    14.597     0.000

Intercepts
    AFFCOM           1.674        0.225     7.422     0.000
    ENAGG            4.753        0.251    18.950     0.000
```

```
Residual Variances
    AFFCOM          0.662      0.032      20.844     0.000
    ENAGG           0.872      0.026      33.946     0.000
```

Note: These are the estimates I would report as the standardized solution.

```
STDY Standardization

                                                    Two-Tailed
                  Estimate     S.E.     Est./S.E.    P-Value

ENAGG    ON
    AFFCOM         -0.100      0.041     -2.402      0.016
    ABUSE           0.467      0.060      7.843      0.000

AFFCOM   ON
    ABUSE          -0.180      0.059     -3.053      0.002
    TFL             0.574      0.038     15.074      0.000

Intercepts
    AFFCOM          1.674      0.225      7.422      0.000
    ENAGG           4.753      0.251     18.950      0.000

Residual Variances
    AFFCOM          0.662      0.032     20.844      0.000
    ENAGG           0.872      0.026     33.946      0.000

STD Standardization

                                                    Two-Tailed
                  Estimate     S.E.     Est./S.E.    P-Value

ENAGG    ON
    AFFCOM         -0.016      0.007     -2.392      0.017
    ABUSE           0.104      0.014      7.377      0.000

AFFCOM   ON
    ABUSE          -0.248      0.082     -3.033      0.002
    TFL             0.791      0.060     13.129      0.000

Intercepts
    AFFCOM          2.305      0.283      8.136      0.000
    ENAGG           1.059      0.044     24.158      0.000

Residual Variances
    AFFCOM          1.255      0.073     17.146      0.000
    ENAGG           0.043      0.003     17.146      0.000
```

R-SQUARE

```
    Observed                                          Two-Tailed
    Variable      Estimate      S.E.    Est./S.E.      P-Value
    AFFCOM         0.338        0.032    10.659         0.000
    ENAGG          0.128        0.026     4.964         0.000
```

QUALITY OF NUMERICAL RESULTS

```
Condition Number for the Information Matrix     0.429E-04
(ratio of smallest to largest eigenvalue)
```

MODEL MODIFICATION INDICES

Minimum M.I. value for printing the modification index   10.000

```
                 M.I.       E.P.C.     Std E.P.C.     StdYX E.P.C.
```

No modification indices above the minimum value.

Note: As would be expected with a well-fitting model, there are no modifications that would result in an improvement to model fit.

Mediation

As previously discussed, the models tested above differ in their conceptualizations of how affective commitment mediates the relationship between abusive supervision and enacted aggression (i.e., I tested a fully mediated and a partially mediated model). The use of structural equation modeling techniques for testing mediated relationships is very common in the organizational (e.g., James, Mulaik, & Brett, 2006) and psychological (MacKinnon, Fairchild, & Fritz, 2007) research literatures. As the popularity of these techniques has grown, so has our understanding of how to test for mediated relationships.

For many years, the "gold standard" for testing mediation was the four-step process outlined by Baron and Kenny (1986). However, this approach became controversial for two reasons. First, not all researchers agreed with the first requirement: that there be a significant zero-order relationship between the predictor and the outcome (James et al., 2006). Indeed, following Sewall Wright's rules, a mediated effect is a compound path and is computed as the cross-product of the two simple paths constituting the effect. In the current example, it is possible to have quite substantial effects between abusive supervision and affective commitment and between commitment and enacted aggression. Even if both of these paths are .3 (for example), the indirect effect is .3 × .3 = .09, which may not be significant. Equally important, a study with sufficient statistical power to detect the simple effects may not be able to detect a compound or mediated effect. Second, reviewers have pointed to the fact that Baron and Kenny's approach to mediation tests the indirect effect by inference rather than by providing a specific test of the indirect effect.

Current approaches to testing mediation typically involve two strategies. First, researchers are encouraged to estimate the confidence interval around the indirect effect. By definition, confidence intervals that do not include zero indicate that there is a significant indirect effect. Because indirect effects are multiplicative, the appropriate confidence intervals may not be symmetric (i.e., having the same range above and below the estimate), and it is now common to estimate what Mplus calls the bias-corrected confidence intervals, which allow for different ranges above and below the estimate (MacKinnon et al., 2007). It is also now common to use a bootstrap method to obtain these confidence intervals. Bootstrapping involves repeated sampling from the observed data to generate the required sampling distributions (MacKinnon et al., 2007).

In Mplus, we can estimate the indirect effects with the use of the MODEL INDIRECT subcommand. MODEL INDIRECT appears in the MODEL command and takes one of two forms. In the first form, we specify the indirect effect we want to estimate, in our case the effect of abusive supervision on enacted aggression via the mediator affective commitment:

```
MODEL:     Enagg ON Affcom;
           Affcom ON Abuse;
           MODEL INDIRECT: Enagg VIA Affcom Abuse;
```

The second form is more useful when you have multiple mediators (for the example I have introduced, a second mediator called M); use of this form will generate a separate indirect effect for each possible compound path from the predictor (Abuse) to the outcome (Enagg):

```
MODEL:     Enagg ON Affcom M;
           Affcom M ON Abuse;
           MODEL INDIRECT: Enagg IND Abuse;
```

To specify bootstrapping of the estimates, we would add an ANALYSIS command to our code; in this case, I am requesting 5,000 bootstrapped samples:

```
ANALYSIS:   BOOTSTRAP = 5000;
```

To generate the bias-corrected confidence intervals and to bootstrap the estimates, we would add the relevant keywords to the OUTPUT command. Thus,

```
OUTPUT:     STANDARDIZED MODINDICES (ALL) CINTERVAL (BCBOOTSTRAP)
```

Putting the whole thing together, our revised code for the partially mediated model previously tested would be as follows:

```
TITLE:      Example of observed variable path analysis
DATA:       FILE IS apws.dat;
VARIABLE:   NAMES ARE ID Gender TFL Abuse GHQ Affcom Enagg;
            usevariables are tfl abuse affcom enagg;
ANALYSIS:   BOOTSTRAP = 5000;
MODEL:      Enagg ON Affcom Abuse;
            Affcom ON Abuse TFL;
OUTPUT:     STANDARDIZED MODINDICES (ALL) CINTERVAL (BCBOOTSTRAP);
```

Running this code results in the following output:

```
Mplus VERSION 7 (Mac)
MUTHEN & MUTHEN

INPUT INSTRUCTIONS

TITLE:      Example of observed variable path analysis
DATA:       FILE IS apws.dat;
VARIABLE:   NAMES ARE ID Gender TFL Abuse GHQ Affcom Enagg;
            USEVARIABLES ARE TFL Abuse Affcom Enagg;
ANALYSIS:   BOOTSTRAP = 5000;
MODEL:      Enagg ON Affcom Abuse;
            Affcom ON Abuse TFL;
            MODEL INDIRECT: Enagg IND Abuse;
OUTPUT:     STANDARDIZED MODINDICES (ALL) CINTERVAL (BCBOOTSTRAP);

*** WARNING in OUTPUT command
MODINDICES option is not available with BOOTSTRAP.
Request for MODINDICES is ignored.
1 WARNING(S) FOUND IN THE INPUT INSTRUCTIONS
```

Note: Mplus repeats the command file. Note that although a warning is generated because we asked for the modification indices, which are not available when bootstrapping, this does not cause an error (the analysis will still run correctly).

Example of observed variable path analysis

SUMMARY OF ANALYSIS

Number of groups	1
Number of observations	588
Number of dependent variables	2
Number of independent variables	2
Number of continuous latent variables	0

Observed dependent variables
  Continuous
    AFFCOM   ENAGG

Observed independent variables
    TFL   ABUSE

Estimator	ML
Information matrix	OBSERVED
Maximum number of iterations	1000
Convergence criterion	0.500D-04
Maximum number of steepest descent iterations	20
Number of bootstrap draws	
Requested	5000
Completed	5000

Input data file(s)
apws.dat

Input data format FREE

Note: The details of the data and the analysis are as previously specified.

THE MODEL ESTIMATION TERMINATED NORMALLY

MODEL FIT INFORMATION

MODEL FIT INFORMATION

Number of Free Parameters	8
Loglikelihood	
H0 Value	-812.599
H1 Value	-812.061
Information Criteria	
Akaike (AIC)	1641.198
Bayesian (BIC)	1676.212

```
                Sample-Size Adjusted BIC                        1650.815
                    (n* = (n + 2) / 24)

Chi-Square Test of Model Fit
                Value                                              1.077
                Degrees of Freedom                                     1
                P-Value                                           0.2994

RMSEA (Root Mean Square Error Of Approximation)
                Estimate                                           0.011
                90 Percent C.I.                            0.000   0.111
                Probability RMSEA <= .05                           0.582

CFI/TLI
                CFI                                                1.000
                TLI                                                0.999

Chi-Square Test of Model Fit for the Baseline Model
                Value                                            324.176
                Degrees of Freedom                                     5
                P-Value                                           0.0000

SRMR (Standardized Root Mean Square Residual)
                Value                                      0.008
```

Note: Because we have not changed the model, the fit indices are as previously estimated.

MODEL RESULTS

	Estimate	S.E.	Est./S.E.	Two-Tailed P-Value
ENAGG ON				
AFFCOM	-0.016	0.006	-2.629	0.009
ABUSE	0.104	0.022	4.719	0.000
AFFCOM ON				
ABUSE	-0.248	0.083	-2.975	0.003
TFL	0.791	0.068	11.595	0.000
Intercepts				
AFFCOM	2.305	0.321	7.190	0.000
ENAGG	1.059	0.048	21.871	0.000
Residual Variances				
AFFCOM	1.255	0.075	16.712	0.000
ENAGG	0.043	0.008	5.482	0.000

STANDARDIZED MODEL RESULTS

	StdYX Estimate	StdY Estimate	Std Estimate
ENAGG ON			
AFFCOM	-0.100	-0.100	-0.016
ABUSE	0.307	0.467	0.104
AFFCOM ON			
ABUSE	-0.118	-0.180	-0.248
TFL	0.512	0.574	0.791
Intercepts			
AFFCOM	1.674	1.674	2.305
ENAGG	4.753	4.753	1.059
Residual Variances			
AFFCOM	0.662	0.662	1.255
ENAGG	0.872	0.872	0.043

R-SQUARE

Observed Variable	Estimate
AFFCOM	0.338
ENAGG	0.128

TOTAL, TOTAL INDIRECT, SPECIFIC INDIRECT, AND DIRECT EFFECTS

	Estimate	S.E.	Est./S.E.	Two-Tailed P-Value
Effects from ABUSE to ENAGG				
Total	0.108	0.022	4.953	0.000
Total indirect	0.004	0.002	1.991	0.047
Specific indirect				
ENAGG				
AFFCOM				
ABUSE	0.004	0.002	1.991	0.047
Direct				
ENAGG				
ABUSE	0.104	0.022	4.719	0.000

STANDARDIZED TOTAL, TOTAL INDIRECT, SPECIFIC INDIRECT, AND DIRECT EFFECTS

STDYX Standardization

	Estimate	S.E.	Est./S.E.	Two-Tailed P-Value
Effects from ABUSE to ENAGG				
Total	0.319	0.058	5.507	0.000
Total indirect	0.012	0.006	2.058	0.040

112 USING MPLUS FOR STRUCTURAL EQUATION MODELING

```
Specific indirect
    ENAGG
    AFFCOM
    ABUSE              0.012      0.006      2.058      0.040

Direct
    ENAGG
    ABUSE              0.307      0.059      5.167      0.000
```

Note: This is part of the new information. Estimates of the total, direct, and indirect effects are provided. Although it is clear that the direct effect is greater than the indirect effect, it is also the case that both effects are significant (suggesting partial mediation). These are the unstandardized effects; the standardized effects follow.

```
STDY Standardization

                                                     Two-Tailed
                    Estimate      S.E.     Est./S.E.   P-Value

Effects from ABUSE to ENAGG
    Total            0.485       0.098      4.953      0.000
    Total indirect   0.018       0.009      1.991      0.047

    Specific indirect
        ENAGG
        AFFCOM
        ABUSE        0.018       0.009      1.991      0.047

    Direct
        ENAGG
        ABUSE        0.467       0.099      4.719      0.000

STD Standardization

                                                     Two-Tailed
                    Estimate      S.E.     Est./S.E.   P-Value

Effects from ABUSE to ENAGG
    Total            0.108       0.022      4.953      0.000
    Total indirect   0.004       0.002      1.991      0.047

    Specific indirect
        ENAGG
        AFFCOM
        ABUSE        0.004       0.002      1.991      0.047

    Direct
        ENAGG
        ABUSE        0.104       0.022      4.719      0.000
```

Chapter 6: Observed Variable Path Analysis

CONFIDENCE INTERVALS OF MODEL RESULTS

	Lower .5%	Lower 2.5%	Lower 5%	Estimate	Upper 5%	Upper 2.5%	Upper .5%
ENAGG ON							
AFFCOM	-0.034	-0.030	-0.027	-0.016	-0.007	-0.005	-0.002
ABUSE	0.054	0.063	0.069	0.104	0.142	0.149	0.164
AFFCOM ON							
ABUSE	-0.483	-0.422	-0.393	-0.248	-0.117	-0.093	-0.046
TFL	0.623	0.654	0.678	0.791	0.903	0.923	0.966
Intercepts							
AFFCOM	1.503	1.672	1.777	2.305	2.840	2.935	3.128
ENAGG	0.935	0.965	0.982	1.059	1.143	1.157	1.186
Residual Variances							
AFFCOM	1.066	1.114	1.137	1.255	1.382	1.406	1.455
ENAGG	0.028	0.031	0.033	0.043	0.060	0.063	0.071

CONFIDENCE INTERVALS OF TOTAL, TOTAL INDIRECT, SPECIFIC INDIRECT, AND DIRECT EFFECTS

	Lower .5%	Lower 2.5%	Lower 5%	Estimate	Upper 5%	Upper 2.5%	Upper .5%
Effects from ABUSE to ENAGG							
Total	0.059	0.067	0.073	0.108	0.145	0.153	0.167
Total indirect	0.000	0.001	0.002	0.004	0.008	0.009	0.012
Specific indirect							
ENAGG							
AFFCOM							
ABUSE	0.000	0.001	0.002	0.004	0.008	0.009	0.012
Direct							
ENAGG							
ABUSE	0.054	0.063	0.069	0.104	0.142	0.149	0.164

Note: These are the bias-corrected confidence intervals. Note that they are bias corrected because they are not symmetric about the estimate (e.g., the upper 5% minus the estimate is not equal to the estimate minus the lower 5%). The boundaries are provided for the 90%, 95%, and 99% confidence intervals. These are the unstandardized estimates; the standardized estimates follow.

CONFIDENCE INTERVALS OF STANDARDIZED TOTAL, TOTAL INDIRECT, SPECIFIC INDIRECT, AND DIRECT EFFECTS

STDYX Standardization

```
              Lower .5%  Lower 2.5%  Lower 5%  Estimate  Upper 5%  Upper 2.5%  Upper .5%

Effects from ABUSE to ENAGG
Total          0.170     0.205      0.224     0.319     0.414     0.433       0.468
Total
indirect      -0.003     0.001      0.002     0.012     0.021     0.023       0.027

Specific indirect
   ENAGG
   AFFCOM
   ABUSE     -0.003     0.001      0.002     0.012     0.021     0.023       0.027

   Direct
   ENAGG
   ABUSE      0.154     0.191      0.209     0.307     0.405     0.424       0.460

STDY Standardization

              Lower .5%  Lower 2.5%  Lower 5%  Estimate  Upper 5%  Upper 2.5%  Upper .5%

Effects from ABUSE to ENAGG

Total          0.233     0.293      0.324     0.485     0.646     0.677       0.737
Total
indirect      -0.005     0.000      0.003     0.018     0.033     0.036       0.041

   Specific indirect
   ENAGG
   AFFCOM
   ABUSE     -0.005     0.000      0.003     0.018     0.033     0.036       0.041
   Direct
   ENAGG
   ABUSE      0.212     0.273      0.304     0.467     0.630     0.661       0.722

STD Standardization
              Lower .5%  Lower 2.5%  Lower 5%  Estimate  Upper 5%  Upper 2.5%  Upper .5%

Effects from ABUSE to ENAGG

Total          0.052     0.065      0.072     0.108     0.144     0.151       0.164
Total
indirect      -0.001     0.000      0.001     0.004     0.007     0.008       0.009

   Specific indirect
   ENAGG
   AFFCOM
   ABUSE     -0.001     0.000      0.001     0.004     0.007     0.008       0.009

   Direct
   ENAGG
   ABUSE      0.047     0.061      0.068     0.104     0.140     0.147       0.161
```

Using Equality Constraints

In many applications of structural equation modeling, we are simply interested in whether the parameters are significant; that is, do they differ from zero? In some applications, we may want to compare parameters. For example, I am interested in the effect of leadership on individual well-being (e.g., Kelloway, Turner, Barling, & Loughlin, 2012) and have recently developed a scale of positive leadership behaviors (Kelloway, Weigand, McKee, & Das, 2013). I am interested in determining whether positive leadership as measured by my scale has the same effect as does transformational leadership on employee well-being. The model I am using is shown in Figure 6.2. As shown, the model hypothesizes that both transformational leadership and positive leadership predict affective commitment. In turn, affective commitment is hypothesized to predict well-being.

The code corresponding to this model is shown below.

```
TITLE:      Example of observed variable path analysis
DATA:       FILE IS apws.dat;
VARIABLE:   NAMES ARE ID Gender TFL Pos Abuse GHQ Affcom Enagg;
            USEVARIABLES ARE TFL Affcom Pos GHQ;
MODEL:      Affcom ON Pos;
            Affcom on TFL;
            GHQ on Affcom;
OUTPUT:     STANDARDIZED MODINDICES (ALL);
```

The procedure for testing whether two parameters differ (in this case Affcom ON Pos and Affcom ON TFL) involves estimating two models. First, we estimate the model shown in Figure 6.2 by running the code shown above. Inspection of the output suggests that the model fits the data, $\chi^2(2) = 4.112$, *ns*,

Figure 6.2

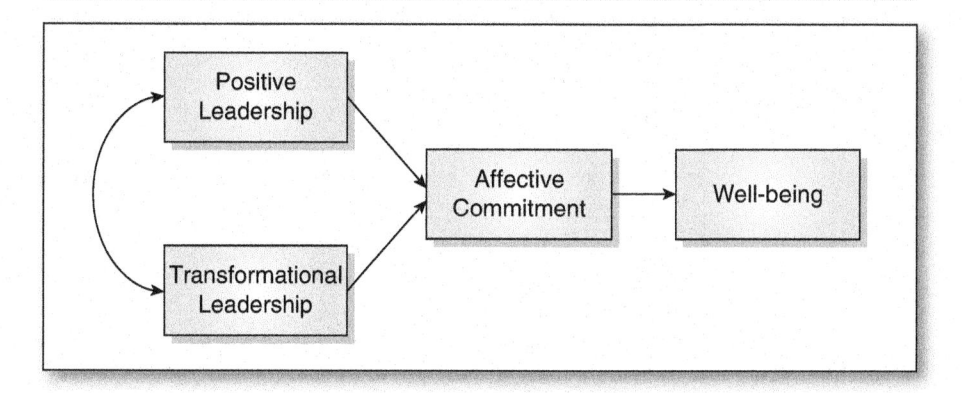

CFI = .99, RMSEA = .04, and that both parameters of interest were significant (Affcom on Pos = .20, $p < .01$, and Affcom ON TFL = .64, $p < .01$).

Next, we constrain the parameters to equality. In Mplus, we can do this by assigning the parameters the same label. Thus,

```
MODEL:     Affcom ON Pos (A);
           Affcom ON TFL (A);
```

When we rerun the model with this additional constraint, we obtain the output shown below. Note that the relevant parameters are now both constrained to equality (both now equal .434). The constrained model still provides a reasonable fit to the data but has 1 fewer degree of freedom (because of the constraint we imposed) and now has a χ^2 value of 11.17. Because the models are nested, we can use a chi-square difference test to test the null hypothesis that the parameters are equal. Subtracting our initial value from the constrained value model results in a value of 7.04 with 1 degree of freedom, which would lead us to reject the hypothesis of equality.

```
Mplus VERSION 7 (Mac)
MUTHEN & MUTHEN

INPUT INSTRUCTIONS

TITLE:       Example of observed variable path analysis
DATA:        FILE IS apws.dat;
VARIABLE:    NAMES ARE ID Gender TFL Pos Abuse GHQ Affcom Enagg;
             USEVARIABLES ARE TFL Affcom Pos GHQ;
MODEL:       Affcom ON Pos (A);
             Affcom ON TFL (A);
             GHQ ON Affcom;
OUTPUT:      STANDARDIZED MODINDICES (ALL)

INPUT READING TERMINATED NORMALLY
```

Note: Mplus repeats the input file. When parameters are given the same label (A), they are constrained to equality.

```
Example of observed variable path analysis

SUMMARY OF ANALYSIS

Number of groups                                      1
Number of observations                              585
Number of dependent variables                         2
Number of independent variables                       2
Number of continuous latent variables                 0
```

Chapter 6: Observed Variable Path Analysis

```
Observed dependent variables
  Continuous
    AFFCOM     GHQ

Observed independent variables
  TFL     POS
```

Note: Two exogenous (TFL and Pos) and two endogenous (Affcom and GHQ) variables are read from each of 585 observations in the data file.

```
Estimator                                                    ML
Information matrix                                     OBSERVED
Maximum number of iterations                               1000
Convergence criterion                                 0.500D-04
Maximum number of steepest descent iterations                20

Input data file(s)
apws.dat

Input data format FREE

THE MODEL ESTIMATION TERMINATED NORMALLY

MODEL FIT INFORMATION

Number of Free Parameters                                     6

Loglikelihood
       H0 Value                                      -1486.315
       H1 Value                                      -1480.726

Information Criteria
       Akaike (AIC)                                    2984.630
       Bayesian (BIC)                                  3010.859
       Sample-Size Adjusted BIC                        2991.811
         (n* = (n + 2) / 24)

Chi-Square Test of Model Fit
       Value                                             11.179
       Degrees of Freedom                                     3
       P-Value                                           0.0108

RMSEA (Root Mean Square Error Of Approximation)
       Estimate                                           0.068
       90 Percent C.I.                          0.029    0.113
       Probability RMSEA <= .05                           0.193

CFI/TLI
       CFI                                                0.975
       TLI                                                0.959
```

118   USING MPLUS FOR STRUCTURAL EQUATION MODELING

```
Chi-Square Test of Model Fit for the Baseline Model
         Value                                        337.507
         Degrees of Freedom                                 5
         P-Value                                       0.0000

SRMR (Standardized Root Mean Square Residual)
         Value                                          0.023
```

Note: The model provides a good fit by most of the indices. The CFI and TLI are both greater than .95, and the SRMR is close to zero. The RMSEA is less than .08, and the test of close fit is nonsignificant. Note, however, that the χ^2 value is nonsignificant and is increased from that obtained in the unconstrained model.

MODEL RESULTS

	Estimate	S.E.	Est./S.E.	Two-Tailed P-Value
AFFCOM ON				
POS	0.434	0.025	17.197	0.000
TFL	0.434	0.025	17.197	0.000
GHQ ON				
AFFCOM	0.194	0.020	9.684	0.000
Intercepts				
AFFCOM	1.727	0.171	10.120	0.000
GHQ	3.802	0.095	39.994	0.000
Residual Variances				
AFFCOM	1.252	0.073	17.103	0.000
GHQ	0.441	0.026	17.103	0.000

Note: Notice that the parameters predicting Affcom (i.e., Affcom ON Pos, Affcom ON TFL) are now constrained to equality. Other parameters in the model are freely estimated.

STANDARDIZED MODEL RESULTS

STDYX Standardization

	Estimate	S.E.	Est./S.E.	Two-Tailed P-Value
AFFCOM ON				
POS	0.333	0.016	20.847	0.000
TFL	0.282	0.014	20.750	0.000

```
GHQ       ON
    AFFCOM              0.372         0.036        10.431         0.000

Intercepts
    AFFCOM              1.258         0.151         8.352         0.000
    GHQ                 5.316         0.247        21.502         0.000
Residual Variances
    AFFCOM              0.664         0.032        20.870         0.000
    GHQ                 0.862         0.026        32.536         0.000
```

Note: As previously discussed, the different versions of the standardized solution rely on different sampling distributions. As a result, the STDYX estimates for the prediction of Affcom are not equal to one another, but they are for the STDY and the STD estimates.

```
STDY Standardization

                                                             Two-Tailed
                       Estimate        S.E.     Est./S.E.      P-Value

AFFCOM    ON
    POS                 0.316         0.014        22.557         0.000
    TFL                 0.316         0.014        22.557         0.000

GHQ       ON
    AFFCOM              0.372         0.036        10.431         0.000

Intercepts
    AFFCOM              1.258         0.151         8.352         0.000
    GHQ                 5.316         0.247        21.502         0.000

Residual Variances
    AFFCOM              0.664         0.032        20.870         0.000
    GHQ                 0.862         0.026        32.536         0.000

STD Standardization

                                                             Two-Tailed
                       Estimate        S.E.     Est./S.E.      P-Value

AFFCOM    ON
    POS                 0.434         0.025        17.197         0.000
    TFL                 0.434         0.025        17.197         0.000

GHQ       ON
    AFFCOM              0.194         0.020         9.684         0.000

Intercepts
    AFFCOM              1.727         0.171        10.120         0.000
    GHQ                 3.802         0.095        39.994         0.000
```

```
Residual Variances
    AFFCOM            1.252         0.073         17.103         0.000
    GHQ               0.441         0.026         17.103         0.000
```

R-SQUARE

```
    Observed                                                  Two-Tailed
    Variable       Estimate        S.E.       Est./S.E.        P-Value
    AFFCOM           0.336         0.032         10.550          0.000
    GHQ              0.138         0.026          5.216          0.000
```

QUALITY OF NUMERICAL RESULTS

```
Condition Number for the Information Matrix      0.978E-03
(ratio of smallest to largest eigenvalue)
```

MODEL MODIFICATION INDICES

```
Minimum M.I. value for printing the modification index   10.000

                 M.I.      E.P.C.      Std E.P.C.      StdYX E.P.C.

No modification indices above the minimum value.
```

Note: There are no modifications that would substantially improve the fit of the model

Multisample Analysis

We can use this same logic to test for the equality of parameters across multiple samples. To do this, we need a variable in the data file that indicates which group the case belongs to. For our purposes, we will test model parameters across gender. To do so, we need to introduce a grouping variable in the VARIABLE command. Thus,

```
TITLE:        Example of observed variable path analysis
DATA:         FILE IS apws.dat;
VARIABLE:     NAMES ARE ID Gender TFL Pos Abuse GHQ Affcom Enagg;
              USEVARIABLES ARE TFL Affcom Pos GHQ;
              GROUPING IS Gender (1 = Female,2 = Male);
MODEL:        Affcom ON TFL;
              Affcom ON Pos;
              GHQ ON Affcom;
OUTPUT:       STANDARDIZED MODINDICES (ALL)
```

Running this unconstrained model estimates the same model freely within each of the two groups defined on the grouping variable. The output is as follows:

```
Mplus VERSION 7 (Mac)
MUTHEN & MUTHEN

INPUT INSTRUCTIONS

TITLE:      Example of observed variable path analysis
DATA:       FILE IS apws.dat;
VARIABLE:   NAMES ARE ID Gender TFL Pos Abuse GHQ Affcom Enagg;
            USEVARIABLES ARE TFL Affcom Pos GHQ;
            GROUPING IS Gender (1 = Female,2 = Male);
MODEL:      Affcom ON TFL;
            Affcom ON Pos;
            GHQ ON Affcom;
OUTPUT:     STANDARDIZED MODINDICES (ALL)
```

Note: The input file is repeated.

```
INPUT READING TERMINATED NORMALLY

Example of observed variable path analysis

SUMMARY OF ANALYSIS

Number of groups                                               2
Number of observations
   Group FEMALE                                              371
   Group MALE                                               214

Number of dependent variables                                  2
Number of independent variables                                2
Number of continuous latent variables                          0

Observed dependent variables
  Continuous
     AFFCOM     GHQ

Observed independent variables
   TFL     POS

Variables with special functions
   Grouping variable     GENDER
```

Note: Mplus has read two endogenous (Affcom and GHQ) and two exogenous (TFL and Pos) variables from the file. It has recognized two groups of data in the file, female (n = 371) and male (n = 214) participants.

```
Estimator                                                          ML
Information matrix                                           OBSERVED
Maximum number of iterations                                     1000
Convergence criterion                                       0.500D-04
Maximum number of steepest descent iterations                      20

Input data file(s)
  apws.dat

Input data format  FREE

THE MODEL ESTIMATION TERMINATED NORMALLY

MODEL FIT INFORMATION

Number of Free Parameters                                          14

Loglikelihood
        H0 Value                                            -1478.017
        H1 Value                                            -1474.145

Information Criteria
        Akaike (AIC)                                         2984.034
        Bayesian (BIC)                                       3045.237
        Sample-Size Adjusted BIC                             3000.792
           (n* = (n + 2) / 24)

Chi-Square Test of Model Fit
        Value                                                   7.744
        Degrees of Freedom                                          4
        P-Value                                                0.1014

Chi-Square Contributions From Each Group
        FEMALE                                                  0.733
        MALE                                                    7.011

RMSEA (Root Mean Square Error Of Approximation)
        Estimate                                                0.057
        90 Percent C.I.                             0.000       0.116
        Probability RMSEA <= .05                                0.354

CFI/TLI
        CFI                                                     0.989
        TLI                                                     0.972

Chi-Square Test of Model Fit for the Baseline Model
        Value                                                 346.475
        Degrees of Freedom                                         10
        P-Value                                                0.0000


SRMR (Standardized Root Mean Square Residual)
        Value                                                   0.028
```

Note: The model as a whole fits the data (the χ^2 value is nonsignificant, the CFI and TLI exceed .95, the RMSEA is less than .08 and the test of close fit is nonsignificant, and the SRMR is less than .06). Note, however, that Mplus now reports the contribution to the χ^2 value from each group. Although the model fits in each group, it is clear that it provides a better fit ($\chi^2 = 0.73$) for female than for male participants ($\chi^2 = 7.01$).

```
MODEL RESULTS

                                                        Two-Tailed
                     Estimate      S.E.    Est./S.E.     P-Value

Group FEMALE

AFFCOM   ON
    TFL               0.562       0.104      5.388        0.000
    POS               0.322       0.086      3.730        0.000

GHQ      ON
    AFFCOM            0.174       0.024      7.167        0.000

Intercepts
    AFFCOM            1.604       0.222      7.208        0.000
    GHQ               3.870       0.115     33.675        0.000

Residual Variances
    AFFCOM            1.304       0.096     13.620        0.000
    GHQ               0.435       0.032     13.620        0.000

Group MALE

AFFCOM   ON
    TFL               0.780       0.126      6.170        0.000
    POS               0.160       0.112      1.425        0.154

GHQ      ON
    AFFCOM            0.232       0.035      6.623        0.000

Intercepts
    AFFCOM            1.565       0.290      5.403        0.000
    GHQ               3.663       0.168     21.848        0.000

Residual Variances
    AFFCOM            1.093       0.106     10.344        0.000
    GHQ               0.445       0.043     10.344        0.000
```

Note: The unstandardized parameters are reported separately for each group (as are the standardized estimates reported below). All of the estimated parameters for the female participants are significant. For the male participants, the prediction of Affcom from Pos is not significant. However, this may be attributable to the sample sizes, as the absolute value of the parameter for male participants (i.e., .16) is very close to the value for female participants (.17).

```
STANDARDIZED MODEL RESULTS

STDYX Standardization

                                                        Two-Tailed
                    Estimate       S.E.    Est./S.E.     P-Value

Group FEMALE

AFFCOM  ON
    TFL              0.367        0.066       5.526       0.000
    POS              0.254        0.067       3.772       0.000

GHQ  ON
    AFFCOM           0.349        0.046       7.647       0.000

Intercepts
    AFFCOM           1.136        0.187       6.084       0.000
    GHQ              5.497        0.311      17.701       0.000

Residual Variances
    AFFCOM           0.655        0.040      16.396       0.000
    GHQ              0.878        0.032      27.616       0.000

Group MALE

AFFCOM  ON
    TFL              0.504        0.077       6.554       0.000
    POS              0.116        0.082       1.429       0.153

GHQ  ON
    AFFCOM           0.412        0.057       7.270       0.000

Intercepts
    AFFCOM           1.203        0.264       4.550       0.000
    GHQ              5.004        0.409      12.223       0.000
Residual Variances
    AFFCOM           0.645        0.053      12.281       0.000
    GHQ              0.830        0.047      17.735       0.000

STDY Standardization
```

	Estimate	S.E.	Est./S.E.	Two-Tailed P-Value
Group FEMALE				
AFFCOM ON				
TFL	0.398	0.072	5.567	0.000
POS	0.228	0.060	3.787	0.000
GHQ ON				
AFFCOM	0.349	0.046	7.647	0.000
Intercepts				
AFFCOM	1.136	0.187	6.084	0.000
GHQ	5.497	0.311	17.701	0.000
Residual Variances				
AFFCOM	0.655	0.040	16.396	0.000
GHQ	0.878	0.032	27.616	0.000
Group MALE				
AFFCOM ON				
TFL	0.599	0.090	6.656	0.000
POS	0.123	0.086	1.431	0.153
GHQ ON				
AFFCOM	0.412	0.057	7.270	0.000
Intercepts				
AFFCOM	1.203	0.264	4.550	0.000
GHQ	5.004	0.409	12.223	0.000
Residual Variances				
AFFCOM	0.645	0.053	12.281	0.000
GHQ	0.830	0.047	17.735	0.000

STD Standardization

	Estimate	S.E.	Est./S.E.	Two-Tailed P-Value
Group FEMALE				
AFFCOM ON				
TFL	0.562	0.104	5.388	0.000
POS	0.322	0.086	3.730	0.000
GHQ ON				
AFFCOM	0.174	0.024	7.167	0.000

```
Intercepts
    AFFCOM          1.604       0.222       7.208       0.000
    GHQ             3.870       0.115      33.675       0.000

Residual Variances
    AFFCOM          1.304       0.096      13.620       0.000
    GHQ             0.435       0.032      13.620       0.000

Group MALE

AFFCOM ON
    TFL             0.780       0.126       6.170       0.000
    POS             0.160       0.112       1.425       0.154

GHQ ON
    AFFCOM          0.232       0.035       6.623       0.000

Intercepts
    AFFCOM          1.565       0.290       5.403       0.000
    GHQ             3.663       0.168      21.848       0.000

Residual Variances
    AFFCOM          1.093       0.106      10.344       0.000
    GHQ             0.445       0.043      10.344       0.000
```

R-SQUARE

Group FEMALE

```
    Observed                                            Two-Tailed
    Variable       Estimate     S.E.     Est./S.E.      P-Value
    AFFCOM          0.345       0.040       8.636       0.000
    GHQ             0.122       0.032       3.824       0.000
```

Group MALE

```
    Observed                                            Two-Tailed
    Variable       Estimate     S.E.     Est./S.E.      P-Value
    AFFCOM          0.355       0.053       6.750       0.000
    GHQ             0.170       0.047       3.635       0.000
```

QUALITY OF NUMERICAL RESULTS

Condition Number for the Information Matrix   0.511E-03
(ratio of smallest to largest eigenvalue)

MODEL MODIFICATION INDICES

Minimum M.I. value for printing the modification index   10.000

```
                    M.I.       E.P.C.      Std E.P.C.      StdYX E.P.C.
Group FEMALE
No modification indices above the minimum value.
```

Chapter 6: Observed Variable Path Analysis   127

```
Group MALE
No modification indices above the minimum value.
```

Note: No modifications that would improve the fit of the model were noted for either sample.

You can add the equality constraints by simply labeling each parameter in the model as shown in this code:

```
TITLE:      Example of observed variable path analysis
DATA:       FILE IS apws.dat;
VARIABLE:   NAMES ARE ID Gender TFL Pos Abuse GHQ Affcom Enagg;
            USEVARIABLES ARE TFL Affcom Pos GHQ;
            GROUPING IS Gender (1 = Female,2 = Male);
MODEL:      Affcom ON TFL (A);
            Affcom ON Pos (B);
            GHQ ON Affcom (C);
OUTPUT:     STANDARDIZED MODINDICES (ALL)
```

Each of the three parameters in the model is constrained to equality across groups. Running this model results in $\chi^2(7) = 11.40$. Therefore, the chi-square difference test suggests that the two models (constrained and constrained) are not significantly different, $\chi^2_{difference}(3) = 3.36$, *ns*, and we can conclude that the parameters do not differ across groups. If this initial test were significant, we would proceed with further testing, constraining each parameter to equality one at a time to identify exactly which parameters differ across the groups.

Although this is the simplest and most common application of multisample analysis, one can also use a more flexible alternative specification. Having identified the grouping variable in the VARIABLES command, you can specify separate models for each of the groups in the MODEL statement. For example, an equivalent specification of the unconstrained model used above would be to specify the overall model and then specify separate models for each group, as shown below. This might be a useful approach when one wants to estimate different models across the groups or when one is working with more than 2 groups and wants to constrain specific parameters (e.g., constrain parameter X in to equality in groups 2 and 3 but freely estimate it in group 1).

```
MODEL:          Affcom ON TFL;
                Affcom ON Pos;
                GHQ ON Affcom;
MODEL Female:   Affcom ON TFL;
                Affcom ON Pos;
                GHQ ON Affcom;
MODEL Male:     Affcom ON TFL;
                Affcom ON Pos;
                GHQ ON Affcom;
```

Note

1. Rank-and-order conditions refer to the identification of nonrecursive structural models and will not be dealt with further.

7

Latent Variable Path Analysis

The true power of structural equation modeling is the ability to estimate a complete model incorporating both measurement and structural considerations. In this chapter, we consider such a latent variable path analysis. Thus, in conducting the analysis, we will be equally concerned with assessing the proposed measurement relations (i.e., through confirmatory factor analysis) and the proposed structural relations (i.e., through path analysis). Although latent variable models can be complex, in actuality we are merely combining techniques we have covered in previous chapters. Moreover, although I will not be repeating this material, testing equality constraints, mediation, and multi-sample models can all be implemented with latent variables, just as they were with observed variable path analyses in the preceding chapter.

Model Specification

To illustrate the use of latent variable path analysis, we will consider the model presented in Figure 7.1. There are two components to the model. First, the structural model specifies the predictive relationships among the latent variables. Second, the measurement model defines how the latent variables are measured (i.e., represented by indicators).

The structural model we were interested in was based on the hypotheses that individuals who experience injustice in the workplace would be less affectively committed to the organization. In turn, organizational commitment would predict employees' participation in the safety program. Each of these constructs is represented by three indicator (or observed) variables.

In addition to the structural relations, we also were interested in using latent variables; that is, each construct in the model would be represented by multiple indicators. Bentler (1980) noted that "choosing the right number of

Figure 7.1

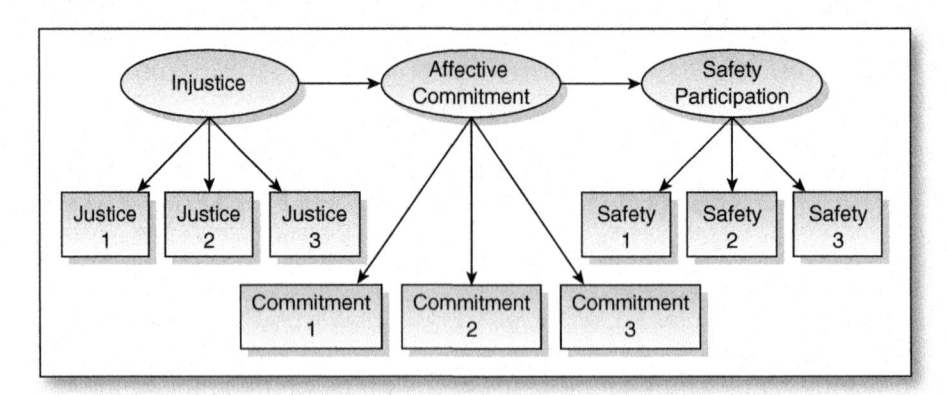

[Figure 7.1: Path diagram showing Injustice → Affective Commitment → Safety Participation, with Injustice measured by Justice 1, Justice 2, Justice 3; Affective Commitment measured by Commitment 1, Commitment 2, Commitment 3; and Safety Participation measured by Safety 1, Safety 2, Safety 3.]

indicators for each LV [latent variable] is something of an art; in principle, the more the better; in practice, too many indicators make it difficult if not impossible to fit a model to data" (p. 425).

Moreover, as noted in Chapter 5, Bollen (1989) suggested that a confirmatory factor analysis model (which uses indicators to represent latent variables or factors) should incorporate at least two, preferably three, indicators per latent variable. Researchers can mix "levels" of operationalization in choosing indicators for their models. In the current example, the three justice indicators are measures of distributive, procedural, and interactional injustice. The indicators of affective commitment are item parcels (see Chapter 5) formed from Allen and Meyer's (1990) affective commitment measure. The three safety indicators are single items, each assessing participation in a particular aspect of the safety program (e.g., attend training, attend meetings).

ALTERNATIVE MODEL SPECIFICATIONS

The central hypothesis of our model is that commitment mediates the relationship between injustice and safety participation. Consistent with the discussion of mediated relationships in the previous chapter, two plausible rival model specifications are the partially mediated (which adds a path from injustice to safety participation; see Figure 7.2) and nonmediated (which deletes the path from affective commitment to safety participation; see Figure 7.3) models.

MODEL TESTING STRATEGY

There is a major complication in testing latent variable models. If the model does not fit, the lack of fit can be attributable to an ill-fitting measurement

Figure 7.2

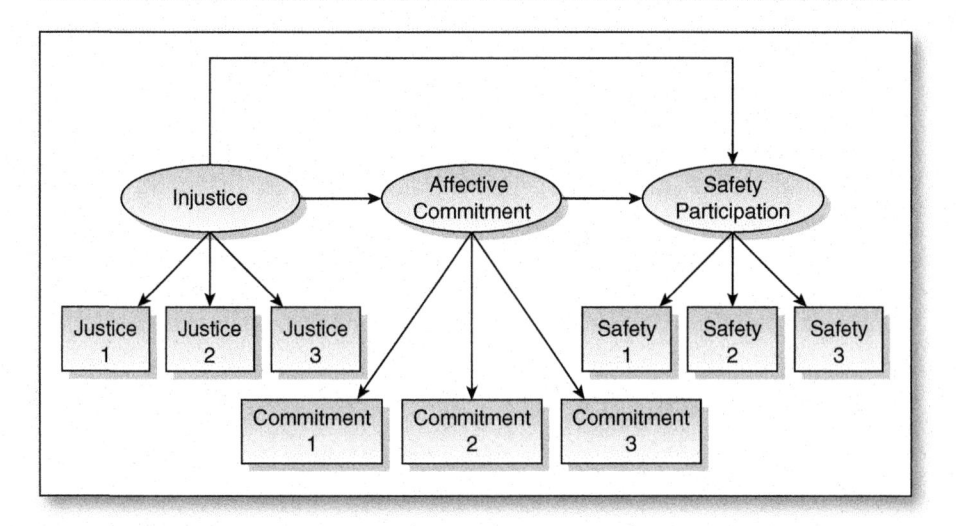

Figure 7.3

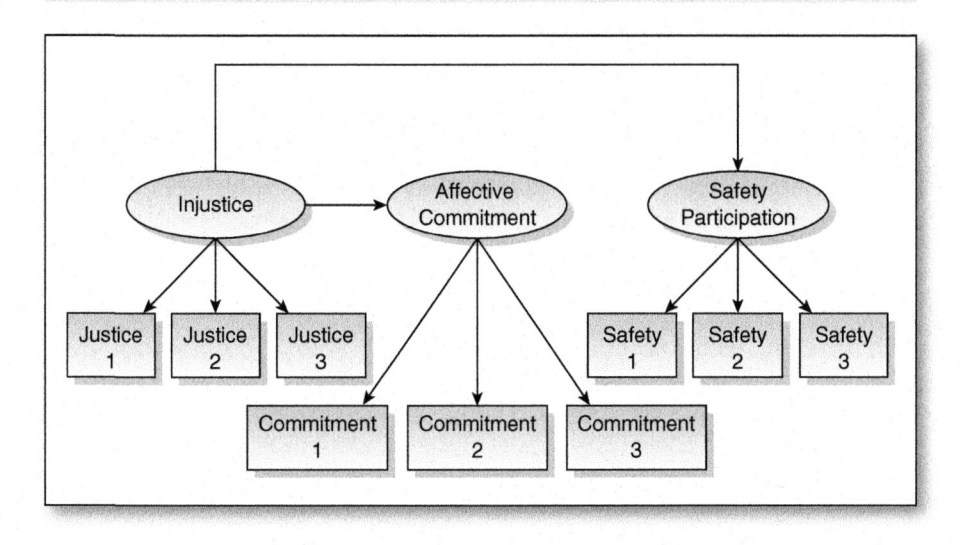

model, an ill-fitting structural model, or both (Anderson & Gerbing, 1988). Accordingly, Anderson and Gerbing (1988) recommended a strategy of two-stage modeling in which one first assesses the fit of the measurement model and then moves to a consideration of the structural model (see Williams, Vandenberg, & Edwards, 2009, for a similar view).

The strategy is based on the observation that the latent variable structural model incorporates the measurement model. In fact, at least with respect to the relationships among the latent variables, one can think of the measurement model as a saturated or just-identified model. That is, the measurement model allows a relationship (i.e., a correlation; see Figure 7.2) between each pair of latent variables.

This being the case, the fit of the measurement model provides a baseline for the fit of the full latent variable model. The full model, incorporating both structural and measurement relationships, cannot provide a better fit to the data than does the measurement model.

Incorporating Anderson and Gerbing's (1988) suggestions with our three hypothesized structural models suggests a sequence of model tests in which we first establish the fit of the measurement model and then move to a consideration of the structural parameters of interest. The remainder of this chapter, therefore, provides the assessment of the measurement model, followed by assessment of the full model.

The Mplus code for the measurement model simply defines three latent variables, each indicated by three observed variables:

```
TITLE:      Example of latent variable path analysis;
DATA:       FILE IS Chapter7.data;
VARIABLE:   NAMES ARE SATT1 SATT2 SATT3 JUST1 JUST2 JUST3 ACOM1
ACOM2 ACOM3;
MODEL:      Safety BY SATT1-SATT3;
            Justice BY JUST1-JUST3;
            Affcom BY ACOM1-ACOM3;
OUTPUT:     STANDARDIZED MODINDICES (ALL);
```

The output from this file is shown below. As you will see, the measurement model provides a reasonable fit to the data. The comparative fit index (CFI) exceeds .95, and the root mean square error of approximation (RMSEA) test of close fit is nonsignificant.

```
Mplus VERSION 7 (Mac)
MUTHEN & MUTHEN

INPUT INSTRUCTIONS

TITLE:      Example of latent variable path analysis;
DATA:       FILE IS Chapter7.dat;
VARIABLE:   NAMES ARE SATT1 SATT2 SATT3 JUST1 JUST2 JUST3 ACOM1 ACOM2 ACOM3;

MODEL:      Safety BY SATT1-SATT3;
            Justice BY JUST1-JUST3;
            Affcom BY ACOM1-ACOM3;
OUTPUT:     STANDARDIZED MODINDICES (ALL);

INPUT READING TERMINATED NORMALLY

Example of latent variable path analysis;
```

SUMMARY OF ANALYSIS

Number of groups	1
Number of observations	298
Number of dependent variables	9
Number of independent variables	0
Number of continuous latent variables	3

Observed dependent variables
  Continuous
    SATT1   SATT2   SATT3   JUST1   JUST2   JUST3
    ACOM1   ACOM2   ACOM3

Continuous latent variables
  SAFETY   JUSTICE   AFFCOM

Estimator	ML
Information matrix	OBSERVED
Maximum number of iterations	1000
Convergence criterion	0.500D-04
Maximum number of steepest descent iterations	20

Input data file(s)
Chapter7.dat

Input data format FREE

THE MODEL ESTIMATION TERMINATED NORMALLY

Note: Mplus repeats the command file and reports on the data read into the program. As shown, there are 298 cases in one group. The model comprises three latent and nine observed variables.

MODEL FIT INFORMATION

Number of Free Parameters	30

Loglikelihood
        H0 Value   -4526.556
        H1 Value   -4498.229

Information Criteria
        Akaike (AIC)   9113.112
        Bayesian (BIC)   9224.025
        Sample-Size Adjusted BIC   9128.884
          (n* = (n + 2) / 24)

Chi-Square Test of Model Fit
        Value   56.653
        Degrees of Freedom   24
        P-Value   0.0002

```
RMSEA (Root Mean Square Error Of Approximation)
        Estimate                                              0.068
        90 Percent C.I.                           0.045       0.091
        Probability RMSEA <= .05                              0.096

CFI/TLI
        CFI                                                   0.972
        TLI                                                   0.958

Chi-Square Test of Model Fit for the Baseline Model
        Value                                              1199.615
        Degrees of Freedom                                       36
        P-Value                                              0.0000

SRMR (Standardized Root Mean Square Residual)
        Value                                                 0.051
```

Note: The measurement model provides quite a reasonable fit to the data. Both the CFI and the Tucker-Lewis index (TLI) exceed .95, the SRMR and the RMSEA are both less than .08, and the test for close fit is nonsignificant. Although the χ^2 value is significant, it is not overly large, and the other indices suggest a good-fitting model.

MODEL RESULTS

	Estimate	S.E.	Est./S.E.	Two-Tailed P-Value
SAFETY BY				
SATT1	1.000	0.000	999.000	999.000
SATT2	1.219	0.114	10.699	0.000
SATT3	6.235	0.813	7.673	0.000
JUSTICE BY				
JUST1	1.000	0.000	999.000	999.000
JUST2	1.339	0.103	12.980	0.000
JUST3	1.194	0.094	12.698	0.000
AFFCOM BY				
ACOM1	1.000	0.000	999.000	999.000
ACOM2	1.022	0.067	15.228	0.000
ACOM3	-0.682	0.071	-9.554	0.000
JUSTICE WITH				
SAFETY	0.220	0.045	4.932	0.000
AFFCOM WITH				
SAFETY	0.254	0.063	4.015	0.000
JUSTICE	0.931	0.133	7.004	0.000

```
Intercepts
    SATT1            3.965       0.040       99.548       0.000
    SATT2            3.964       0.053       75.480       0.000
    SATT3           26.248       0.440       59.634       0.000
    JUST1            4.868       0.083       58.390       0.000
    JUST2            4.551       0.086       52.931       0.000
    JUST3            4.942       0.082       60.374       0.000
    ACOM1            3.356       0.100       33.515       0.000
    ACOM2            3.646       0.099       36.649       0.000
    ACOM3            3.302       0.104       31.630       0.000

Variances
    SAFETY           0.349       0.047        7.462       0.000
    JUSTICE          0.985       0.153        6.445       0.000
    AFFCOM           2.189       0.260        8.426       0.000

Residual Variances
    SATT1            0.124       0.030        4.161       0.000
    SATT2            0.304       0.048        6.342       0.000
    SATT3           44.181       3.877       11.396       0.000
    JUST1            1.086       0.102       10.650       0.000
    JUST2            0.438       0.080        5.497       0.000
    JUST3            0.592       0.074        7.943       0.000
    ACOM1            0.798       0.127        6.280       0.000
    ACOM2            0.664       0.126        5.266       0.000
    ACOM3            2.229       0.196       11.371       0.000
```

Note: Consistent with the fit of the model, all of the estimated parameters are significant. Recall that Mplus fixes the first factor loading on each latent variable to be 1.00 to establish a metric for the latent variable.

```
STANDARDIZED MODEL RESULTS

STDYX Standardization
                                                          Two-Tailed
                    Estimate       S.E.     Est./S.E.      P-Value
SAFETY BY
    SATT1            0.859       0.038       22.759       0.000
    SATT2            0.794       0.038       20.924       0.000
    SATT3            0.485       0.051        9.534       0.000

JUSTICE BY
    JUST1            0.690       0.035       19.685       0.000
    JUST2            0.895       0.021       41.794       0.000
    JUST3            0.839       0.024       34.846       0.000

AFFCOM BY
    ACOM1            0.856       0.026       32.499       0.000
    ACOM2            0.880       0.025       34.555       0.000
    ACOM3           -0.560       0.044      -12.637       0.000
```

```
JUSTICE WITH
   SAFETY            0.375      0.061      6.141      0.000

AFFCOM WITH
   SAFETY            0.291      0.065      4.460      0.000
   JUSTICE           0.634      0.044     14.288      0.000

Intercepts
   SATT1             5.767      0.243     23.711      0.000
   SATT2             4.372      0.188     23.228      0.000
   SATT3             3.454      0.153     22.594      0.000
   JUST1             3.382      0.150     22.524      0.000
   JUST2             3.066      0.138     22.169      0.000
   JUST3             3.497      0.155     22.633      0.000
   ACOM1             1.941      0.098     19.733      0.000
   ACOM2             2.123      0.104     20.318      0.000
   ACOM3             1.832      0.095     19.326      0.000

Variances
   SAFETY            1.000      0.000    999.000    999.000
   JUSTICE           1.000      0.000    999.000    999.000
   AFFCOM            1.000      0.000    999.000    999.000

Residual Variances
   SATT1             0.263      0.065      4.051      0.000
   SATT2             0.369      0.060      6.130      0.000
   SATT3             0.765      0.049     15.541      0.000
   JUST1             0.524      0.048     10.854      0.000
   JUST2             0.199      0.038      5.190      0.000
   JUST3             0.296      0.040      7.336      0.000
   ACOM1             0.267      0.045      5.925      0.000
   ACOM2             0.225      0.045      5.016      0.000
   ACOM3             0.686      0.050     13.823      0.000
```

Note: These are the standardized parameters I would report in a results section. Note that because the STDYX estimates standardize the latent variables, the variances of the latent variables are fixed to 1.00, and the first factor loading on each latent variable is estimated.

```
STDY Standardization
                                                     Two-Tailed
                   Estimate     S.E.    Est./S.E.     P-Value

SAFETY BY
   SATT1             0.859      0.038     22.759      0.000
   SATT2             0.794      0.038     20.924      0.000
   SATT3             0.485      0.051      9.534      0.000

JUSTICE BY
   JUST1             0.690      0.035     19.685      0.000
   JUST2             0.895      0.021     41.794      0.000
   JUST3             0.839      0.024     34.846      0.000
```

```
AFFCOM BY
    ACOM1           0.856      0.026       32.499       0.000
    ACOM2           0.880      0.025       34.555       0.000
    ACOM3          -0.560      0.044      -12.637       0.000

JUSTICE WITH
    SAFETY          0.375      0.061        6.141       0.000

AFFCOM WITH
    SAFETY          0.291      0.065        4.460       0.000
    JUSTICE         0.634      0.044       14.288       0.000

Intercepts
    SATT1           5.767      0.243       23.711       0.000
    SATT2           4.372      0.188       23.228       0.000
    SATT3           3.454      0.153       22.594       0.000
    JUST1           3.382      0.150       22.524       0.000
    JUST2           3.066      0.138       22.169       0.000
    JUST3           3.497      0.155       22.633       0.000
    ACOM1           1.941      0.098       19.733       0.000
    ACOM2           2.123      0.104       20.318       0.000
    ACOM3           1.832      0.095       19.326       0.000

Variances
    SAFETY          1.000      0.000      999.000      999.000
    JUSTICE         1.000      0.000      999.000      999.000
    AFFCOM          1.000      0.000      999.000      999.000

Residual Variances
    SATT1           0.263      0.065        4.051       0.000
    SATT2           0.369      0.060        6.130       0.000
    SATT3           0.765      0.049       15.541       0.000
    JUST1           0.524      0.048       10.854       0.000
    JUST2           0.199      0.038        5.190       0.000
    JUST3           0.296      0.040        7.336       0.000
    ACOM1           0.267      0.045        5.925       0.000
    ACOM2           0.225      0.045        5.016       0.000
    ACOM3           0.686      0.050       13.823       0.000

STD Standardization

                                                   Two-Tailed
                  Estimate    S.E.    Est./S.E.     P-Value

SAFETY BY
    SATT1           0.590      0.040       14.925       0.000
    SATT2           0.720      0.052       13.865       0.000
    SATT3           3.681      0.455        8.099       0.000

JUSTICE BY
    JUST1           0.992      0.077       12.890       0.000
    JUST2           1.329      0.072       18.512       0.000
    JUST3           1.185      0.070       16.914       0.000
```

AFFCOM BY				
ACOM1	1.480	0.088	16.852	0.000
ACOM2	1.512	0.086	17.486	0.000
ACOM3	-1.009	0.102	-9.881	0.000
JUSTICE WITH				
SAFETY	0.375	0.061	6.141	0.000
AFFCOM WITH				
SAFETY	0.291	0.065	4.460	0.000
JUSTICE	0.634	0.044	14.288	0.000
Intercepts				
SATT1	3.965	0.040	99.548	0.000
SATT2	3.964	0.053	75.480	0.000
SATT3	26.248	0.440	59.634	0.000
JUST1	4.868	0.083	58.390	0.000
JUST2	4.551	0.086	52.931	0.000
JUST3	4.942	0.082	60.374	0.000
ACOM1	3.356	0.100	33.515	0.000
ACOM2	3.646	0.099	36.649	0.000
ACOM3	3.302	0.104	31.630	0.000
Variances				
SAFETY	1.000	0.000	999.000	999.000
JUSTICE	1.000	0.000	999.000	999.000
AFFCOM	1.000	0.000	999.000	999.000
Residual Variances				
SATT1	0.124	0.030	4.161	0.000
SATT2	0.304	0.048	6.342	0.000
SATT3	44.181	3.877	11.396	0.000
JUST1	1.086	0.102	10.650	0.000
JUST2	0.438	0.080	5.497	0.000
JUST3	0.592	0.074	7.943	0.000
ACOM1	0.798	0.127	6.280	0.000
ACOM2	0.664	0.126	5.266	0.000
ACOM3	2.229	0.196	11.371	0.000

R-SQUARE

Observed Variable	Estimate	S.E.	Est./S.E.	Two-Tailed P-Value
SATT1	0.737	0.065	11.380	0.000
SATT2	0.631	0.060	10.462	0.000
SATT3	0.235	0.049	4.767	0.000
JUST1	0.476	0.048	9.842	0.000
JUST2	0.801	0.038	20.897	0.000

```
    JUST3              0.704       0.040      17.423         0.000
    ACOM1              0.733       0.045      16.249         0.000
    ACOM2              0.775       0.045      17.277         0.000
    ACOM3              0.314       0.050       6.319         0.000
```

QUALITY OF NUMERICAL RESULTS

```
Condition Number for the Information Matrix          0.207E-02
(ratio of smallest to largest eigenvalue)
```

MODEL MODIFICATION INDICES

```
Minimum M.I. value for printing the modification index    10.000

                    M.I.      E.P.C.    Std E.P.C.   StdYX E.P.C.

ON/BY Statements


SATT3     ON JUSTICE   /
JUSTICE   BY SATT3     13.860    1.764        1.751         0.230

ON Statements

SAFETY    ON SATT3     14.319   -0.053       -0.089        -0.678
SATT1     ON SATT2     14.329    1.500        1.500         1.978
SATT2     ON SATT1     14.333    3.672        3.672         2.785
SATT3     ON JUST2     18.698    1.253        1.253         0.245
JUST2     ON SATT3     12.067    0.025        0.025         0.127

WITH Statements

SATT2     WITH SATT1   14.333    0.456        0.456         2.347
SATT3     WITH SAFETY  14.320   -2.329       -3.945        -0.593
JUST2     WITH SATT3   12.637    1.257        1.257         0.286
```

Note: The modification indices suggest several changes to improve the fit of the model. Although most of these changes would likely reduce the χ^2 value to nonsignificance, I am not likely to incorporate any of the suggestions. Consideration of the changes suggests that they are not consistent with any theory; they largely involve the estimation of residual correlations or predictive relationships among the observed variables. Because the model provides an acceptable fit, and the changes do not make conceptual sense, I opt not to change the model.

Note that in the measurement model, the three latent variables are simply correlated with one another. That is, Mplus treats the three latent variables as exogenous variables and, by default, estimates the correlations among the latent variables. To test the structural model, we need only to add the ON statements to the MODEL command, as shown below. Doing so removes the correlations estimated in the previous analyses (because two of the latent variables are now endogenous) and adds the predictive relationships we specify.

```
Mplus VERSION 7 (Mac)
MUTHEN & MUTHEN

INPUT INSTRUCTIONS

TITLE:     Example of latent variable path analysis;
DATA:      FILE IS Chapter7.dat;
VARIABLE:  NAMES ARE SATT1 SATT2 SATT3 JUST1 JUST2 JUST3 ACOM1 ACOM2 ACOM3;
MODEL:     Safety BY SATT1-SATT3;
           Justice BY JUST1-JUST3;
           Affcom BY ACOM1-ACOM3;
           Safety ON Affcom;
           Affcom ON Justice;
OUTPUT:    STANDARDIZED MODINDICES (ALL)

INPUT READING TERMINATED NORMALLY
```

Note: The command file first defines the three latent variables (the BY statements) and then specifies the structural relationships (the ON statements). This analysis estimates the fully mediated model.

```
Example of latent variable path analysis;

SUMMARY OF ANALYSIS

Number of groups                                                 1
Number of observations                                         298
Number of dependent variables                                    9
Number of independent variables                                  0
Number of continuous latent variables                            3

Observed dependent variables
  Continuous
     SATT1       SATT2       SATT3       JUST1       JUST2       JUST3
     ACOM1       ACOM2       ACOM3
Continuous latent variables
     SAFETY      JUSTICE     AFFCOM
```

```
Estimator                                                    ML
Information matrix                                     OBSERVED
Maximum number of iterations                               1000
Convergence criterion                                 0.500D-04
Maximum number of steepest descent iterations                20

Input data file(s)
  CHAPTER7.DAT

Input data format FREE

THE MODEL ESTIMATION TERMINATED NORMALLY

MODEL FIT INFORMATION

Number of Free Parameters                                    29

Loglikelihood
        H0 Value                                      -4532.639
        H1 Value                                      -4498.229

Information Criteria
        Akaike (AIC)                                   9123.277
        Bayesian (BIC)                                 9230.493
        Sample-Size Adjusted BIC                       9138.523
          (n* = (n + 2) / 24)

Chi-Square Test of Model Fit
        Value                                            68.819
        Degrees of Freedom                                   25
        P-Value                                          0.0000

RMSEA (Root Mean Square Error Of Approximation)
        Estimate                                          0.077
        90 Percent C.I.                         0.055     0.099
        Probability RMSEA <= .05                          0.021

CFI/TLI
        CFI                                               0.962
        TLI                                               0.946

Chi-Square Test of Model Fit for the Baseline Model
        Value                                          1199.615
        Degrees of Freedom                                   36
        P-Value                                          0.0000

SRMR (Standardized Root Mean Square Residual)
        Value                                             0.072
```

142 USING MPLUS FOR STRUCTURAL EQUATION MODELING

Note: The model provides an "okay" but not outstanding fit to the data. The CFI and TLI exceed or equal .95, and the RMSEA is less than .08. However, the χ^2 value is significant, as is the test of close fit.

```
MODEL RESULTS
                                                        Two-Tailed
                    Estimate      S.E.    Est./S.E.     P-Value

 SAFETY  BY
    SATT1              1.000     0.000      999.000       999.000
    SATT2              1.214     0.122        9.968         0.000
    SATT3              6.124     0.813        7.531         0.000

 JUSTICE BY
    JUST1              1.000     0.000      999.000       999.000
    JUST2              1.337     0.103       12.941         0.000
    JUST3              1.206     0.095       12.651         0.000

 AFFCOM  BY
    ACOM1              1.000     0.000      999.000       999.000
    ACOM2              1.007     0.064       15.711         0.000
    ACOM3             -0.675     0.071       -9.519         0.000
```

Note: This is the measurement part of the model. All estimated parameters are significant.

```
 SAFETY  ON
    AFFCOM             0.126     0.027        4.725         0.000

 AFFCOM  ON
    JUSTICE            0.970     0.108        8.979         0.000
```

Note: This is the structural component of the model. Again, both estimated parameters are significant.

```
 Intercepts
    SATT1              3.965     0.040       99.548         0.000
    SATT2              3.964     0.053       75.480         0.000
    SATT3             26.248     0.440       59.632         0.000
    JUST1              4.868     0.083       58.390         0.000
    JUST2              4.551     0.086       52.931         0.000
    JUST3              4.942     0.082       60.374         0.000
    ACOM1              3.356     0.100       33.514         0.000
    ACOM2              3.646     0.099       36.649         0.000
    ACOM3              3.302     0.104       31.630         0.000

 Variances
    JUSTICE            0.979     0.152        6.422         0.000
```

Chapter 7: Latent Variable Path Analysis   143

```
Residual Variances
    SATT1        0.121      0.033      3.730      0.000
    SATT2        0.304      0.051      5.908      0.000
    SATT3       44.554      3.894     11.442      0.000
    JUST1        1.092      0.102     10.682      0.000
    JUST2        0.454      0.081      5.593      0.000
    JUST3        0.573      0.075      7.619      0.000
    ACOM1        0.774      0.122      6.358      0.000
    ACOM2        0.705      0.121      5.844      0.000
    ACOM3        2.238      0.197     11.363      0.000
    SAFETY       0.317      0.047      6.790      0.000
    AFFCOM       1.293      0.169      7.654      0.000

STANDARDIZED MODEL RESULTS

STDYX Standardization
                                                Two-Tailed
                 Estimate      S.E.   Est./S.E.   P-Value

SAFETY BY
    SATT1        0.862      0.041     21.150      0.000
    SATT2        0.794      0.041     19.538      0.000
    SATT3        0.478      0.051      9.367      0.000

JUSTICE BY
    JUST1        0.687      0.035     19.558      0.000
    JUST2        0.891      0.022     40.658      0.000
    JUST3        0.844      0.024     35.053      0.000

AFFCOM BY
    ACOM1        0.861      0.025     34.192      0.000
    ACOM2        0.872      0.025     35.189      0.000
    ACOM3       -0.557      0.045    -12.500      0.000

SAFETY ON
    AFFCOM       0.315      0.064      4.886      0.000

AFFCOM ON
    JUSTICE      0.645      0.044     14.816      0.000

Intercepts
    SATT1        5.767      0.243     23.711      0.000
    SATT2        4.372      0.188     23.228      0.000
    SATT3        3.454      0.153     22.593      0.000
    JUST1        3.382      0.150     22.524      0.000
    JUST2        3.066      0.138     22.169      0.000
    JUST3        3.497      0.155     22.633      0.000
    ACOM1        1.941      0.098     19.733      0.000
    ACOM2        2.123      0.104     20.318      0.000
    ACOM3        1.832      0.095     19.326      0.000

Variances
    JUSTICE      1.000      0.000    999.000    999.000
```

Residual Variances

SATT1	0.256	0.070	3.648	0.000
SATT2	0.370	0.064	5.736	0.000
SATT3	0.772	0.049	15.829	0.000
JUST1	0.527	0.048	10.913	0.000
JUST2	0.206	0.039	5.276	0.000
JUST3	0.287	0.041	7.056	0.000
ACOM1	0.259	0.043	5.979	0.000
ACOM2	0.239	0.043	5.523	0.000
ACOM3	0.689	0.050	13.860	0.000
SAFETY	0.901	0.041	22.180	0.000
AFFCOM	0.584	0.056	10.408	0.000

STDY Standardization

	Estimate	S.E.	Est./S.E.	Two-Tailed P-Value
SAFETY BY				
SATT1	0.862	0.041	21.150	0.000
SATT2	0.794	0.041	19.538	0.000
SATT3	0.478	0.051	9.367	0.000
JUSTICE BY				
JUST1	0.687	0.035	19.558	0.000
JUST2	0.891	0.022	40.658	0.000
JUST3	0.844	0.024	35.053	0.000
AFFCOM BY				
ACOM1	0.861	0.025	34.192	0.000
ACOM2	0.872	0.025	35.189	0.000
ACOM3	-0.557	0.045	-12.500	0.000
SAFETY ON				
AFFCOM	0.315	0.064	4.886	0.000
AFFCOM ON				
JUSTICE	0.645	0.044	14.816	0.000
Intercepts				
SATT1	5.767	0.243	23.711	0.000
SATT2	4.372	0.188	23.228	0.000
SATT3	3.454	0.153	22.593	0.000
JUST1	3.382	0.150	22.524	0.000
JUST2	3.066	0.138	22.169	0.000
JUST3	3.497	0.155	22.633	0.000
ACOM1	1.941	0.098	19.733	0.000
ACOM2	2.123	0.104	20.318	0.000
ACOM3	1.832	0.095	19.326	0.000
Variances				
JUSTICE	1.000	0.000	999.000	999.000

Residual Variances

SATT1	0.256	0.070	3.648	0.000
SATT2	0.370	0.064	5.736	0.000
SATT3	0.772	0.049	15.829	0.000
JUST1	0.527	0.048	10.913	0.000
JUST2	0.206	0.039	5.276	0.000
JUST3	0.287	0.041	7.056	0.000
ACOM1	0.259	0.043	5.979	0.000
ACOM2	0.239	0.043	5.523	0.000
ACOM3	0.689	0.050	13.860	0.000
SAFETY	0.901	0.041	22.180	0.000
AFFCOM	0.584	0.056	10.408	0.000

STD Standardization

	Estimate	S.E.	Est./S.E.	Two-Tailed P-Value
SAFETY BY				
SATT1	0.593	0.041	14.473	0.000
SATT2	0.720	0.054	13.436	0.000
SATT3	3.631	0.454	7.990	0.000
JUSTICE BY				
JUST1	0.989	0.077	12.844	0.000
JUST2	1.323	0.072	18.336	0.000
JUST3	1.193	0.070	17.013	0.000
AFFCOM BY				
ACOM1	1.488	0.087	17.143	0.000
ACOM2	1.498	0.086	17.442	0.000
ACOM3	-1.005	0.102	-9.810	0.000
SAFETY ON				
AFFCOM	0.315	0.064	4.886	0.000
AFFCOM ON				
JUSTICE	0.645	0.044	14.816	0.000
Intercepts				
SATT1	3.965	0.040	99.548	0.000
SATT2	3.964	0.053	75.480	0.000
SATT3	26.248	0.440	59.632	0.000
JUST1	4.868	0.083	58.390	0.000
JUST2	4.551	0.086	52.931	0.000
JUST3	4.942	0.082	60.374	0.000
ACOM1	3.356	0.100	33.514	0.000
ACOM2	3.646	0.099	36.649	0.000
ACOM3	3.302	0.104	31.630	0.000
Variances				
JUSTICE	1.000	0.000	999.000	999.000

Residual Variances

SATT1	0.121	0.033	3.730	0.000
SATT2	0.304	0.051	5.908	0.000
SATT3	44.554	3.894	11.442	0.000
JUST1	1.092	0.102	10.682	0.000
JUST2	0.454	0.081	5.593	0.000
JUST3	0.573	0.075	7.619	0.000
ACOM1	0.774	0.122	6.358	0.000
ACOM2	0.705	0.121	5.844	0.000
ACOM3	2.238	0.197	11.363	0.000
SAFETY	0.901	0.041	22.180	0.000
AFFCOM	0.584	0.056	10.408	0.000

R-SQUARE

Observed Variable	Estimate	S.E.	Est./S.E.	Two-Tailed P-Value
SATT1	0.744	0.070	10.575	0.000
SATT2	0.630	0.064	9.769	0.000
SATT3	0.228	0.049	4.683	0.000
JUST1	0.473	0.048	9.779	0.000
JUST2	0.794	0.039	20.329	0.000
JUST3	0.713	0.041	17.527	0.000
ACOM1	0.741	0.043	17.096	0.000
ACOM2	0.761	0.043	17.594	0.000
ACOM3	0.311	0.050	6.250	0.000

Latent Variable	Estimate	S.E.	Est./S.E.	Two-Tailed P-Value
SAFETY	0.099	0.041	2.443	0.015
AFFCOM	0.416	0.056	7.408	0.000

QUALITY OF NUMERICAL RESULTS

Condition Number for the Information Matrix   0.209E-02
(ratio of smallest to largest eigenvalue)

MODEL MODIFICATION INDICES

Minimum M.I. value for printing the modification index   10.000

	M.I.	E.P.C.	Std E.P.C.	StdYX E.P.C.

ON/BY Statements

SATT3   ON JUSTICE   /
JUSTICE   BY SATT3   14.237   1.661   1.644   0.216

```
SAFETY   ON JUSTICE    /
JUSTICE  BY SAFETY          11.878      0.193       0.321       0.321
JUSTICE  ON SAFETY     /
SAFETY   BY JUSTICE         11.878      0.595       0.357       0.357
AFFCOM   ON SAFETY     /
SAFETY   BY AFFCOM          11.878     -0.811      -0.323      -0.323

ON Statements

SAFETY   ON JUST1           10.351      0.092       0.156       0.224
SAFETY   ON JUST2           12.777      0.111       0.187       0.278
JUSTICE  ON SATT3           20.970      0.041       0.041       0.314
AFFCOM   ON SATT1           13.874     -0.639      -0.430      -0.295
SATT3    ON JUST2           19.308      1.202       1.202       0.235
JUST2    ON SATT3           16.072      0.028       0.028       0.142

WITH Statements

JUSTICE  WITH SAFETY        11.878      0.188       0.339       0.339
AFFCOM   WITH SAFETY        11.878     -0.257      -0.401      -0.401
SATT3    WITH JUSTICE       14.237      1.626       1.644       0.246
JUST2    WITH SATT3         13.067      1.288       1.288       0.286
```

I proceeded to test the partially mediated and nonmediated models (Figures 7.2 and 7.3), and the fit indices for all tested models are shown in Table 7.1. The measurement model and the partially mediated model provide, in this case, exactly the same fit to the data. This is because the structural component of the model is saturated or just identified. Although the model as a whole is overidentified, the overidentification comes from the measurement component of the model rather than from the structural elements of the model.

The fully mediated model is nested within the partially mediated model, so we can assess the difference in model fit using a chi-square difference test. In this case, the partially mediated model provides a better fit to the data, $\chi^2_{\text{difference}}(1) = 12.17$, $p < .01$. The nonmediated model is also nested within the partially mediated model, and the two models provide the same level of fit to the data, $\chi^2_{\text{difference}}(1) = 0.93$, ns. Although the models fit the data equally well, the nonmediated model has 1 fewer degree of freedom (i.e., has one fewer estimated parameter in the model), making it the more parsimonious model. Therefore, this is the model I would choose to retain.

The command file for the nonmediated model is presented below. Note that I had to specify that the correlation between affective commitment and

Table 7.1 Fit Indices for the Four Models

Model	χ^2	df	CFI	TLI	RMSEA	SRMR
Measurement	56.65**	24	.97	.96	.07	.05
Fully mediated	68.82**	25	.96	.95	.08*	.07
Partially mediated	56.65**	24	.97	.96	.07	.05
Nonmediated	57.58**	25	.97	.96	.07	.05

*$p < .05$. **$p < .01$.

safety participation was zero. By default, Mplus will estimate this correlation, resulting in a different version of the saturated model. It is always important to check the output file to ensure that the model being estimated is the one you think is being estimated.

```
TITLE:     Example of latent variable path analysis;
DATA:      FILE IS Chapter7.dat;
VARIABLE:  NAMES ARE SATT1 SATT2 SATT3 JUST1 JUST2 JUST3 ACOM1 ACOM2 ACOM3;
MODEL:     Safety BY SATT1-SATT3;
           Justice BY JUST1-JUST3;
           Affcome BY ACOM1 - ACOM3;
           Affcom ON Justice;
           Safety ON Justice;
           Affcom WITH Safety @ 0; ! This declares the correlation to be zero
OUTPUT:    STANDARDIZED MODINDICES (ALL)
```

Sample Results

Descriptive statistics and intercorrelations for all study variables are presented in Table 7.2. All models were estimated using Mplus 7.1 (Muthén & Muthén, 1998-2013) and were based on maximum likelihood estimation.

Four models were estimated. First the measurement model defined three latent variables, each indicated by three observed variables. Then the structural models previously described as the fully mediated (Figure 7.1), partially mediated (Figure 7.2), and nonmediated (Figure 7.3) models were estimated.

Table 7.2 Descriptive Statistics and Intercorrelations for All Study Variables

Variable	M	SD	1	2	3	4	5	6	7	8
Safety 1	3.97	0.69	1.00							
Safety 2	3.97	0.91	.69	1.00						
Safety 3	26.25	7.60	.42	.35	1.00					
Justice 1	4.87	1.44	.28	.24	.26	1.00				
Justice 2	4.55	1.48	.27	.27	.36	.61	1.00			
Justice 3	4.94	1.41	.19	.23	.22	.56	.76	1.00		
Commitment 1	3.36	1.73	.23	.23	.26	.45	.50	.45	1.00	
Commitment 2	3.65	1.72	.16	.22	.23	.40	.46	.46	.76	1.00
Commitment 3	3.30	1.80	−.05	−.12	−.10	−.32	−.33	−.36	−.44	−.51

Note: $r > .10$, $p < .01$.

Results of these analyses are presented in Table 7.1. As shown, the measurement model, partially mediated model, and nonmediated models all provided acceptable fits to the data. The fully mediated model provided a worse fit to the data than did the partially mediated model, $\chi^2_{\text{difference}}(1) = 12.17$, $p < .01$. The nonmediated and partially mediated models provided the same level of fit to the data, $\chi^2_{\text{difference}}(1) = 0.93$, ns. Therefore, the latter was retained as the best fitting, most parsimonious model. Standardized results for the nonmediated model are presented in Figure 7.4. As shown, perceptions of organizational injustice predicted both affective commitment to the organization ($\beta = .64$, $p < .01$) and participation in safety programs ($\beta = .38$, $p < .01$)

150 USING MPLUS FOR STRUCTURAL EQUATION MODELING

Figure 7.4

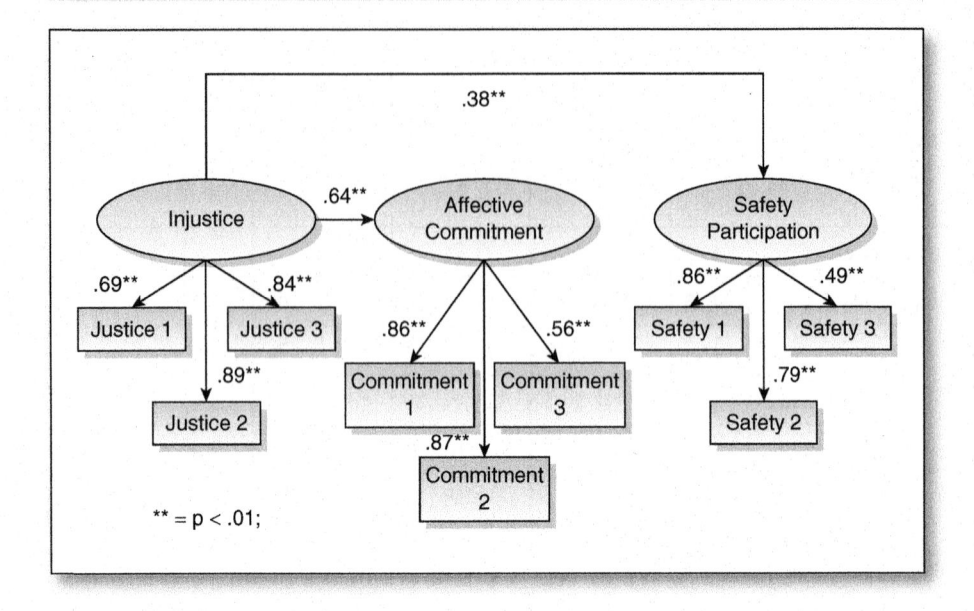

```
                        .38**
         ┌─────────────────────────────────────────┐
         │         .64**                           │
         ▼                                         ▼
    ┌─────────┐         ┌──────────┐         ┌──────────────┐
    │Injustice│────────▶│ Affective│         │    Safety    │
    │         │         │Commitment│         │Participation │
    └─────────┘         └──────────┘         └──────────────┘
   .69**  .84**        .86**   .56**        .86**      .49**
    │  .89** │          │       │            │   .79**   │
    ▼    ▼   ▼          ▼       ▼            ▼    ▼      ▼
 ┌──────┐┌──────┐  ┌──────────┐┌──────────┐┌──────┐┌──────┐┌──────┐
 │Justice││Justice│ │Commitment││Commitment││Safety ││Safety││Safety│
 │  1   ││  3   │ │    1     ││    3     ││  1   ││  2   ││  3   │
 └──────┘└──────┘  └──────────┘└──────────┘└──────┘└──────┘└──────┘
         │                  .87**
         ▼                    │
     ┌────────┐           ┌──────────┐
     │Justice │           │Commitment│
     │   2    │           │    2     │
     └────────┘           └──────────┘

** = p < .01;
```

8

Longitudinal Analysis

Researchers are constantly exhorted to move beyond cross-sectional analysis to the use of longitudinal designs. It has long been recognized that cross-sectional data may result in biased parameter estimates (Maxwell & Cole, 2007) and does not allow causal inference (Taris, 2003). Moreover, our conceptualization of what constitutes longitudinal data has changed (Kelloway & Francis, 2012); increasingly, researchers recognize the need for at least three waves of data. Although two-wave studies are still common, we now recognize that such designs are inadequate for describing the process of change (Singer & Willett, 2003) and may confound measurement change with substantive change (Ployhart & Vandenberg, 2010; Singer & Willett, 2003).

In this chapter, we consider three common models for longitudinal analysis, recognizing that there are many other possible combinations and ways to analyze change data. First, we consider tests of measurement equivalence, a longitudinal extension of confirmatory factor analysis (for a complete review, see Vandenberg & Lance, 2000) designed to establish measurement equivalence over time. Such tests are often a valuable precursor to models aimed at establishing substantive change. Second, we illustrate the testing of cross-lagged models that examine predictor-criterion relations across waves of data. Finally, we take a different approach in looking at the testing of latent growth curves, with the potential to examine predictor-criterion relations using cross-domain latent growth curves (McArdle & Hamagami, 1996; see also Pitariu & Ployhart, 2010).

Measurement Equivalence Across Time

Following our established convention of three indicators for each latent variable, and recognizing the desirability of at least three waves of data collection in our longitudinal study, Figure 8.1 presents a hypothesized measurement structure for psychological well-being. Each of the latent variables (i.e., well-being at each time point) is indicated by three observed variables, and the latent variables are allowed to correlate with one another.

Figure 8.1

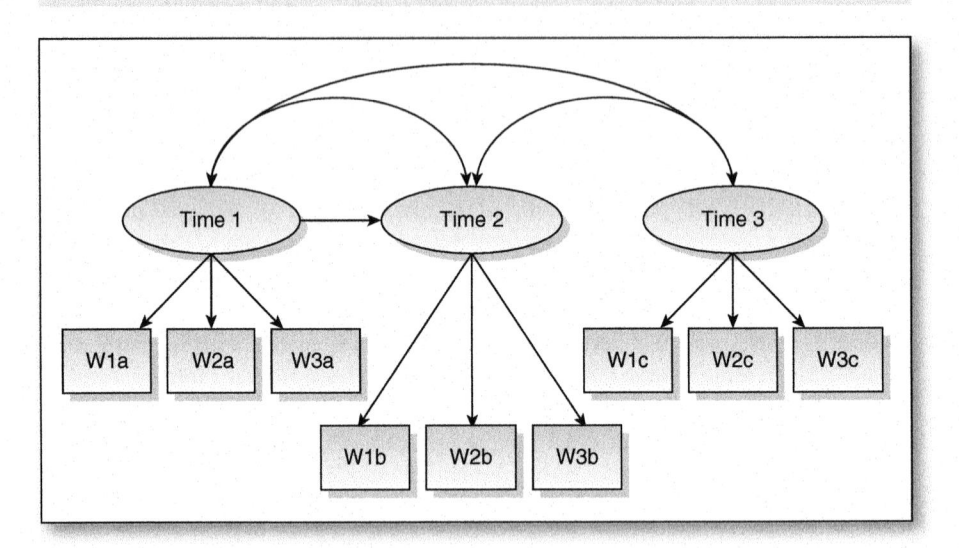

You will recognize this as the confirmatory factor analysis model introduced in Chapter 5. The Mplus code to generate the model is as follows:

```
TITLE:     Measurement invariance over time;
DATA:      FILE IS ch8a.dat;
VARIABLE:  NAMES ARE W1B W2B W3B W1C W2C W3C W1A W2A W3A;
MODEL:     TIME3 BY W1C;
           TIME3 BY W2C;
           TIME3 BY W3C;
           TIME2 BY W1B;
           TIME2 BY W2B;
           TIME2 BY W3B;
           TIME1 BY W1A;
           TIME1 BY W2A;
           TIME1 BY W3A;
OUTPUT:    STANDARDIZED MODINDICES (ALL);
```

We wish to establish the equivalence of factor loadings (i.e., the parameters linking the latent and observed variables) across time. To do so, we will use the procedure for testing equality constraints introduced in Chapter 6. That is, we will first estimate the confirmatory factor analysis and then impose the required equality constraints, constraining similar parameters from each time wave to equality. The relevant Mplus code is as follows:

```
TITLE:     Measurement invariance over time;
DATA:      FILE IS ch8a.dat;
VARIABLE:  NAMES ARE W1B w2B W3B W1C W2C W3C W1A W2A W3A;
MODEL:     TIME3 BY W1C;
           TIME3 BY W2C (B);
           TIME3 BY W3C (C);
           TIME2 BY W1B;
           TIME2 BY W2B (B);
           TIME2 BY W3B (C);
           TIME1 BY W1A;
           TIME1 BY W2A (B);
           TIME1 BY W3A (C);
OUTPUT:    STANDARDIZED MODINDICES (ALL);
```

Recall that the first parameter defining each latent variable is fixed to 1.0 in order to assign a scale of measurement to the latent variable. Therefore, there is no need to fix these parameters to equality (as they are already equal). Doing so will have no effect on the analysis, but it is not necessary. Therefore, we are imposing two equality constraints on the model: declaring the second parameter on each latent variable to be equal across the three time periods to one another and then constraining the third parameter or factor loading to equality across the three time periods.

Estimating the original confirmatory factor analysis model resulted in $\chi^2(24) = 656.14$, $p < .01$. Adding the equality constraints described above resulted in $\chi^2(28) = 657.69$, $p < .01$, resulting in $\chi^2_{\text{difference}}(4) = 1.55$, ns. Because the test is not significant, it can be interpreted as support for the hypothesis of measurement equivalence in that constraining the parameters to equality did not significantly worsen the fit of the model. It is instructive on several counts to examine the results of running the code with the equality constraints.

```
Mplus VERSION 7 (Mac)
MUTHEN & MUTHEN

INPUT INSTRUCTIONS

TITLE:     Measurement invariance over time;
DATA:      FILE IS ch8a.dat;
VARIABLE:  NAMES ARE W1B w2B W3B W1C W2C W3C W1A W2A W3A;
MODEL:     TIME3 BY W1C;
           TIME3 BY W2C (B);
           TIME3 BY W3C (C);
```

```
            TIME2 BY W1B;
            TIME2 BY W2B (B);
            TIME2 BY W3B (C);
            TIME1 BY W1A;
            TIME1 BY W2A (B);
            TIME1 BY W3A (C);
OUTPUT:     STANDARDIZED MODINDICES (ALL);
```

INPUT READING TERMINATED NORMALLY

Measurement invariance over time;

SUMMARY OF ANALYSIS
Number of groups   1
Number of observations   627
Number of dependent variables   9
Number of independent variables   0
Number of continuous latent variables   3

Observed dependent variables
  Continuous
     W1B   W2B   W3B   W1C   W2C   W3C
     W1A   W2A   W3A

Continuous latent variables
     TIME3   TIME2   TIME1

Estimator   ML
Information matrix   OBSERVED
Maximum number of iterations   1000
Convergence criterion   0.500D-04
Maximum number of steepest descent iterations   20

Input data file(s)
  ch8a.dat

Input data format FREE

THE MODEL ESTIMATION TERMINATED NORMALLY

MODEL FIT INFORMATION

Number of Free Parameters   26

Loglikelihood
          H0 Value   -6348.568
          H1 Value   -6019.721

Information Criteria
          Akaike (AIC)   12749.136
          Bayesian (BIC)   12864.601
          Sample-Size Adjusted BIC   12782.054
             (n* = (n + 2) / 24)

```
Chi-Square Test of Model Fit
        Value                                            657.694
        Degrees of Freedom                                    28
        P-Value                                           0.0000

RMSEA (Root Mean Square Error Of Approximation)
        Estimate                                           0.189
        90 Percent C.I.                            0.177   0.202
        Probability RMSEA <= .05                           0.000

CFI/TLI
        CFI                                                0.895
        TLI                                                0.865

Chi-Square Test of Model Fit for the Baseline Model
        Value                                           6021.872
        Degrees of Freedom                                    36
        P-Value                                           0.0000

SRMR (Standardized Root Mean Square Residual)
        Value                                              0.036
```

Note: Although there was no difference between the constrained and unconstrained model, the model does not provide an absolute good fit to the data.

```
MODEL RESULTS

                                                       Two-Tailed
                     Estimate     S.E.    Est./S.E.      P-Value

  TIME3   BY
    W1C                 1.000    0.000      999.000      999.000
    W2C                 1.162    0.022       52.467        0.000
    W3C                 1.463    0.027       54.596        0.000

  TIME2   BY
    W1B                 1.000    0.000      999.000      999.000
    W2B                 1.162    0.022       52.467        0.000
    W3B                 1.463    0.027       54.596        0.000

  TIME1   BY
    W1A                 1.000    0.000      999.000      999.000
    W2A                 1.162    0.022       52.467        0.000
    W3A                 1.463    0.027       54.596        0.000

  TIME2   WITH
    TIME3               0.630    0.045       13.957        0.000

  TIME1   WITH
    TIME3               0.630    0.045       13.892        0.000
    TIME2               0.705    0.049       14.491        0.000
```

```
Intercepts
    W1B              2.881      0.041      70.564      0.000
    W2B              2.850      0.047      60.321      0.000
    W3B              3.202      0.058      54.736      0.000
    W1C              2.805      0.040      70.252      0.000
    W2C              2.738      0.045      60.313      0.000
    W3C              3.070      0.056      55.146      0.000
    W1A              2.907      0.042      69.929      0.000
    W2A              2.870      0.048      60.257      0.000
    W3A              3.298      0.059      56.266      0.000

Variances
    TIME3            0.749      0.050      15.107      0.000
    TIME2            0.822      0.054      15.323      0.000
    TIME1            0.837      0.055      15.269      0.000

Residual Variances
    W1B              0.223      0.017      13.008      0.000
    W2B              0.290      0.022      12.903      0.000
    W3B              0.387      0.032      12.009      0.000
    W1C              0.251      0.019      13.466      0.000
    W2C              0.281      0.022      12.860      0.000
    W3C              0.341      0.030      11.257      0.000
    W1A              0.247      0.018      13.345      0.000
    W2A              0.293      0.023      12.904      0.000
    W3A              0.365      0.032      11.556      0.000

STANDARDIZED MODEL RESULTS

STDYX Standardization
                                                    Two-Tailed
                  Estimate    S.E.   Est./S.E.     P-Value

TIME3 BY
    W1C              0.866      0.011      76.872      0.000
    W2C              0.885      0.010      88.162      0.000
    W3C              0.908      0.009      99.193      0.000

TIME2 BY
    W1B              0.887      0.010      89.649      0.000
    W2B              0.890      0.010      91.344      0.000
    W3B              0.905      0.009     101.032      0.000

TIME1 BY
    W1A              0.879      0.010      85.640      0.000
    W2A              0.891      0.010      91.995      0.000
    W3A              0.911      0.009     105.118      0.000

TIME2 WITH
    TIME3            0.803      0.018      44.212      0.000
```

```
TIME1 WITH
    TIME3              0.795      0.019      42.970      0.000
    TIME2              0.850      0.015      56.689      0.000

Intercepts
    W1B                2.818      0.084      33.406      0.000
    W2B                2.409      0.075      32.198      0.000
    W3B                2.186      0.071      30.930      0.000
    W1C                2.806      0.082      34.038      0.000
    W2C                2.409      0.075      32.127      0.000
    W3C                2.202      0.071      30.910      0.000
    W1A                2.793      0.083      33.525      0.000
    W2A                2.406      0.075      32.173      0.000
    W3A                2.247      0.072      31.058      0.000

Variances
    TIME3              1.000      0.000     999.000     999.000
    TIME2              1.000      0.000     999.000     999.000
    TIME1              1.000      0.000     999.000     999.000

Residual Variances
    W1B                0.214      0.018      12.185      0.000
    W2B                0.207      0.017      11.942      0.000
    W3B                0.180      0.016      11.120      0.000
    W1C                0.251      0.019      12.856      0.000
    W2C                0.217      0.018      12.249      0.000
    W3C                0.175      0.017      10.545      0.000
    W1A                0.228      0.018      12.623      0.000
    W2A                0.206      0.017      11.913      0.000
    W3A                0.169      0.016      10.705      0.000

STDY Standardization
                                                     Two-Tailed
                    Estimate      S.E.   Est./S.E.    P-Value

TIME3 BY
    W1C                0.866      0.011      76.872      0.000
    W2C                0.885      0.010      88.162      0.000
    W3C                0.908      0.009      99.193      0.000

TIME2 BY
    W1B                0.887      0.010      89.649      0.000
    W2B                0.890      0.010      91.344      0.000
    W3B                0.905      0.009     101.032      0.000

TIME1 BY
    W1A                0.879      0.010      85.640      0.000
    W2A                0.891      0.010      91.995      0.000
    W3A                0.911      0.009     105.118      0.000
```

TIME2 WITH
    TIME3   0.803   0.018   44.212   0.000

TIME1 WITH
    TIME3   0.795   0.019   42.970   0.000
    TIME2   0.850   0.015   56.689   0.000

Intercepts
    W1B   2.818   0.084   33.406   0.000
    W2B   2.409   0.075   32.198   0.000
    W3B   2.186   0.071   30.930   0.000
    W1C   2.806   0.082   34.038   0.000
    W2C   2.409   0.075   32.127   0.000
    W3C   2.202   0.071   30.910   0.000
    W1A   2.793   0.083   33.525   0.000
    W2A   2.406   0.075   32.173   0.000
    W3A   2.247   0.072   31.058   0.000

Variances
    TIME3   1.000   0.000   999.000   999.000
    TIME2   1.000   0.000   999.000   999.000
    TIME1   1.000   0.000   999.000   999.000

Residual Variances
    W1B   0.214   0.018   12.185   0.000
    W2B   0.207   0.017   11.942   0.000
    W3B   0.180   0.016   11.120   0.000
    W1C   0.251   0.019   12.856   0.000
    W2C   0.217   0.018   12.249   0.000
    W3C   0.175   0.017   10.545   0.000
    W1A   0.228   0.018   12.623   0.000
    W2A   0.206   0.017   11.913   0.000
    W3A   0.169   0.016   10.705   0.000

STD Standardization

                                                    Two-Tailed
                   Estimate   S.E.   Est./S.E.   P-Value

TIME3 BY
    W1C   0.865   0.029   30.214   0.000
    W2C   1.006   0.033   30.739   0.000
    W3C   1.266   0.041   31.150   0.000

TIME2 BY
    W1B   0.907   0.030   30.647   0.000
    W2B   1.053   0.034   30.776   0.000
    W3B   1.326   0.043   31.165   0.000

TIME1 BY
    W1A   0.915   0.030   30.538   0.000
    W2A   1.063   0.035   30.786   0.000
    W3A   1.338   0.043   31.293   0.000

```
TIME2 WITH
    TIME3                    0.803      0.018        44.212          0.000

TIME1 WITH
    TIME3                    0.795      0.019        42.970          0.000
    TIME2                    0.850      0.015        56.689          0.000

Intercepts
    W1B                      2.881      0.041        70.564          0.000
    W2B                      2.850      0.047        60.321          0.000
    W3B                      3.202      0.058        54.736          0.000
    W1C                      2.805      0.040        70.252          0.000
    W2C                      2.738      0.045        60.313          0.000
    W3C                      3.070      0.056        55.146          0.000
    W1A                      2.907      0.042        69.929          0.000
    W2A                      2.870      0.048        60.257          0.000
    W3A                      3.298      0.059        56.266          0.000

Variances
    TIME3                    1.000      0.000       999.000        999.000
    TIME2                    1.000      0.000       999.000        999.000
    TIME1                    1.000      0.000       999.000        999.000

Residual Variances
    W1B                      0.223      0.017        13.008          0.000
    W2B                      0.290      0.022        12.903          0.000
    W3B                      0.387      0.032        12.009          0.000
    W1C                      0.251      0.019        13.466          0.000
    W2C                      0.281      0.022        12.860          0.000
    W3C                      0.341      0.030        11.257          0.000
    W1A                      0.247      0.018        13.345          0.000
    W2A                      0.293      0.023        12.904          0.000
    W3A                      0.365      0.032        11.556          0.000

R-SQUARE
    Observed                                                     Two-Tailed
    Variable      Estimate       S.E.     Est./S.E.              P-Value
    W1B              0.786       0.018        44.825               0.000
    W2B              0.793       0.017        45.672               0.000
    W3B              0.820       0.016        50.516               0.000
    W1C              0.749       0.019        38.436               0.000
    W2C              0.783       0.018        44.081               0.000
    W3C              0.825       0.017        49.597               0.000
    W1A              0.772       0.018        42.820               0.000
    W2A              0.794       0.017        45.997               0.000
    W3A              0.831       0.016        52.559               0.000

QUALITY OF NUMERICAL RESULTS

Condition Number for the Information Matrix            0.628E-02
(ratio of smallest to largest eigenvalue)
```

MODEL MODIFICATION INDICES

Minimum M.I. value for printing the modification index   10.000

	M.I.	E.P.C.	Std E.P.C.	StdYX E.P.C.

ON Statements

	M.I.	E.P.C.	Std E.P.C.	StdYX E.P.C.
TIME2 ON W1B	14.502	-0.255	-0.282	-0.288
TIME2 ON W3B	10.232	0.180	0.199	0.291
TIME2 ON W1C	15.770	0.203	0.224	0.224
TIME1 ON W1A	17.991	-0.266	-0.290	-0.302
W1B ON W1C	57.579	0.190	0.190	0.186
W1B ON W1A	40.429	0.157	0.157	0.160
W2B ON W1C	10.574	-0.093	-0.093	-0.078
W2B ON W2C	14.627	0.097	0.097	0.094
W2B ON W2A	23.674	0.120	0.120	0.121
W3B ON W2C	17.660	-0.128	-0.128	-0.099
W3B ON W1A	13.935	-0.125	-0.125	-0.089
W3B ON W2A	12.483	-0.104	-0.104	-0.085
W1C ON W1B	68.548	0.208	0.208	0.212
W1C ON W1A	31.592	0.138	0.138	0.143
W2C ON W1B	10.867	-0.091	-0.091	-0.082
W2C ON W3B	20.907	-0.088	-0.088	-0.114
W3C ON W1B	12.352	-0.115	-0.115	-0.084
W1A ON W1B	38.541	0.160	0.160	0.158
W1A ON W1C	33.452	0.149	0.149	0.143
W2A ON W2B	16.773	0.103	0.103	0.102
W2A ON W2C	10.596	0.083	0.083	0.079

WITH Statements

	M.I.	E.P.C.	Std E.P.C.	StdYX E.P.C.
W1B WITH TIME2	14.502	-0.057	-0.063	-0.133
W2B WITH W1B	10.232	-0.055	-0.055	-0.218
W3B WITH TIME2	10.233	0.070	0.077	0.124
W3B WITH W2B	14.500	0.097	0.097	0.289
W1C WITH TIME2	15.770	0.051	0.056	0.112
W1C WITH W1B	158.095	0.154	0.154	0.650
W1C WITH W2B	37.116	-0.085	-0.085	-0.317
W2C WITH W1B	12.411	-0.047	-0.047	-0.187
W2C WITH W2B	72.182	0.130	0.130	0.455
W2C WITH W3B	48.493	-0.127	-0.127	-0.385
W3C WITH W1B	36.583	-0.094	-0.094	-0.341
W3C WITH W2B	12.342	-0.063	-0.063	-0.199
W3C WITH W3B	63.523	0.170	0.170	0.468
W1A WITH TIME1	17.992	-0.066	-0.072	-0.144
W1A WITH W1B	119.622	0.134	0.134	0.570
W1A WITH W2B	13.159	-0.051	-0.051	-0.190
W1A WITH W3B	23.914	-0.082	-0.082	-0.265
W1A WITH W1C	80.707	0.114	0.114	0.458
W1A WITH W3C	19.467	-0.071	-0.071	-0.245
W2A WITH W1B	26.876	-0.070	-0.070	-0.276
W2A WITH W2B	88.735	0.147	0.147	0.505

```
W2A WITH W3B      22.473    -0.088    -0.088    -0.262
W2A WITH W1C      22.339    -0.067    -0.067    -0.246
W2A WITH W2C      72.467     0.131     0.131     0.456
W2A WITH W3C      26.242    -0.092    -0.092    -0.291
W3A WITH W1B      11.253    -0.054    -0.054    -0.187
W3A WITH W2B      24.108    -0.090    -0.090    -0.276
W3A WITH W3B      45.539     0.148     0.148     0.394
W3A WITH W1C      19.517    -0.073    -0.073    -0.241
W3A WITH W2C      26.694    -0.093    -0.093    -0.291
W3A WITH W3C      70.481     0.177     0.177     0.502
W3A WITH W2A      17.995     0.111     0.111     0.341
```

Although these results support the hypothesis of measurement equivalence, the model as a whole does not provide a good fit to the data according to any of the measures of fit. As noted above, inspection of the modification indices suggests that allowing the residuals of similar measures across time to correlate (e.g., W1A with W1B with W1C) would substantially improve the fit of the model. Some might argue that this is a "wastebasket" parameter, but there is also an argument that allowing these correlations simply recognizes and incorporates the method covariance that results from using exactly the same measures over time. For the sake of exploration, I added the suggested modifications with a substantial change in model fit (see below).

```
Mplus VERSION 7 (Mac)
MUTHEN & MUTHEN

INPUT INSTRUCTIONS

TITLE:      Measurement invariance over time;
DATA:       FILE IS ch8a.dat;
VARIABLE:   NAMES ARE W1B W2B W3B W1C W2C W3C W1A W2A W3A;
MODEL:      TIME3 BY W1C;
            TIME3 BY W2C (B);
            TIME3 BY W3C (C);
            TIME2 BY W1B;
            TIME2 BY W2B (B);
            TIME2 BY W3B (C);
            TIME1 BY W1A;
            TIME1 BY W2A (B);
            TIME1 BY W3A (C);
            w1c WITH W1B W1A;
            w1b WITH W1A;
            w2c WITH W2B W2A;
            w2b WITH W2A;
            w3c WITH W3B W3A;
            w3b WITH W3A;
OUTPUT:     STANDARDIZED MODINDICES (ALL);
```

162 USING MPLUS FOR STRUCTURAL EQUATION MODELING

INPUT READING TERMINATED NORMALLY

Measurement invariance over time;

SUMMARY OF ANALYSIS

Number of groups   1
Number of observations   627
Number of dependent variables   9
Number of independent variables   0
Number of continuous latent variables   3

Observed dependent variables
   Continuous
      W1B   W2B   W3B   W1C   W2C   W3C
      W1A   W2A   W3A

Continuous latent variables
      TIME3   TIME2   TIME1

Estimator   ML
Information matrix   OBSERVED
Maximum number of iterations   1000
Convergence criterion   0.500D-04
Maximum number of steepest descent iterations   20

Input data file(s)
ch8a.dat
Input data format FREE

THE MODEL ESTIMATION TERMINATED NORMALLY

MODEL FIT INFORMATION

Number of Free Parameters   35

Loglikelihood
      H0 Value   -6055.843
      H1 Value   -6019.721

Information Criteria
      Akaike (AIC)   12181.685
      Bayesian (BIC)   12337.119
      Sample-Size Adjusted BIC   12225.998
         (n* = (n + 2) / 24)

Chi-Square Test of Model Fit
      Value   72.244
      Degrees of Freedom   19
      P-Value   0.0000

```
RMSEA (Root Mean Square Error Of Approximation)
        Estimate                                               0.067
        90 Percent C.I.                                0.051   0.084
        Probability RMSEA <= .05                               0.041

CFI/TLI
        CFI                                                    0.991
        TLI                                                    0.983

Chi-Square Test of Model Fit for the Baseline Model
        Value                                               6021.872
        Degrees of Freedom                                        36
        P-Value                                               0.0000

SRMR (Standardized Root Mean Square Residual)
        Value                                                  0.035
```

Note: The model now provides quite a reasonable fit to the data.

```
MODEL RESULTS

                                                        Two-Tailed
                    Estimate       S.E.    Est./S.E.       P-Value

TIME3 BY
    W1C                1.000      0.000      999.000       999.000
    W2C                1.250      0.031       40.211         0.000
    W3C                1.583      0.038       41.420         0.000

TIME2 BY
    W1B                1.000      0.000      999.000       999.000
    W2B                1.250      0.031       40.211         0.000
    W3B                1.583      0.038       41.420         0.000

TIME1 BY
    W1A                1.000      0.000      999.000       999.000
    W2A                1.250      0.031       40.211         0.000
    W3A                1.583      0.038       41.420         0.000

TIME2 WITH
    TIME3              0.532      0.043       12.466         0.000

TIME1 WITH
    TIME3              0.531      0.043       12.460         0.000
    TIME2              0.600      0.046       12.995         0.000

W1C WITH
    W1B                0.147      0.016        9.405         0.000
    W1A                0.111      0.016        7.124         0.000

W1B WITH
    W1A                0.128      0.015        8.297         0.000
```

164 USING MPLUS FOR STRUCTURAL EQUATION MODELING

```
W2C    WITH
   W2B                 0.107       0.019       5.693       0.000
   W2A                 0.108       0.019       5.829       0.000

W2B    WITH
   W2A                 0.122       0.019       6.414       0.000

W3C    WITH
   W3B                 0.110       0.026       4.133       0.000
   W3A                 0.122       0.026       4.724       0.000

W3B    WITH
   W3A                 0.091       0.027       3.385       0.001

Intercepts
   W1B                 2.881       0.040      72.910       0.000
   W2B                 2.850       0.048      59.877       0.000
   W3B                 3.202       0.059      54.429       0.000
   W1C                 2.805       0.039      72.320       0.000
   W2C                 2.738       0.046      59.752       0.000
   W3C                 3.070       0.056      54.777       0.000
   W1A                 2.907       0.040      71.981       0.000
   W2A                 2.870       0.048      59.822       0.000
   W3A                 3.298       0.059      55.815       0.000

Variances
   TIME3               0.665       0.048      13.981       0.000
   TIME2               0.727       0.051      14.179       0.000
   TIME1               0.744       0.053      14.120       0.000

Residual Variances
   W1B                 0.252       0.019      13.247       0.000
   W2B                 0.285       0.024      11.670       0.000
   W3B                 0.349       0.036       9.729       0.000
   W1C                 0.279       0.020      13.741       0.000
   W2C                 0.278       0.024      11.440       0.000
   W3C                 0.305       0.033       9.126       0.000
   W1A                 0.279       0.020      13.618       0.000
   W2A                 0.281       0.024      11.532       0.000
   W3A                 0.326       0.035       9.354       0.000
```

STANDARDIZED MODEL RESULTS

STDYX Standardization

```
                                                         Two-Tailed
                    Estimate       S.E.    Est./S.E.      P-Value

TIME3  BY
   W1C                 0.839       0.014      61.438       0.000
   W2C                 0.888       0.011      83.512       0.000
   W3C                 0.919       0.010      96.289       0.000
```

TIME2 BY				
W1B	0.862	0.012	69.887	0.000
W2B	0.894	0.010	87.700	0.000
W3B	0.916	0.009	97.680	0.000
TIME1 BY				
W1A	0.853	0.013	67.255	0.000
W2A	0.897	0.010	89.317	0.000
W3A	0.922	0.009	102.954	0.000
TIME2 WITH				
TIME3	0.765	0.019	39.811	0.000
TIME1 WITH				
TIME3	0.756	0.020	38.302	0.000
TIME2	0.816	0.016	51.250	0.000
W1C WITH				
W1B	0.555	0.036	15.283	0.000
W1A	0.398	0.043	9.342	0.000
W1B WITH				
W1A	0.483	0.040	12.163	0.000
W2C WITH				
W2B	0.381	0.051	7.493	0.000
W2A	0.388	0.050	7.695	0.000
W2B WITH				
W2A	0.430	0.048	8.901	0.000
W3C WITH				
W3B	0.336	0.063	5.321	0.000
W3A	0.388	0.061	6.327	0.000
W3B WITH				
W3A	0.270	0.066	4.111	0.000
Intercepts				
W1B	2.912	0.087	33.558	0.000
W2B	2.391	0.076	31.457	0.000
W3B	2.174	0.072	30.381	0.000
W1C	2.888	0.084	34.265	0.000
W2C	2.386	0.076	31.368	0.000
W3C	2.188	0.072	30.292	0.000
W1A	2.875	0.085	33.657	0.000
W2A	2.389	0.076	31.396	0.000
W3A	2.229	0.073	30.429	0.000

166 USING MPLUS FOR STRUCTURAL EQUATION MODELING

```
Variances
    TIME3               1.000      0.000    999.000    999.000
    TIME2               1.000      0.000    999.000    999.000
    TIME1               1.000      0.000    999.000    999.000

Residual Variances
    W1B                 0.258      0.021     12.121      0.000
    W2B                 0.200      0.018     10.983      0.000
    W3B                 0.161      0.017      9.347      0.000
    W1C                 0.295      0.023     12.882      0.000
    W2C                 0.211      0.019     11.184      0.000
    W3C                 0.155      0.018      8.810      0.000
    W1A                 0.273      0.022     12.605      0.000
    W2A                 0.195      0.018     10.788      0.000
    W3A                 0.149      0.017      9.019      0.000
```

STDY Standardization

	Estimate	S.E.	Est./S.E.	Two-Tailed P-Value
TIME3 BY				
W1C	0.839	0.014	61.438	0.000
W2C	0.888	0.011	83.512	0.000
W3C	0.919	0.010	96.289	0.000
TIME2 BY				
W1B	0.862	0.012	69.887	0.000
W2B	0.894	0.010	87.700	0.000
W3B	0.916	0.009	97.680	0.000
TIME1 BY				
W1A	0.853	0.013	67.255	0.000
W2A	0.897	0.010	89.317	0.000
W3A	0.922	0.009	102.954	0.000
TIME2 WITH				
TIME3	0.765	0.019	39.811	0.000
TIME1 WITH				
TIME3	0.756	0.020	38.302	0.000
TIME2	0.816	0.016	51.250	0.000
W1C WITH				
W1B	0.555	0.036	15.283	0.000
W1A	0.398	0.043	9.342	0.000
W1B WITH				
W1A	0.483	0.040	12.163	0.000
W2C WITH				
W2B	0.381	0.051	7.493	0.000
W2A	0.388	0.050	7.695	0.000
W2B WITH				
W2A	0.430	0.048	8.901	0.000

W3C WITH				
W3B	0.336	0.063	5.321	0.000
W3A	0.388	0.061	6.327	0.000
W3B WITH				
W3A	0.270	0.066	4.111	0.000
Intercepts				
W1B	2.912	0.087	33.558	0.000
W2B	2.391	0.076	31.457	0.000
W3B	2.174	0.072	30.381	0.000
W1C	2.888	0.084	34.265	0.000
W2C	2.386	0.076	31.368	0.000
W3C	2.188	0.072	30.292	0.000
W1A	2.875	0.085	33.657	0.000
W2A	2.389	0.076	31.396	0.000
W3A	2.229	0.073	30.429	0.000
Variances				
TIME3	1.000	0.000	999.000	999.000
TIME2	1.000	0.000	999.000	999.000
TIME1	1.000	0.000	999.000	999.000
Residual Variances				
W1B	0.258	0.021	12.121	0.000
W2B	0.200	0.018	10.983	0.000
W3B	0.161	0.017	9.347	0.000
W1C	0.295	0.023	12.882	0.000
W2C	0.211	0.019	11.184	0.000
W3C	0.155	0.018	8.810	0.000
W1A	0.273	0.022	12.605	0.000
W2A	0.195	0.018	10.788	0.000
W3A	0.149	0.017	9.019	0.000

STD Standardization

	Estimate	S.E.	Est./S.E.	Two-Tailed P-Value
TIME3 BY				
W1C	0.815	0.029	27.962	0.000
W2C	1.019	0.034	30.144	0.000
W3C	1.290	0.042	30.966	0.000
TIME2 BY				
W1B	0.853	0.030	28.359	0.000
W2B	1.066	0.035	30.093	0.000
W3B	1.349	0.043	31.074	0.000
TIME1 BY				
W1A	0.862	0.031	28.240	0.000
W2A	1.078	0.036	30.114	0.000
W3A	1.365	0.044	31.248	0.000
TIME2 WITH				
TIME3	0.765	0.019	39.811	0.000

```
TIME1 WITH
    TIME3              0.756      0.020      38.302     0.000
    TIME2              0.816      0.016      51.250     0.000

W1C WITH
    W1B                0.147      0.016       9.405     0.000
    W1A                0.111      0.016       7.124     0.000

W1B WITH
    W1A                0.128      0.015       8.297     0.000

W2C WITH
    W2B                0.107      0.019       5.693     0.000
    W2A                0.108      0.019       5.829     0.000

W2B WITH
    W2A                0.122      0.019       6.414     0.000

W3C WITH
    W3B                0.110      0.026       4.133     0.000
    W3A                0.122      0.026       4.724     0.000

W3B WITH
    W3A                0.091      0.027       3.385     0.001

Intercepts
    W1B                2.881      0.040      72.910     0.000
    W2B                2.850      0.048      59.877     0.000
    W3B                3.202      0.059      54.429     0.000
    W1C                2.805      0.039      72.320     0.000
    W2C                2.738      0.046      59.752     0.000
    W3C                3.070      0.056      54.777     0.000
    W1A                2.907      0.040      71.981     0.000
    W2A                2.870      0.048      59.822     0.000
    W3A                3.298      0.059      55.815     0.000

Variances
    TIME3              1.000      0.000     999.000   999.000
    TIME2              1.000      0.000     999.000   999.000
    TIME1              1.000      0.000     999.000   999.000

Residual Variances
    W1B                0.252      0.019      13.247     0.000
    W2B                0.285      0.024      11.670     0.000
    W3B                0.349      0.036       9.729     0.000
    W1C                0.279      0.020      13.741     0.000
    W2C                0.278      0.024      11.440     0.000
    W3C                0.305      0.033       9.126     0.000
    W1A                0.279      0.020      13.618     0.000
    W2A                0.281      0.024      11.532     0.000
    W3A                0.326      0.035       9.354     0.000
```

R-SQUARE

Observed Variable	Estimate	S.E.	Est./S.E.	Two-Tailed P-Value
W1B	0.742	0.021	34.943	0.000
W2B	0.800	0.018	43.850	0.000
W3B	0.839	0.017	48.840	0.000
W1C	0.705	0.023	30.719	0.000
W2C	0.789	0.019	41.756	0.000
W3C	0.845	0.018	48.144	0.000
W1A	0.727	0.022	33.627	0.000
W2A	0.805	0.018	44.659	0.000
W3A	0.851	0.017	51.477	0.000

QUALITY OF NUMERICAL RESULTS

Condition Number for the Information Matrix   0.375E-02
(ratio of smallest to largest eigenvalue)

MODEL MODIFICATION INDICES

Minimum M.I. value for printing the modification index   10.000

	M.I.	E.P.C.	Std E.P.C.	StdYX E.P.C.

ON/BY Statements

W1C ON TIME2 /
| TIME2 BY W1C | 10.265 | 0.080 | 0.068 | 0.070 |

ON Statements

W1C ON W1B	10.265	0.080	0.080	0.081
W1C ON W3B	15.869	0.055	0.055	0.084
W2C ON W3B	10.911	-0.053	-0.053	-0.069

WITH Statements

W1B WITH TIME2	21.476	-0.056	-0.065	-0.130
W1B WITH TIME1	11.081	0.035	0.041	0.081
W3B WITH W2B	21.475	0.110	0.110	0.349
W1C WITH TIME2	14.764	0.042	0.050	0.094
W1C WITH W3B	17.362	0.067	0.067	0.216
W2C WITH W3B	23.937	-0.094	-0.094	-0.302
W1A WITH TIME1	15.041	-0.050	-0.058	-0.111
W3A WITH W2B	11.432	-0.063	-0.063	-0.207
W3A WITH W2A	15.041	0.100	0.100	0.330

Latent Growth Curves

Another way to describe change in a variable over time is to estimate the latent growth curve. Assuming you have at least three waves of data collection, latent growth curves involve estimating a confirmatory factor analysis model, albeit one with several unique features. As shown in Figure 8.2, latent growth curves use at least three indicators to estimate two latent variables. One latent variable represents the intercept of the variable, which may be thought of as the starting point. The other latent variable is the slope of the curve. The slope represents the rate of change over time.

In most applications of confirmatory factor analysis, we are interested in estimating the parameters linking the latent and the observed variables (i.e., the factor loadings). However, in the case of latent growth curves, we will fix these parameters, because what we are really interested in are the means and variances of the latent variable. The mean of the intercept simply tells us the starting point of the curve and conveys little information. However, a significant variance of the intercept tells us that not all respondents started at the same level, and this may, depending on context, be of considerable interest. We may, for example, be able to identify groups of people who start at different places or identify variables that predict where one starts on the curve. The mean of the slope tells us about the average rate of change in the sample. If significant, the mean indicates that there has been change at the group level. The variance of the slope tells us about whether the rate of change varied across

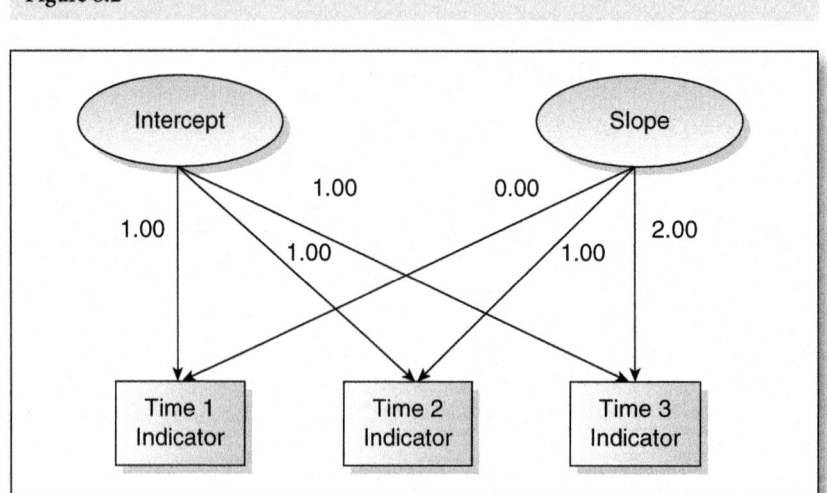

Figure 8.2

individuals. Thus, a significant variance for the slope tells us that not all respondents in our study changed at the same rate; again, this may lead us to explore the potential predictors of differential change.

In the example shown in Figure 8.2, the "factor loadings" for the intercept are all fixed at 1. This simply means that the intercept is the same for each wave of data collection (i.e., the starting point does not change over time). The parameters for the slope are fixed at 0, 1, and 2, indicating a linear change. With enough waves of data collection, one could also estimate a quadratic change, cubic, or any other pattern of change (e.g., an initial change followed by a plateau) by changing the weights.

Mplus has a convention that makes it easy to estimate a latent growth curve. In the MODEL statement, the code

```
I S | X1 @ 1 X2 @ 1 X3 @ 2
```

is used to estimate an intercept (I) and a slope (S). The weights for the slope are defined by the @ keyword, where X1, X2, and X3 are the variables measured at each time period. Note that it is not necessary to estimate the loadings for the intercept, because they are constant across time periods. The output file from a latent growth curve estimation is shown below.

```
Mplus VERSION 7 (Mac)
MUTHEN & MUTHEN

INPUT INSTRUCTIONS

  TITLE:     Measurement invariance over time;
  DATA:      FILE IS ch8a.dat;
  VARIABLE:  NAMES ARE W1B W2B W3B W1C W2C W3C W1A W2A W3A;
             USEVARIABLES ARE W1A W1B W1C;
  MODEL:     I S| w1a @ 0 w1b @ 1 w1c @ 2;
  OUTPUT:    STANDARDIZED MODINDICES (ALL);

INPUT READING TERMINATED NORMALLY

Measurement invariance over time;

SUMMARY OF ANALYSIS

Number of groups                                                 1
Number of observations                                         627
Number of dependent variables                                    3
Number of independent variables                                  0
Number of continuous latent variables                            2

Observed dependent variables
  Continuous
      W1A         W1B         W1C
```

Continuous latent variables
    I   S

Estimator   ML
Information matrix   OBSERVED
Maximum number of iterations   1000
Convergence criterion   0.500D-04
Maximum number of steepest descent iterations   20

Input data file(s)
ch8a.dat

Input data format FREE

THE MODEL ESTIMATION TERMINATED NORMALLY

MODEL FIT INFORMATION

Number of Free Parameters   8

Loglikelihood
        H0 Value   -2131.575
        H1 Value   -2130.978

Information Criteria
        Akaike (AIC)   4279.150
        Bayesian (BIC)   4314.677
        Sample-Size Adjusted BIC   4289.278
          (n* = (n + 2) / 24)

Chi-Square Test of Model Fit
        Value   1.194
        Degrees of Freedom   1
        P-Value   0.2746

RMSEA (Root Mean Square Error Of Approximation)
        Estimate   0.018
        90 Percent C.I.   0.000   0.109
        Probability RMSEA <= .05   0.573

CFI/TLI
        CFI   1.000
        TLI   0.999

Chi-Square Test of Model Fit for the Baseline Model
        Value   1155.364
        Degrees of Freedom   3
        P-Value   0.0000

SRMR (Standardized Root Mean Square Residual)
        Value   0.007

Note: The model provides an excellent fit to the data.

MODEL RESULTS

		Estimate	S.E.	Est./S.E.	Two-Tailed P-Value
I					
	W1A	1.000	0.000	999.000	999.000
	W1B	1.000	0.000	999.000	999.000
	W1C	1.000	0.000	999.000	999.000
S					
	W1A	0.000	0.000	999.000	999.000
	W1B	1.000	0.000	999.000	999.000
	W1C	2.000	0.000	999.000	999.000

Note: These parameters are all fixed and are not estimated.

S WITH				
I	-0.072	0.029	-2.457	0.014

Note: The negative correlation between the slope and intercept is significant. It suggests that those who scored higher on well-being at the beginning (the intercept) changed less over time (the slope).

Means				
I	2.914	0.041	71.277	0.000
S	-0.051	0.016	-3.236	0.001

Note: The mean for the intercept simply tells us that it is different from zero, which in this case is not very informative. The significant mean for the slope tells us that there was a decline in well-being over time.

Intercepts				
W1A	0.000	0.000	999.000	999.000
W1B	0.000	0.000	999.000	999.000
W1C	0.000	0.000	999.000	999.000
Variances				
I	0.885	0.069	12.810	0.000
S	0.055	0.024	2.291	0.022

Note: The variances tell us that not every respondent started at the same level of well-being (the variance of the intercept) and that respondents changed at a different rate (the variance of the slope).

Residual Variances				
W1A	0.186	0.049	3.815	0.000
W1B	0.243	0.026	9.451	0.000
W1C	0.206	0.048	4.303	0.000

STANDARDIZED MODEL RESULTS

STDYX Standardization

	Estimate	S.E.	Est./S.E.	Two-Tailed P-Value
I |				
W1A	0.909	0.024	37.096	0.000
W1B	0.924	0.020	45.208	0.000
W1C	0.931	0.038	24.815	0.000
S |				
W1A	0.000	0.000	999.000	999.000
W1B	0.230	0.048	4.821	0.000
W1C	0.464	0.104	4.452	0.000
S WITH				
I	-0.328	0.075	-4.391	0.000
Means				
I	3.097	0.129	23.943	0.000
S	-0.216	0.082	-2.641	0.008
Intercepts				
W1A	0.000	0.000	999.000	999.000
W1B	0.000	0.000	999.000	999.000
W1C	0.000	0.000	999.000	999.000
Variances				
I	1.000	0.000	999.000	999.000
S	1.000	0.000	999.000	999.000
Residual Variances				
W1A	0.174	0.045	3.907	0.000
W1B	0.234	0.021	11.183	0.000
W1C	0.202	0.045	4.437	0.000

STDY Standardization

	Estimate	S.E.	Est./S.E.	Two-Tailed P-Value
I |				
W1A	0.909	0.024	37.096	0.000
W1B	0.924	0.020	45.208	0.000
W1C	0.931	0.038	24.815	0.000
S |				
W1A	0.000	0.000	999.000	999.000
W1B	0.230	0.048	4.821	0.000
W1C	0.464	0.104	4.452	0.000
S WITH				
I	-0.328	0.075	-4.391	0.000

```
Means
    I                      3.097        0.129       23.943        0.000
    S                     -0.216        0.082       -2.641        0.008

Intercepts
    W1A                    0.000        0.000      999.000      999.000
    W1B                    0.000        0.000      999.000      999.000
    W1C                    0.000        0.000      999.000      999.000

Variances
    I                      1.000        0.000      999.000      999.000
    S                      1.000        0.000      999.000      999.000

Residual Variances
    W1A                    0.174        0.045        3.907        0.000
    W1B                    0.234        0.021       11.183        0.000
    W1C                    0.202        0.045        4.437        0.000

STD Standardization

                                                                Two-Tailed
                        Estimate        S.E.     Est./S.E.      P-Value

I |
    W1A                    0.941        0.037       25.619        0.000
    W1B                    0.941        0.037       25.619        0.000
    W1C                    0.941        0.037       25.619        0.000

S |
    W1A                    0.000        0.000      999.000      999.000
    W1B                    0.235        0.051        4.582        0.000
    W1C                    0.469        0.102        4.582        0.000

S WITH
    I                     -0.328        0.075       -4.391        0.000

Means
    I                      3.097        0.129       23.943        0.000
    S                     -0.216        0.082       -2.641        0.008

Intercepts
    W1A                    0.000        0.000      999.000      999.000
    W1B                    0.000        0.000      999.000      999.000
    W1C                    0.000        0.000      999.000      999.000

Variances
    I                      1.000        0.000      999.000      999.000
    S                      1.000        0.000      999.000      999.000

Residual Variances
    W1A                    0.186        0.049        3.815        0.000
    W1B                    0.243        0.026        9.451        0.000
    W1C                    0.206        0.048        4.303        0.000
```

R-SQUARE

Observed Variable	Estimate	S.E.	Est./S.E.	Two-Tailed P-Value
W1A	0.826	0.045	18.548	0.000
W1B	0.766	0.021	36.665	0.000
W1C	0.798	0.045	17.561	0.000

QUALITY OF NUMERICAL RESULTS

Condition Number for the Information Matrix   0.546E-02
(ratio of smallest to largest eigenvalue)

MODEL MODIFICATION INDICES

Minimum M.I. value for printing the modification index   10.000

                M.I.   E.P.C.   Std E.P.C.   StdYX E.P.C.

No modification indices above the minimum value.

One can extend latent growth curve modeling in several ways. First, note that in our example, we are using observed variables. One could, of course, have estimated a confirmatory factor analysis at each time wave and then used the latent variables from this analysis in a latent growth curve. One could also estimate simultaneous growth curves (i.e., in two variables) and use the change in one to predict the change in the other. For an example of both options, see Ployhart and Vandenberg (2010).

Cross-Lagged Models

Another way of analyzing longitudinal data that focuses on predictor-outcome relationships is to estimate a cross-lagged model. As shown in Figure 8.3, a cross-lagged model incorporates several features. First, it explicitly estimates and controls for the stability or autoregression among variables. That is, each variable is predicted by the same variable at the preceding time wave (i.e., the lags). Once we control for the variance attributable to stability, what is left is the change in the variable. The "cross" in "cross-lagged model" comes from the attempt to predict this change. We can hypothesize that B at Time 1 causes a change in A at Time 2, or that A at Time 1 causes a change in B at Time 2. Each of these predictions would correspond to a substantive interpretation of the data. Moreover, given three waves of data collection, it is possible to estimate these relationships across different lags. For example, A

Figure 8.3

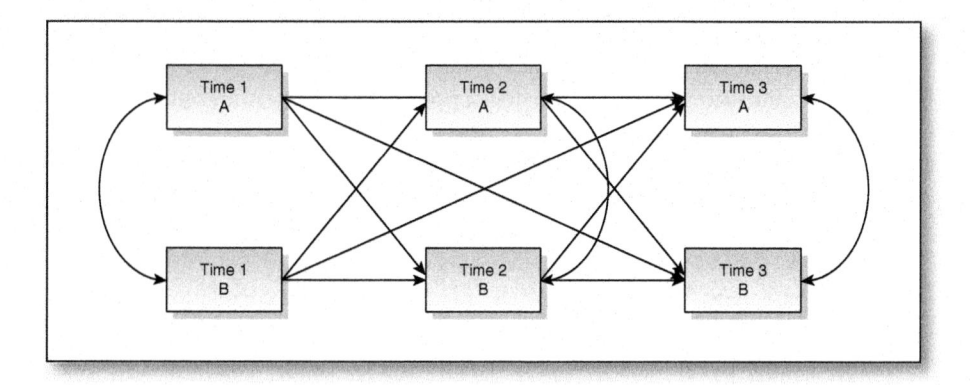

at Time 1 could predict B at Time 2 (e.g., a 3-month lag) or B at Time 3 (e.g., a 6-month lag). Just as we saw with tests of measurement equivalence, the use of the same measures at different time periods may lead to inflated residual correlations, and it is common (see, e.g., Kelloway, Gottlieb, & Barham, 1999) to allow for these in the model.

As is apparent from Figure 8.3, there is a lot going on in even a fairly simple, three-wave model with two variables. I suggest that this is a case in which the use of nested model tests is especially valuable. My logic is that we should begin by estimating the "methods" effects (i.e., the autoregressive effects) as the simplest model (each variable is predicted by the same variable at the preceding wave). The Mplus code for this autoregressive or stability model is shown below.

```
TITLE:      Measurement invariance over time;
DATA:       FILE IS ch8a.dat;
VARIABLE:   NAMES ARE W1B W2B W3B W1C W2C W3C W1A W2A W3A;
            USEVARIABLES ARE W1A W1B W1C W3A W3B W3C;
MODEL:      W1C ON W1B;
            W1B ON W1A;
            W1C ON W1A;
            W3C ON W3B;
            W3B ON W3A;
            W3C ON W3A;
            W3C WITH W1C @ 0;
OUTPUT:     STANDARDIZED MODINDICES (ALL);
```

Aside from the stability effects, note the one additional line, "W3C WITH W1C @ 0." By default, Mplus will estimate a residual correlation for these two

178 USING MPLUS FOR STRUCTURAL EQUATION MODELING

variables, and this code simply sets that correlation to zero. It is always important with Mplus or any other program to check to make sure that the model estimated is exactly the one you specified. In this case, estimating the residual correlation results in a better fitting (but erroneous) model. After correcting this, the autoregressive model provides a poor fit to the data, for example, $\chi^2(8) = 648.72$, comparative fit index = .77, RMSEA = .36, $p < .01$.

Recognizing that the inflated residual correlations may be another source of method effects, I run a second model in which measures taken at the same time wave are allowed to correlate; thus, I remove the specification "W3C WITH W1C @ 0" to allow a residual correlation at Time 3. I also add a new statement, "W3B WITH W1B," to allow a residual correlation at Time 2. Thus,

```
TITLE:      Measurement invariance over time;
DATA:       FILE IS ch8a.dat;
VARIABLE:   NAMES ARE W1B W2B W3B W1C W2C W3C W1A W2A W3A;
            USEVARIABLES ARE W1A W1B W1C W3A W3B W3C;
MODEL:      W1C ON W1B;
            W1B ON W1A;
            W1C ON W1A;
            W3C ON W3B;
            W3B ON W3A;
            W3C ON W3A;
            W3C WITH W1C @ 0;
            W3B WITH W1B;
OUTPUT:     STANDARDIZED MODINDICES (ALL);
```

This model provides a substantially better fit to the data, $\chi^2(6) = 113.02, p < .01$, CFI = .96, RMSEA = .17, $p < .01$, $\chi^2_{difference}(2) = 534.70, p < .01$.

In the next step, I add in the cross-lagged effects that are of interest. As shown below, the resulting model provides an excellent fit to the data, with some interesting cross-lagged effects emerging. The code and output are shown below.

```
Mplus VERSION 7 (Mac)
MUTHEN & MUTHEN

INPUT INSTRUCTIONS

    TITLE:      Measurement invariance over time;
    DATA:       FILE IS ch8a.dat;
    VARIABLE:   NAMES ARE W1B W2B W3B W1C W2C W3C W1A W2A W3A;
                USEVARIABLES ARE W1A W1B W1C W3A W3B W3C;
    MODEL:      W1C ON W1B;
                W1B ON W1A;
                W1C ON W1A;
                W3C ON W3B;
```

```
              W3B ON W3A;
              W3C ON W3A;
              W3C ON W1B;
              W3B ON W1A;
              W1C ON W3B;
              W1B ON W3A;
              ! W3C WITH W1C@0;
              W3B WITH W1B;
              ! W3C ON W1A;
              ! W1C ON W3A;
   OUTPUT:    STANDARDIZED MODINDICES (ALL);
```

INPUT READING TERMINATED NORMALLY

Measurement invariance over time;

SUMMARY OF ANALYSIS

Number of groups	1
Number of observations	627
Number of dependent variables	4
Number of independent variables	2
Number of continuous latent variables	0

Observed dependent variables
   Continuous
      W1B   W1C   W3B   W3C

Observed independent variables
      W1A   W3A

Estimator	ML
Information matrix	OBSERVED
Maximum number of iterations	1000
Convergence criterion	0.500D-04
Maximum number of steepest descent iterations	20

Input data file(s)
  ch8a.dat

Input data format FREE

THE MODEL ESTIMATION TERMINATED NORMALLY

MODEL FIT INFORMATION

Number of Free Parameters   20

Loglikelihood
          H0 Value   -2659.978
          H1 Value   -2656.400

Information Criteria
       Akaike (AIC)   5359.955
       Bayesian (BIC)   5448.774
       Sample-Size Adjusted BIC   5385.277
         (n* = (n + 2) / 24)

Chi-Square Test of Model Fit
       Value   7.155
       Degrees of Freedom   2
       P-Value   0.0279

RMSEA (Root Mean Square Error Of Approximation)
       Estimate   0.064
       90 Percent C.I.   0.018   0.118
       Probability RMSEA <= .05   0.252

CFI/TLI
       CFI   0.998
       TLI   0.987

Chi-Square Test of Model Fit for the Baseline Model
       Value   2736.319
       Degrees of Freedom   14
       P-Value   0.0000

SRMR (Standardized Root Mean Square Residual)
       Value   0.010

MODEL RESULTS

				Two-Tailed
	Estimate	S.E.	Est./S.E.	P-Value
W1C ON				
W1B	0.508	0.047	10.775	0.000
W1A	0.242	0.033	7.432	0.000
W3B	0.046	0.029	1.604	0.109
W1B ON				
W1A	0.617	0.040	15.384	0.000
W3A	0.127	0.028	4.491	0.000
W3C ON				
W3B	0.318	0.045	7.029	0.000
W3A	0.336	0.032	10.569	0.000
W1B	0.161	0.063	2.557	0.011
W3B ON				
W3A	0.521	0.045	11.695	0.000
W1A	0.338	0.063	5.350	0.000

```
W3B    WITH
    W1B              0.389      0.030     12.969     0.000

W3C    WITH
    W1C              0.367      0.028     13.125     0.000

Intercepts
    W1B              0.670      0.076      8.816     0.000
    W1C              0.492      0.079      6.260     0.000
    W3B              0.502      0.120      4.194     0.000
    W3C              0.478      0.114      4.184     0.000
Residual Variances
    W1B              0.408      0.023     17.706     0.000
    W1C              0.398      0.023     17.666     0.000
    W3B              1.011      0.057     17.706     0.000
    W3C              0.885      0.050     17.693     0.000

STANDARDIZED MODEL RESULTS

STDYX Standardization

                                                  Two-Tailed
                     Estimate     S.E.   Est./S.E.   P-Value

W1C    ON
    W1B              0.515      0.046     11.300     0.000
    W1A              0.249      0.034      7.405     0.000
    W3B              0.067      0.042      1.605     0.109

W1B    ON
    W1A              0.627      0.038     16.624     0.000
    W3A              0.183      0.041      4.509     0.000

W3C    ON
    W3B              0.335      0.047      7.187     0.000
    W3A              0.355      0.033     10.624     0.000
    W1B              0.118      0.046      2.565     0.010

W3B    ON
    W3A              0.522      0.042     12.317     0.000
    W1A              0.239      0.044      5.396     0.000

W3B    WITH
    W1B              0.605      0.025     23.937     0.000

W3C    WITH
    W1C              0.619      0.025     24.965     0.000

Intercepts
    W1B              0.658      0.088      7.495     0.000
    W1C              0.490      0.088      5.587     0.000
```

W3B	0.343	0.088	3.899	0.000
W3C	0.344	0.088	3.903	0.000

Residual Variances

W1B	0.393	0.024	16.071	0.000
W1C	0.395	0.025	16.053	0.000
W3B	0.473	0.027	17.245	0.000
W3C	0.459	0.027	17.069	0.000

STDY Standardization

	Estimate	S.E.	Est./S.E.	Two-Tailed P-Value

W1C ON

W1B	0.515	0.046	11.300	0.000
W1A	0.240	0.032	7.414	0.000
W3B	0.067	0.042	1.605	0.109

W1B ON

W1A	0.605	0.037	16.289	0.000
W3A	0.125	0.028	4.512	0.000

W3C ON

W3B	0.335	0.047	7.187	0.000
W3A	0.242	0.023	10.669	0.000
W1B	0.118	0.046	2.565	0.010

W3B ON

W3A	0.356	0.029	12.309	0.000
W1A	0.231	0.043	5.405	0.000

W3B WITH

W1B	0.605	0.025	23.937	0.000

W3C WITH

W1C	0.619	0.025	24.965	0.000

Intercepts

W1B	0.658	0.088	7.495	0.000
W1C	0.490	0.088	5.587	0.000
W3B	0.343	0.088	3.899	0.000
W3C	0.344	0.088	3.903	0.000

Residual Variances

W1B	0.393	0.024	16.071	0.000
W1C	0.395	0.025	16.053	0.000
W3B	0.473	0.027	17.245	0.000
W3C	0.459	0.027	17.069	0.000

STD Standardization

	Estimate	S.E.	Est./S.E.	Two-Tailed P-Value

```
W1C   ON
    W1B                    0.508      0.047     10.775      0.000
    W1A                    0.242      0.033      7.432      0.000
    W3B                    0.046      0.029      1.604      0.109

W1B   ON
    W1A                    0.617      0.040     15.384      0.000
    W3A                    0.127      0.028      4.491      0.000

W3C   ON
    W3B                    0.318      0.045      7.029      0.000
    W3A                    0.336      0.032     10.569      0.000
    W1B                    0.161      0.063      2.557      0.011

W3B   ON
    W3A                    0.521      0.045     11.695      0.000
    W1A                    0.338      0.063      5.350      0.000

W3B   WITH
    W1B                    0.389      0.030     12.969      0.000

W3C   WITH
    W1C                    0.367      0.028     13.125      0.000

Intercepts
    W1B                    0.670      0.076      8.816      0.000
    W1C                    0.492      0.079      6.260      0.000
    W3B                    0.502      0.120      4.194      0.000
    W3C                    0.478      0.114      4.184      0.000

Residual Variances
    W1B                    0.408      0.023     17.706      0.000
    W1C                    0.398      0.023     17.666      0.000
    W3B                    1.011      0.057     17.706      0.000
    W3C                    0.885      0.050     17.693      0.000

R-SQUARE

    Observed                                              Two-Tailed
    Variable       Estimate      S.E.    Est./S.E.       P-Value
    W1B              0.607      0.024     24.813          0.000
    W1C              0.605      0.025     24.630          0.000
    W3B              0.527      0.027     19.221          0.000
    W3C              0.541      0.027     20.150          0.000


QUALITY OF NUMERICAL RESULTS
Condition Number for the Information Matrix       0.529E-03
(ratio of smallest to largest eigenvalue)

MODEL MODIFICATION INDICES
```

```
Minimum M.I. value for printing the modification index    10.000

                    M.I.     E.P.C.     Std E.P.C.    StdYX E.P.C.

No modification indices above the minimum value.
```

9

Multilevel Modeling

Multilevel (also known as hierarchical linear or mixed) models are becoming increasingly prevalent in social science research. The popularity of the technique arises from the recognition that our data often exist in clusters: We study students (who are clustered in classrooms), employees (who are clustered in teams or work groups), or customers (who are clustered in service units). This clustering has some serious consequences for the analytic techniques we use and can have some unexpected effects on our analysis.

Most of our analytic techniques (e.g., regression, analysis of variance) assume that the observations are independent. Obviously, if our data exist in a clustered or nested structure, we are violating the assumption of independence. For example, in a study of leadership, we might have individual employees rate their leader. However, because employees are clustered into work groups that each report to a leader, employees within any given group are all rating the same leader. It is difficult to argue that these are independent observations when everyone within the group is rating the same person. The general result of violating the assumption of independence is that we underestimate the standard errors of our parameters (Cohen, Cohen, West, & Aikem, 2003). Because statistical tests are calculated by dividing a parameter by its standard error, underestimation of the standard errors will result in more lenient statistical tests with an associated inflation of Type I error.

Ignoring clustering can also have unanticipated effects in our data. Consider the data presented in Table 9.1. If we calculate the bivariate correlation between X and Y on the basis of all 15 cases, we would conclude that the variables are very strongly related (i.e., $r = .91$, $p < .01$). If, however, we recognize that the data are clustered into three groups (each with five members), we can calculate the correlation within each group. Doing so will result in a correlation of zero within each group! How can variables that are strongly related in the sample be virtually independent in the groups constituting the sample?

Table 9.1

Respondent	X	Y	Group
1	3	5	1
2	3	3	1
3	3	1	1
4	5	3	1
5	1	3	1
6	8	10	2
7	8	8	2
8	8	6	2
9	10	8	2
10	6	8	2
11	13	15	3
12	13	13	3
13	13	11	3
14	15	13	3
15	11	13	3

The answer is that there is a mean difference between the groups. The mean of the first group is 3, the mean of the second group is 8, and the mean of the third group is 13. The full-sample correlation is based almost entirely on that group difference; once we control for the group difference by doing within-group analysis, the correlation becomes zero.

There are many cases when, in fact, we are interested in both the individual (i.e., within-group) relationships and the between-group relationships. For example, in studies of leadership in organizations, it can be interesting to ask whether the effect of leadership on a given outcome occurs at the individual level or the group level. An individual-level effect might suggest that the effect of leadership is based on the individual relationships between subordinates and their leader. A group-level effect, on the other hand, might be interpreted as a more objective "leadership" effect in that it is based on the experiences of all members in the group.

Multilevel Models in Mplus

Multilevel models in Mplus are implemented through two primary mechanisms. First, one must declare one of the variables as the "cluster" variable. This is the variable that indicates to Mplus which cases belong in each group. The second mechanism is to specify the type of analysis as two level. We will begin with the basic two-level analysis and then move to other forms of two-level analysis as the chapter progresses. The code for an initial two-level analysis is shown below. These data derive from a study of leadership in organizations in which each leader was assigned a code (in the variable Leader). This becomes our cluster variable for the analysis. Mplus provides a TWOLEVEL BASIC option, which is always a good starting point to explore the structure of the data.

```
TITLE:      Multilevel analysis;
DATA:       FILE IS ch9.dat;
VARIABLE:   NAMES ARE Leader TFL GHQ Trust MTFL;
            USEVARIABLES ARE TFL GHQ Trust;
            CLUSTER IS Leader;
ANALYSIS:   TYPE IS TWOLEVEL BASIC;
OUTPUT:     SAMPSTAT STDYX;
```

Running this code produces the output shown below.

```
Mplus VERSION 7 (Mac)
MUTHEN & MUTHEN

INPUT INSTRUCTIONS

TITLE:      Multilevel analysis;
DATA:       FILE IS ch9.dat;
VARIABLE:   NAMES ARE Leader TFL GHQ Trust MTFL;
            USEVARIABLES ARE TFL GHQ Trust;
            CLUSTER IS Leader;
ANALYSIS:   TYPE IS TWOLEVEL BASIC;
OUTPUT:     SAMPSTAT STDYX;

INPUT READING TERMINATED NORMALLY

Multilevel analysis;

SUMMARY OF ANALYSIS

Number of groups                                    1
Number of observations                            236
Number of dependent variables                       3
Number of independent variables                     0
Number of continuous latent variables               0
```

```
Observed dependent variables
  Continuous
    TFL       GHQ       TRUST
```

Note: There are 236 cases (respondents in the file), and I am using three variables: TFL (leadership), General Health Questionnaire (GHQ) score (a measure of psychological well-being), and a measure of trust.

```
Variables with special functions
  Cluster variable      LEADER
```

Note: As described above, Leader is the cluster variable (indicating the nesting structure of the data).

```
Estimator                                               MLR
```

Note: Mplus uses the maximum likelihood with robust errors (MLR) estimator for two-level analyses.

```
Information matrix                                 OBSERVED
Maximum number of iterations                            100
Convergence criterion                              0.100D-05
Maximum number of EM iterations                         500
Convergence criteria for the EM algorithm
  Loglikelihood change                             0.100D-02
  Relative loglikelihood change                    0.100D-05
  Derivative                                       0.100D-03
Minimum variance                                   0.100D-03
Maximum number of steepest descent iterations            20
Maximum number of iterations for H1                    2000
Convergence criterion for H1                       0.100D-03
Optimization algorithm                                  EMA

Input data file(s)
  ch9.dat
Input data format FREE

SUMMARY OF DATA

Number of clusters                                      121

   Size (s)    Cluster ID with Size s

     1          1  3  4  5  8  9 11 21 22 24 27 29 34 36 37 50 57 59 301
                302 308 312 315 316 320 321 325 328 330 331 335 338
                339 413 421 432 434 436 439 443 447 453 601 602 603
                604 606 609 610 616 617 621 625

     2          428 430 327 433 314 53 438 48 332 319 337 454 305 43
                340 341 403 607 409 323 612 613 615 415 418 619 620
                60 622 624 426
```

```
3                  324 444 445 336 448 450 416 309 420 318 422 423 424
                   425 306 427 313 429 307 342 343 303 435 404 333 410
                   441

4                  455 311 407 334 344 437 411 452 401 304

Average cluster size        1.950
```

Note: Mplus recognizes that there are 121 clusters (leaders). Ten of these have four employees providing ratings. A large number have only one employee providing a rating, and this may be a concern for the analysis. One might want to base the analysis only on those leaders with more than one rating.

```
Estimated Intraclass Correlations for the Y Variables

          Intraclass              Intraclass              Intraclass
Variable  Correlation   Variable  Correlation   Variable  Correlation
TFL         0.179         GHQ       0.120         TRUST     0.025
```

Note: The intraclass correlation coefficient (ICC) is calculated for all study variables. The ICC can be interpreted as the percentage of variance that exists at the group level. Thus, for these analyses, 17.9% of the variance in leadership ratings is between-group variance. Twelve percent of the variance in GHQ scores is between-group variance, and only 2.5% of the variance in trust is between-group variance.

```
RESULTS FOR BASIC ANALYSIS

NOTE: The sample statistics for within and between refer to the
      maximum-likelihood estimated within and between covariance
      matrices, respectively.

    ESTIMATED SAMPLE STATISTICS FOR WITHIN

              Means
              TFL          GHQ         TRUST

    1         0.000        0.000       0.000
```

Note: The within-group means are reported as zero because they are a function of the between-group means (i.e., the group mean plus a residual).

```
              Covariances
              TFL          GHQ         TRUST

    TFL       0.497
    GHQ      -0.475       14.905
    TRUST     0.243       -0.753       0.654
```

```
              Correlations
              TFL           GHQ           TRUST

              ───────
TFL           1.000                       ───────
GHQ          -0.175         1.000         ───────
TRUST         0.426        -0.241         1.000

      ESTIMATED SAMPLE STATISTICS FOR BETWEEN

              Means
              TFL           GHQ           TRUST

              ───────       ───────       ───────
1             2.528         22.148        5.003

              Covariances
              TFL           GHQ           TRUST

              ───────       ───────       ───────
TFL           0.109
GHQ          -0.066         2.024
TRUST         0.019        -0.025         0.017

              Correlations
              TFL           GHQ           TRUST

              ───────       ───────       ───────
TFL           1.000
GHQ          -0.141         1.000
TRUST         0.459        -0.135         1.000
```

Note: The TWOLEVEL BASIC option provides sample statistics for both the between-group level and the within-group level. The variances of variables are found on the diagonal of the covariance matrix. One can verify the calculation of ICCs using these values (e.g., for TFL, the ICC is .109/ (.109 + .497))

The first step in many multilevel analyses is to estimate the null model (sometimes called the intercept-only model or unconditional model). Normally one does this to calculate the ICCs. However, Mplus provides these as part of the two-level basic analysis, and there is, strictly speaking, no need to estimate the null model. However, many researchers will still estimate the null model as a baseline for assessing the fit of subsequent models.

To estimate the null model, one would use code similar to that shown below.

```
TITLE:     Multilevel analysis;
DATA:      FILE IS ch9.dat;
```

Chapter 9: Multilevel Modeling   191

```
VARIABLE:   NAMES ARE Leader TFL GHQ Trust MTFL;
            USEVARIABLES ARE GHQ;
            CLUSTER IS Leader;
ANALYSIS:   TYPE IS TWOLEVEL;
OUTPUT:     SAMPSTAT STDYX;
```

Note that this time, I have specified only one outcome variable ("USEVARIABLES ARE GHQ"), and I have changed the type of analysis to TWOLEVEL (not TWOLEVEL BASIC). The resulting output is given below.

```
Mplus VERSION 7 (Mac)
MUTHEN & MUTHEN

INPUT INSTRUCTIONS

TITLE:      Multilevel analysis;
DATA:       FILE IS ch9.dat;
VARIABLE:   NAMES ARE Leader TFL GHQ Trust MTFL;
            USEVARIABLES ARE GHQ;
            CLUSTER IS Leader;
ANALYSIS:   TYPE IS TWOLEVEL;
OUTPUT:     SAMPSTAT STDYX;

*** WARNING in MODEL command
  All variables are uncorrelated with all other variables in the
model.
  Check that this is what is intended.
   1 WARNING(S) FOUND IN THE INPUT INSTRUCTIONS
```

Note: This warning is produced by default because one-variable models, or models that specify variables that are uncorrelated with other variables, are not typical. It does not affect the analysis and is, in this case, what is intended.

```
Multilevel analysis;

SUMMARY OF ANALYSIS

Number of groups                                                 1
Number of observations                                         236
Number of dependent variables                                    1
Number of independent variables                                  0
Number of continuous latent variables                            0

Observed dependent variables
  Continuous
    GHQ

Variables with special functions
  Cluster variable      LEADER
```

```
Estimator                                            MLR

Information matrix                                              OBSERVED
Maximum number of iterations                                         100
Convergence criterion                                          0.100D-05
Maximum number of EM iterations                                      500
Convergence criteria for the EM algorithm
  Loglikelihood change                                         0.100D-02
  Relative loglikelihood change                                0.100D-05
  Derivative                                                   0.100D-03
Minimum variance                                               0.100D-03
Maximum number of steepest descent iterations                         20
Maximum number of iterations for H1                                 2000
Convergence criterion for H1                                   0.100D-03
Optimization algorithm                                               EMA

Input data file(s)
ch9.dat
Input data format FREE

SUMMARY OF DATA

Number of clusters                                                   121

Average cluster size                                               1.950

Estimated Intraclass Correlations for the Y Variables

                 Intraclass
    Variable     Correlation

    GHQ             0.124
```

Note: This is a less detailed examination of the data than obtained with TWOLEVEL BASIC but contains the information required: the number of clusters, the average cluster size, and the ICC.

```
SAMPLE STATISTICS

NOTE: The sample statistics for within and between refer to the
      maximum-likelihood estimated within and between covariance
      matrices, respectively.

    ESTIMATED SAMPLE STATISTICS FOR WITHIN

          Means
          GHQ
          _____
    1     0.000

          Covariances
          GHQ
```

```
    GHQ      14.855

             Correlations
             GHQ

    GHQ      1.000

        ESTIMATED SAMPLE STATISTICS FOR BETWEEN

             Means
             GHQ

    1        22.150

             Covariances
             GHQ

    GHQ      2.097

             Correlations
             GHQ

    GHQ      1.000
```

THE MODEL ESTIMATION TERMINATED NORMALLY

MODEL FIT INFORMATION

Number of Free Parameters   3

Loglikelihood
        H0 Value   -667.580
        H0 Scaling Correction Factor   1.6978
          for MLR
        H1 Value   -667.581
        H1 Scaling Correction Factor   1.6978
          for MLR

Information Criteria
        Akaike (AIC)   1341.159
        Bayesian (BIC)   1351.551
        Sample-Size Adjusted BIC   1342.042
          (n* = (n + 2) / 24)

Chi-Square Test of Model Fit
        Value   0.000*
        Degrees of Freedom   0
        P-Value   1.0000
        Scaling Correction Factor   1.0000
          for MLR

*   The chi-square value for MLM, MLMV, MLR, ULSMV, WLSM and
     WLSMV cannot be used for chi-square difference testing in
     the regular way. MLM, MLR and WLSM chi-square difference

testing is described on the Mplus website. MLMV, WLSMV, and ULSMV difference testing is done using the DIFFTEST option.

```
RMSEA (Root Mean Square Error Of Approximation)

        Estimate                                          0.000

CFI/TLI
        CFI                                               1.000
        TLI                                               1.000

Chi-Square Test of Model Fit for the Baseline Model
        Value                                             0.002
        Degrees of Freedom                                    0
        P-Value                                          0.0000

SRMR (Standardized Root Mean Square Residual)
        Value for Within                                  0.000
        Value for Between                                 0.000
```

Note: These are the model fit statistics. Although not very informative in this case, they (especially the information criteria and the −2 log likelihood value) provide a baseline for assessing model fit. As mentioned in Chapter 2, the use of the MLR estimator requires special calculation to do nested chi-square comparisons.

MODEL RESULTS

	Estimate	S.E.	Est./S.E.	Two-Tailed P-Value
Within Level				
Variances				
GHQ	14.902	2.401	6.206	0.000
Between Level				
Means				
GHQ	22.153	0.287	77.148	0.000
Variances				
GHQ	2.032	1.483	1.370	0.171

Note: Again we obtain estimates of the within-level and between-level variances as well as the grand mean. Note that the between-group variance is not significant.

STANDARDIZED MODEL RESULTS

```
STDYX Standardization
                                                              Two-Tailed
                        Estimate        S.E.     Est./S.E.     P-Value

Within Level

  Variances
    GHQ                  1.000         0.000      999.000      999.000

Between Level

  Means
    GHQ                 15.539         5.611        2.769        0.006

  Variances
    GHQ                  1.000         0.000      999.000      999.000

R-SQUARE
Within Level
Between Level

QUALITY OF NUMERICAL RESULTS

Condition Number for the Information Matrix               0.382E-03
(ratio of smallest to largest eigenvalue)
```

Conditional Models

In contrast to the intercepts-only or unconditional model that did not incorporate predictors, we now move to consideration of multilevel regression models that do incorporate predictive relationships. Because we have been making a distinction between "between group" and "within group," it follows that we can introduce predictors at either of these two levels. First, we will introduce a predictor at the within-group level with no predictors at the between-group level; models of this form are known as random-intercepts models or conditional models. Then we will consider the case of a between-group predictor with no within group predictor; models of this form are often referred to as "means as outcomes" models because one is trying to predict the between-group differences (i.e., the differences in the group means).

When we start to introduce predictors into our models, we need to briefly discuss the issue of centering. Centering a predictor simply refers to subtracting the mean of the predictor from each score. In general, centering aids in interpreting the results. Centering creates a distribution of deviation scores with a mean of zero. Because centering imposes a common scale of measurement (i.e., all scores are centered around zero) for the predictors, centering may help the program converge during estimation.

Essentially, two types of centering are used in multilevel analysis: grand mean centering and group mean centering. In grand mean centering, one subtracts the sample mean from each score; in grand mean centering, each score is transformed in the same way. In group mean centering, the group mean is subtracted from each score; thus, scores in different groups are subject to different transformations. Hofmann and Gavin (1998; see also Enders & Tofighi, 2007) noted that grand mean centering might be the most generally applicable form of centering, with group mean centering being useful in cases in which one is testing cross-level interactions.

In the current case, we will predict GHQ score from the leadership variable, TFL. We will use grand mean centering of the predictor. In older versions of Mplus, this was done in the VARIABLE command with a line such as "CENTERING = GRANDMEAN (TFL)." In Version 7 of Mplus, this syntax was changed to the DEFINE command, as shown below. To specify the relationships of interest, we will use the regression syntax (i.e., "Y ON X") we have previously used. The only other new feature of our analysis is to indicate in the MODEL command whether the relationships specified are at the between level or the within level. Using the keywords %WITHIN% and %BETWEEN% allows us to specify these levels. Correspondingly, we have specified that TFL is a within-level variable in the VARIABLE command. The code for running a conditional model is shown below.

```
TITLE:      Multilevel analysis;
DATA:       FILE IS ch9.dat;
VARIABLE:   NAMES ARE Leader TFL GHQ Trust MTFL;
            USEVARIABLES ARE GHQ TFL;
            CLUSTER IS Leader;
            WITHIN = TFL;
DEFINE:     CENTER TFL (GRANDMEAN);
ANALYSIS:   TYPE IS TWOLEVEL;
MODEL:      %WITHIN%
            GHQ ON TFL;
OUTPUT:     SAMPSTAT stdyx;
```

This code results in the output shown below.

```
Mplus VERSION 7 (Mac)
MUTHEN & MUTHEN

INPUT INSTRUCTIONS

TITLE:      Multilevel analysis;
DATA:       FILE IS ch9.dat;
```

```
VARIABLE:    NAMES ARE Leader TFL GHQ Trust MTFL;
             USEVARIABLES ARE GHQ TFL;
             CLUSTER IS Leader;
             WITHIN = TFL;
DEFINE:      CENTER TFL (GRANDMEAN);
ANALYSIS:    TYPE IS TWOLEVEL;
MODEL:       %WITHIN%
             GHQ ON TFL;
OUTPUT:      SAMPSTAT stdyx;

*** WARNING in DEFINE command
  The CENTER transformation is done after all other DEFINE transformations
  have been completed.
     1 WARNING(S) FOUND IN THE INPUT INSTRUCTIONS
```

Note: This warning is for informational purposes only and does not affect our analyses.

```
Multilevel analysis;

SUMMARY OF ANALYSIS

Number of groups                                                  1
Number of observations                                          236
Number of dependent variables                                     1
Number of independent variables                                   1
Number of continuous latent variables                             0

Observed dependent variables
  Continuous
     GHQ

Observed independent variables
     TFL

Variables with special functions
  Cluster variable      LEADER

  Within variables
     TFL

  Centering (GRANDMEAN)
     TFL

Estimator         MLR

Information matrix                                         OBSERVED
Maximum number of iterations                                    100
Convergence criterion                                     0.100D-05
Maximum number of EM iterations                                 500
```

Convergence criteria for the EM algorithm
  Loglikelihood change   0.100D-02
  Relative loglikelihood change   0.100D-05
  Derivative   0.100D-03
Minimum variance   0.100D-03
Maximum number of steepest descent iterations   20
Maximum number of iterations for H1   2000
Convergence criterion for H1   0.100D-03
Optimization algorithm   EMA

Input data file(s)
ch9.dat
Input data format FREE

SUMMARY OF DATA

Number of clusters   121

Average cluster size   1.950

Estimated Intraclass Correlations for the Y Variables

                 Intraclass
    Variable   Correlation
    GHQ   0.121

SAMPLE STATISTICS

Note: The sample statistics for within and between refer to the maximum-likelihood estimated within- and between-covariance matrices, respectively.

   ESTIMATED SAMPLE STATISTICS FOR WITHIN

           Means
           GHQ   TFL

   1   0.000   0.000

           Covariances
           GHQ   TFL

   GHQ   14.911
   TFL   -0.547   0.606

           Correlations
           GHQ   TFL

   GHQ   1.000
   TFL   -0.182   1.000

   ESTIMATED SAMPLE STATISTICS FOR BETWEEN

```
          Means
          GHQ          TFL
          _____       _____
    1     22.156       0.000

          Covariances
          GHQ          TFL
          _____       _____
    GHQ   2.047
    TFL   0.000        0.000

          Correlations
          GHQ          TFL
          _____       _____
    GHQ   1.000
    TFL   0.000        0.000
```

THE MODEL ESTIMATION TERMINATED NORMALLY

MODEL FIT INFORMATION

```
Number of Free Parameters                                    4

Loglikelihood
        H0 Value                                      -664.115
        H0 Scaling Correction Factor                    1.6170
            for MLR
        H1 Value                                      -664.116
        H1 Scaling Correction Factor                    1.6170
            for MLR

Information Criteria
        Akaike (AIC)                                  1336.230
        Bayesian (BIC)                                1350.085
        Sample-Size Adjusted BIC                      1337.407
            (n* = (n + 2) / 24)
```

Note: Comparison of these values with the preceding output file suggests a slight improvement in fit, as the −2 log likelihood and information criteria have all declined slightly from the previous estimates.

```
Chi-Square Test of Model Fit
        Value                                           0.000*
        Degrees of Freedom                                   0
        P-Value                                         1.0000
        Scaling Correction Factor                       1.0000
            for MLR

*    The chi-square value for MLM, MLMV, MLR, ULSMV, WLSM and
     WLSMV cannot be used for chi-square difference testing in
```

the regular way. MLM, MLR and WLSM chi-square difference testing is described on the Mplus website. MLMV, WLSMV, and ULSMV difference testing is done using the DIFFTEST option.

```
RMSEA (Root Mean Square Error Of Approximation)
        Estimate                                        0.000

CFI/TLI
        CFI                                             1.000
        TLI                                             1.000

Chi-Square Test of Model Fit for the Baseline Model
        Value                                           5.216
        Degrees of Freedom                                  1
        P-Value                                        0.0224

SRMR (Standardized Root Mean Square Residual)
        Value for Within                       0.000
        Value for Between                      0.000

MODEL RESULTS

                                                    Two-Tailed
                    Estimate      S.E.    Est./S.E.   P-Value

Within Level

  GHQ ON
    TFL             -0.903       0.331      -2.731     0.006

  Residual Variances
    GHQ             14.451       2.375       6.085     0.000
```

Note: There is a significant effect of leadership on GHQ score. As a result, the residual variance for GHQ score is slightly smaller than the variance estimate shown in the preceding output file.

```
Between Level

  Means
    GHQ             22.159       0.283      78.425     0.000

  Variances
    GHQ              2.000       1.589       1.258     0.208
```

Note: Mplus estimates the mean and variance at the between level by default (even though we did not specify a between-level model).

STANDARDIZED MODEL RESULTS

STDYX Standardization

	Estimate	S.E.	Est./S.E.	Two-Tailed P-Value
Within Level				
GHQ ON				
TFL	-0.182	0.068	-2.675	0.007
Residual Variances				
GHQ	0.967	0.025	39.086	0.000
Between Level				
Means				
GHQ	15.670	6.146	2.550	0.011
Variances				
GHQ	1.000	0.000	999.000	999.000

R-SQUARE

Within Level

Observed Variable	Estimate	S.E.	Est./S.E.	Two-Tailed P-Value
GHQ	0.033	0.025	1.337	0.181

Between Level

QUALITY OF NUMERICAL RESULTS

Condition Number for the Information Matrix   0.368E-03
(ratio of smallest to largest eigenvalue)

The means-as-outcomes model follows a similar setup. I will again use TFL as the predictor. However, this time I will not declare it as a within-group variable. Declaring it as a between-group variable will result in an error because Mplus will detect that there is within-group variance on a variable specified as between group. A third option is simply not to specify the variable as either within or between; in this case, Mplus will apportion the variance in the predictor to the appropriate levels and use the predictor as specified.

TFL will be centered as in the preceding example.

We will not specify a within-group model; therefore, the within-group variance will be estimated by default. The code for a means-as-outcomes model is as follows:

```
TITLE:      Multilevel analysis;
DATA:       FILE IS ch9.dat;
```

```
VARIABLE:    NAMES ARE Leader TFL GHQ Trust MTFL;
             USEVARIABLES ARE GHQ TFL;
             CLUSTER IS Leader;
DEFINE:      CENTER TFL (GRANDMEAN);
ANALYSIS:    TYPE IS TWOLEVEL;
MODEL:       %BETWEEN%
             GHQ ON TFL;
OUTPUT:      SAMPSTAT STDYX;
```

Running this analysis results in the following output:

```
Mplus VERSION 7 (Mac)
MUTHEN & MUTHEN

INPUT INSTRUCTIONS

TITLE:       Multilevel analysis;
DATA:        FILE IS ch9.dat;
VARIABLE:    NAMES ARE Leader TFL GHQ Trust MTFL;
             USEVARIABLES ARE GHQ TFL;
             CLUSTER IS Leader;
DEFINE:      CENTER TFL (GRANDMEAN);
ANALYSIS:    TYPE IS TWOLEVEL;
MODEL:       %BETWEEN%
             GHQ ON TFL;
OUTPUT:      SAMPSTAT STDYX;

*** WARNING in DEFINE command
   The CENTER transformation is done after all other DEFINE transformations
   have been completed.
   1 WARNING(S) FOUND IN THE INPUT INSTRUCTIONS
```

Note: Again, this warning can be disregarded.

```
Multilevel analysis;

SUMMARY OF ANALYSIS

Number of groups                                                 1
Number of observations                                         236
Number of dependent variables                                    1
Number of independent variables                                  1
Number of continuous latent variables                            0

Observed dependent variables
  Continuous
     GHQ

Observed independent variables
     TFL
```

```
Variables with special functions
  Cluster variable     LEADER

  Centering (GRANDMEAN)
    TFL

Estimator      MLR

Information matrix                                    OBSERVED
Maximum number of iterations                               100
Convergence criterion                                0.100D-05
Maximum number of EM iterations                            500
Convergence criteria for the EM algorithm
  Loglikelihood change                               0.100D-02
  Relative loglikelihood change                      0.100D-05
  Derivative                                         0.100D-03
Minimum variance                                     0.100D-03
Maximum number of steepest descent iterations               20
Maximum number of iterations for H1                       2000
Convergence criterion for H1                         0.100D-03
Optimization algorithm                                     EMA

Input data file(s)
  ch9.dat
Input data format  FREE

SUMMARY OF DATA

Number of clusters                                         121

Average cluster size                                     1.950

Estimated Intraclass Correlations for the Y Variables

                Intraclass
    Variable    Correlation
    GHQ         0.123

SAMPLE STATISTICS

NOTE: The sample statistics for within and between refer to the
      maximum-likelihood estimated within and between covariance
      matrices, respectively.

    ESTIMATED SAMPLE STATISTICS FOR WITHIN

            Means
            GHQ         TFL
            _____      _____
    1       0.000       0.000
```

```
              Covariances
              GHQ          TFL
              _____       _____
    GHQ       14.859
    TFL       -0.475       0.498

              Correlations
              GHQ          TFL
              _____       _____
    GHQ       1.000
    TFL       -0.175       1.000
```

ESTIMATED SAMPLE STATISTICS FOR BETWEEN

```
              Means
              GHQ          TFL
              _____       _____
    1         22.150       0.010

              Covariances
              GHQ          TFL
              _____       _____
    GHQ       2.093
    TFL       -0.068       0.109

              Correlations
              GHQ          TFL
              _____       _____
    GHQ       1.000
    TFL       -0.142       1.000
```

THE MODEL ESTIMATION TERMINATED NORMALLY

MODEL FIT INFORMATION

Number of Free Parameters   4

Loglikelihood
        H0 Value   -939.450
        H0 Scaling Correction Factor   1.5713
          for MLR
        H1 Value   -937.397
        H1 Scaling Correction Factor   1.4245
          for MLR

Information Criteria
        Akaike (AIC)   1886.900
        Bayesian (BIC)   1900.755
        Sample-Size Adjusted BIC   1888.076
          (n* = (n + 2) / 24)

```
Chi-Square Test of Model Fit
        Value                                        4.903*
        Degrees of Freedom                                1
        P-Value                                      0.0268
        Scaling Correction Factor                    0.8373
            for MLR

*   The chi-square value for MLM, MLMV, MLR, ULSMV, WLSM and
    WLSMV cannot be used for chi-square difference testing in
    the regular way. MLM, MLR and WLSM chi-square difference
    testing is described on the Mplus website. MLMV, WLSMV, and
    ULSMV difference testing is done using the DIFFTEST option.

RMSEA (Root Mean Square Error Of Approximation)

        Estimate                                      0.129

CFI/TLI
        CFI                                           0.173
        TLI                                          -0.654

Chi-Square Test of Model Fit for the Baseline Model
        Value                                         6.719
        Degrees of Freedom                                2
        P-Value                                      0.0347

SRMR (Standardized Root Mean Square Residual)
        Value for Within                              0.101
        Value for Between                             0.253

MODEL RESULTS
                                                   Two-Tailed
                    Estimate      S.E.   Est./S.E.   P-Value

Within Level
  Variances
    GHQ              14.883      2.369      6.281     0.000

Between Level

  GHQ  ON
    TFL              -2.531      1.375     -1.841     0.066

  Intercepts
    GHQ              22.160      0.280     79.156     0.000

  Residual Variances
    GHQ               1.369      1.798      0.762     0.446
```

Note: The effect of TFL is nonsignificant as a predictor of group means.

STANDARDIZED MODEL RESULTS

STDYX Standardization

	Estimate	S.E.	Est./S.E.	Two-Tailed P-Value
Within Level				
Variances				
GHQ	1.000	0.000	999.000	999.000
Between Level				
GHQ ON				
TFL	-0.579	0.411	-1.408	0.159
Intercepts				
GHQ	15.447	5.560	2.778	0.005
Residual Variances				
GHQ	0.665	0.476	1.399	0.162

R-SQUARE

Within Level

Between Level

Observed Variable	Estimate	S.E.	Est./S.E.	Two-Tailed P-Value
GHQ	0.335	0.476	0.704	0.482

QUALITY OF NUMERICAL RESULTS

Condition Number for the Information Matrix   0.265E-03
(ratio of smallest to largest eigenvalue)

Of course, you might have already gathered that the relationship of interest (i.e., leadership as a predictor of well-being) could be estimated at both levels simultaneously. Again in this estimation, we would simply not specify the predictor as either a within or a between variable and rely on Mplus to apportion the variance appropriately. However, the predictive relationship would be specified in both the %WITHIN% and the %BETWEEN% models. Here is the code and output for that analysis:

```
Mplus VERSION 7 (Mac)
MUTHEN & MUTHEN

INPUT INSTRUCTIONS
```

```
TITLE:        Multilevel analysis;
DATA:         FILE IS ch9.dat;
VARIABLE:     NAMES ARE Leader TFL GHQ Trust MTFL;
              USEVARIABLES ARE GHQ TFL;
              CLUSTER IS Leader;
DEFINE:       CENTER TFL (GRANDMEAN);
ANALYSIS:     TYPE IS TWOLEVEL;
MODEL:        %WITHIN%
              GHQ ON TFL;
              %BETWEEN%
              GHQ ON TFL;
OUTPUT:       SAMPSTAT STDYX;
```

*** WARNING in DEFINE command
  The CENTER transformation is done after all other DEFINE transformations
have been completed.
  1 WARNING(S) FOUND IN THE INPUT INSTRUCTIONS

Multilevel analysis;

SUMMARY OF ANALYSIS

Number of groups
Number of observations   236
Number of dependent variables   1
Number of independent variables   1
Number of continuous latent variables   0

Observed dependent variables
  Continuous
    GHQ

Observed independent variables
    TFL

Variables with special functions
  Cluster variable   LEADER

  Centering (GRANDMEAN)
    TFL

Estimator   MLR

Information matrix   OBSERVED
Maximum number of iterations   100
Convergence criterion   0.100D-05
Maximum number of EM iterations   500
Convergence criteria for the EM algorithm
  Loglikelihood change   0.100D-02
  Relative loglikelihood change   0.100D-05
  Derivative   0.100D-03
Minimum variance   0.100D-03

```
Maximum number of steepest descent iterations              20
Maximum number of iterations for H1                      2000
Convergence criterion for H1                         0.100D-03
Optimization algorithm                                    EMA

Input data file(s)
  ch9.dat
Input data format  FREE

SUMMARY OF DATA

Number of clusters              121

Average cluster size          1.950

Estimated Intraclass Correlations for the Y Variables

                      Intraclass
        Variable     Correlation
        GHQ            0.123

SAMPLE STATISTICS

NOTE: The sample statistics for within and between refer to the
      maximum-likelihood estimated within and between covariance
      matrices, respectively.

    ESTIMATED SAMPLE STATISTICS FOR WITHIN


              Means
              GHQ          TFL
              _____        _____
    1         0.000        0.000


              Covariances
              GHQ          TFL
              _____        _____
    GHQ       14.859
    TFL       -0.475       0.498

              Correlations
              GHQ          TFL
              _____        _____
    GHQ       1.000
    TFL       -0.175       1.000

    ESTIMATED SAMPLE STATISTICS FOR BETWEEN

              Means
              GHQ          TFL
              _____        _____
    1         22.150       0.010
```

```
           Covariances
           GHQ            TFL
           _____         _____
    GHQ    2.093
    TFL   -0.068          0.109

           Correlations
           GHQ            TFL
           _____         _____
    GHQ    1.000
    TFL   -0.142          1.000
```

THE MODEL ESTIMATION TERMINATED NORMALLY

MODEL FIT INFORMATION

```
Number of Free Parameters                                          5

Loglikelihood
        H0 Value                                           -937.397
        H0 Scaling Correction Factor                          1.4373
            for MLR
        H1 Value                                           -937.397
        H1 Scaling Correction Factor                          1.4373
            for MLR

Information Criteria
        Akaike (AIC)                                       1884.793
        Bayesian (BIC)                                     1902.112
        Sample-Size Adjusted BIC                           1886.264
           (n* = (n + 2) / 24)

Chi-Square Test of Model Fit
        Value                                                 0.000*
        Degrees of Freedom                                        0
        P-Value                                              1.0000
        Scaling Correction Factor                            1.0000
            for MLR
```

*   The chi-square value for MLM, MLMV, MLR, ULSMV, WLSM and
    WLSMV cannot be used for chi-square difference testing in
    the regular way. MLM, MLR and WLSM chi-square difference
    testing is described on the Mplus website. MLMV, WLSMV, and
    ULSMV difference testing is done using the DIFFTEST option.

```
RMSEA (Root Mean Square Error Of Approximation)
        Estimate                                              0.000

CFI/TLI
        CFI                                                   1.000
        TLI                                                   1.000

Chi-Square Test of Model Fit for the Baseline Model
        Value                                                 6.720
```

```
                Degrees of Freedom                                  2
                P-Value                                        0.0347

SRMR (Standardized Root Mean Square Residual)
                Value for Within                                0.000
                Value for Between                               0.001
```

MODEL RESULTS

	Estimate	S.E.	Est./S.E.	Two-Tailed P-Value
Within Level				
GHQ ON				
TFL	-0.958	0.414	-2.314	0.021
Residual Variances				
GHQ	14.442	2.371	6.090	0.000
Between Level				
GHQ ON				
TFL	-0.609	1.535	-0.396	0.692
Intercepts				
GHQ	22.155	0.281	78.730	0.000
Residual Variances				
GHQ	1.998	1.581	1.263	0.206

Note: Consistent with our previous analyses, the prediction of GHQ score by TFL is significant at the individual level (i.e., within groups or Level 1) but not significant at Level 2 or the between-group level.

STANDARDIZED MODEL RESULTS

STDYX Standardization

	Estimate	S.E.	Est./S.E.	Two-Tailed P-Value
Within Level				
GHQ ON				
TFL	-0.175	0.076	-2.316	0.021
Residual Variances				
GHQ	0.969	0.026	36.704	0.000
Between Level				

```
        GHQ  ON
            TFL               -0.141         0.376        -0.377         0.706

        Intercepts
            GHQ               15.518         5.674         2.735         0.006

        Residual Variances
            GHQ                0.980         0.106         9.223         0.000

R-SQUARE

Within Level
    Observed                                                          Two-Tailed
    Variable           Estimate         S.E.      Est./S.E.           P-Value
    GHQ                   0.031         0.026          1.158             0.247

Between Level
    Observed                                                          Two-Tailed
    Variable           Estimate         S.E.      Est./S.E.           P-Value
    GHQ                   0.020         0.106          0.188             0.851

QUALITY OF NUMERICAL RESULTS

Condition Number for the Information Matrix      0.116E-03
(ratio of smallest to largest eigenvalue)
```

Random-Slope Models

The models we have been estimating thus far are multilevel regression models. Like all regression models, they have both a slope and an intercept. We have been focusing on allowing the intercepts to vary (i.e., to recognize that there are mean level differences between the groups). What about allowing the slopes to vary across groups? That would suggest something like a moderation hypothesis, in which we are proposing that the relationship we are investigating can be different for each group. Just as we attempted to predict intercept differences in the means-as-outcomes model, we can then ask whether we can predict the differences in relationships across groups. When we allow the relationship between X and Y to be different for every group, we are estimating a random-slope model.

Random-slope models in Mplus use "TWOLEVEL RANDOM" as the type of analysis and allow both the intercept and slopes to vary across the groups. Using the random option means that we are not able to calculate the standardized solution for random-slope models. We also use the DEFINE feature in the MODEL command to define the random slope. Although the random slope appears in the %WITHIN% model specification, it is, of course, part of the %BETWEEN% model; that is, the slopes are allowed to vary between the groups, not within the groups. Mplus does not estimate the correlation between the random intercept and random slope by default, so we will also include that in our code. In effect, we are calculating a slope for each group and an intercept for each group and allowing the two to correlate across groups. The relevant code and output are shown below.

```
Mplus VERSION 7 (Mac)
MUTHEN & MUTHEN

INPUT INSTRUCTIONS

    TITLE:      Multilevel analysis;
    DATA:       FILE IS ch9.dat;
    VARIABLE:   NAMES ARE Leader TFL GHQ Trust MTFL;
                USEVARIABLES ARE GHQ TFL;
                WITHIN IS TFL;
                CLUSTER IS LEADER;
    DEFINE:     CENTER TFL (GRANDMEAN);
    ANALYSIS:   TYPE IS TWOLEVEL RANDOM;
    MODEL:      %WITHIN%
                RSlope | GHQ ON TFL;
                %BETWEEN%
                GHQ WITH Rslope;
    OUTPUT:

*** WARNING in DEFINE command
    The CENTER transformation is done after all other DEFINE
transformation shave been completed.
    1 WARNING(S) FOUND IN THE INPUT INSTRUCTIONS

Multilevel analysis;

SUMMARY OF ANALYSIS

Number of groups                                                 1
Number of observations                                         236
Number of dependent variables                                    1
Number of independent variables                                  1
Number of continuous latent variables                            1

Observed dependent variables
  Continuous
    GHQ

Observed independent variables
    TFL

Continuous latent variables
    RSLOPE
```

```
Variables with special functions
  Cluster variable     LEADER

  Within variables
    TFL

  Centering (GRANDMEAN)
    TFL

Estimator       MLR

Information matrix                                          OBSERVED
Maximum number of iterations                                     100
Convergence criterion                                      0.100D-05
Maximum number of EM iterations                                  500
Convergence criteria for the EM algorithm
  Loglikelihood change                                     0.100D-02
  Relative loglikelihood change                            0.100D-05
  Derivative                                               0.100D-03
Minimum variance                                           0.100D-03
Maximum number of steepest descent iterations                     20
Maximum number of iterations for H1                             2000
Convergence criterion for H1                               0.100D-03
Optimization algorithm                                           EMA

Input data file(s)
ch9.dat
Input data format FREE

SUMMARY OF DATA

Number of clusters                                               121

Average cluster size                                           1.950

Estimated Intraclass Correlations for the Y Variables

              Intraclass                   Intraclass
   Variable   Correlation      Variable    Correlation
     GHQ        0.121

THE MODEL ESTIMATION TERMINATED NORMALLY

MODEL FIT INFORMATION

Number of Free Parameters                                          6

Loglikelihood
        H0 Value                                            -663.606
        H0 Scaling Correction Factor                          1.8923
          for MLR
```

Information Criteria
    Akaike (AIC)   1339.213
    Bayesian (BIC)   1359.996
    Sample-Size Adjusted BIC   1340.978
        (n* = (n + 2) / 24)

MODEL RESULTS

	Estimate	S.E.	Est./S.E.	Two-Tailed P-Value
Within Level				
Residual Variances				
GHQ	14.228	2.568	5.541	0.000
Between Level				
GHQ WITH				
RSLOPE	0.854	2.480	0.344	0.731
Means				
GHQ	22.158	0.277	80.014	0.000
RSLOPE	-0.868	0.357	-2.431	0.015
Variances				
GHQ	1.700	2.786	0.610	0.542
RSLOPE	0.838	3.088	0.271	0.786

QUALITY OF NUMERICAL RESULTS

Condition Number for the Information Matrix   0.110E-03
(ratio of smallest to largest eigenvalue)

It is a small step from estimating a random slope to trying to understand what might cause that variation in slopes. In the code shown below, I use a variable, Trust, which is hypothesized to have three roles in our multilevel model:

1. Trust is hypothesized as a within-level predictor of GHQ score,
2. Trust is hypothesized to be a predictor of the random intercept (i.e., means as outcomes) on the between group level, and
3. Trust is hypothesized to be a predictor of the random slope (i.e., slopes as outcomes).

Putting all of these predictions together leads to the following model specification and output:

Mplus VERSION 7 (Mac)
MUTHEN & MUTHEN

Chapter 9: Multilevel Modeling 215

```
INPUT INSTRUCTIONS

  TITLE:      Multilevel analysis;
  DATA:       FILE IS ch9.dat;
  VARIABLE:   NAMES ARE Leader TFL GHQ Trust MTFL;
              USEVARIABLES ARE GHQ TFL Trust;
              WITHIN IS TFL;
              CLUSTER IS Leader;
  DEFINE:     CENTER TFL (GRANDMEAN);
  ANALYSIS:   TYPE IS TWOLEVEL RANDOM;
  MODEL:      %WITHIN%
              RSlope | GHQ ON TFL;
              GHQ ON Trust;
              %BETWEEN%
              GHQ WITH RSlope;
              RSlope ON Trust;
              GHQ ON Trust;
  OUTPUT:

*** WARNING in DEFINE command
  The CENTER transformation is done after all other DEFINE transformations
have been completed.
   1 WARNING(S) FOUND IN THE INPUT INSTRUCTIONS

Multilevel analysis;

SUMMARY OF ANALYSIS

Number of groups                                                 1
Number of observations                                         236
Number of dependent variables                                    1
Number of independent variables                                  2
Number of continuous latent variables                            1

Observed dependent variables
  Continuous
    GHQ

Observed independent variables
    TFL         TRUST

Continuous latent variables
    RSLOPE

Variables with special functions
  Cluster variable      LEADER

  Within variables
    TFL

  Centering (GRANDMEAN)
    TFL
```

```
Estimator                                            MLR

Information matrix                              OBSERVED
Maximum number of iterations                         100
Convergence criterion                          0.100D-05
Maximum number of EM iterations                      500
Convergence criteria for the EM algorithm
  Loglikelihood change                         0.100D-02
  Relative loglikelihood change                0.100D-05
  Derivative                                   0.100D-03
Minimum variance                               0.100D-03
Maximum number of steepest descent iterations         20
Maximum number of iterations for H1                 2000
Convergence criterion for H1                   0.100D-03
Optimization algorithm                               EMA

Input data file(s)
ch9.dat
Input data format FREE

SUMMARY OF DATA

Number of clusters                                   121

Average cluster size                               1.950

Estimated Intraclass Correlations for the Y Variables

              Intraclass                    Intraclass
  Variable    Correlation       Variable    Correlation
    GHQ         0.117

THE MODEL ESTIMATION TERMINATED NORMALLY

MODEL FIT INFORMATION

Number of Free Parameters                              9

Loglikelihood
        H0 Value                                -923.921
        H0 Scaling Correction Factor              1.4452
          for MLR

Information Criteria
        Akaike (AIC)                            1865.843
        Bayesian (BIC)                          1897.017
        Sample-Size Adjusted BIC                1868.491
          (n* = (n + 2) / 24)

MODEL RESULTS
```

	Estimate	S.E.	Est./S.E.	Two-Tailed P-Value
Within Level				
GHQ ON				
TRUST	-0.900	0.356	-2.528	0.011
Residual Variances				
GHQ	13.341	2.547	5.238	0.000
Between Level				
RSLOPE ON				
TRUST	-5.520	2.600	-2.123	0.034
GHQ ON				
TRUST	-1.933	3.067	-0.630	0.529
GHQ WITH				
RSLOPE	0.530	2.963	0.179	0.858
Intercepts				
GHQ	31.800	15.423	2.062	0.039
RSLOPE	27.113	13.119	2.067	0.039
Residual Variances				
GHQ	1.360	2.372	0.573	0.566
RSLOPE	0.512	2.244	0.228	0.819

QUALITY OF NUMERICAL RESULTS

Condition Number for the Information Matrix   0.931E-05
(ratio of smallest to largest eigenvalue)

Multilevel Modeling and Mediation

Thus far, we have been talking about multilevel regression analyses in which we define only one outcome. However, as we have seen in previous chapters, it is a small step to move from regressions to estimating more than one regression equation in the same analysis (i.e., an observed variable path analysis). Similarly, one could define a measurement model for latent variables and proceed to estimate a latent variable structural equation model, as we discussed in Chapter 7. Indeed, as I have noted frequently throughout this book, the true power of Mplus comes from its ability to combine analyses to answer substantively complex questions. If one is trying to predict a dichotomous outcome using nested data, then simply declaring the variable as categorical and implementing the techniques discussed in this chapter will result in a multilevel logistic regression; this same analysis can be expressed in a series of regression analyses with different types of outcomes to result in increasingly complex models.

Of course, the temptation is always to test every possible model or configuration and then to choose the best fitting or most interesting to present.

This is a bad strategy both conceptually and empirically. Conceptually, the goal of multilevel analysis is not just to treat clustered data as an artifact that needs to be dealt with by a more complex analysis. Rather, the goal is to articulate and test multilevel theory. That is, as researchers, we need to think about at what "level" the variables we are interested in exert their effects. Is the effect of leadership individual—being based on one-to-one relationships? Or are leaders consistent in treating all group members the same? This is a substantive question but translates readily into implications for how we model the effect of leadership on the outcomes in which we are interested..

Consider the simple model presented in Figure 9.1. The model suggests that employees who perceive their leaders as engaging in transformational leadership will experience greater trust in their leaders, which, in turn, has implications for individual mental health. Although this is a simple mediation model (see Chapter 5), the introduction of multiple levels also introduces several complications.

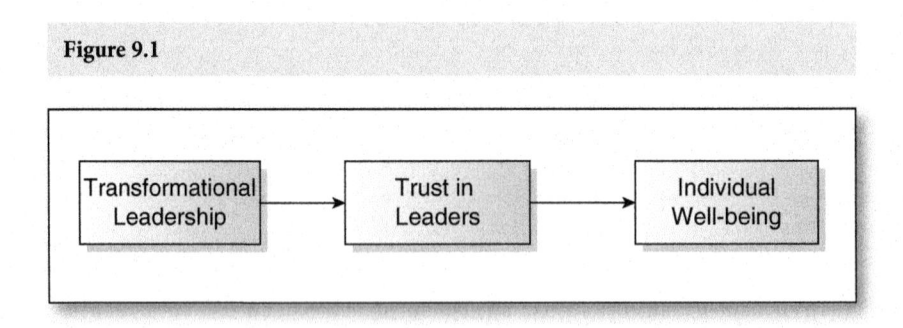

Figure 9.1

Transformational Leadership → Trust in Leaders → Individual Well-being

First, each of these variables can exist at the level of the group (Level 2) or the individual (Level 1). This means there are at least eight basic ways in which the proposed mediated relationship can manifest (see Table 9.2). Moreover, the models are not necessarily mutually exclusive; one can have both a Level 1 model and a Level 2 model or a cross-level model operating at the same time. Clearly there is a need for theory to limit our options and direct our testing to the most plausible and interesting hypotheses.

A second complication quickly ensues. Although many researchers become interested in Mplus because of their desire to test multilevel mediation, in fact Mplus does not calculate these effects. That is, when using a two-level analysis, the MODEL INDIRECT subcommand we used previously to calculate the indirect effects (see Chapter 5) is not operable. Nor is the bootstrap implemented in two-level analysis. There is, however, a workaround that will allow us to calculate and estimate the indirect effect in a hypothesized mediated model (for a thorough discussion of multilevel mediation see

Table 9.2

	Predictor	Mediator	Outcome
Level 1 model	1	1	1
Cross levels	2	1	1
Cross levels	1	2	1
Cross level	1	1	2
Cross level	2	2	1
Cross level	2	2	2
Cross level	2	1	1
Level 2 model	2	2	2

Preacher, Zhang, & Zyphur, 2011; Preacher, Zyphur, & Zhang, 2010). In essence, the solution is to have Mplus calculate the indirect effect and then estimate it as a model parameter. The source code and output that follow show an example of such an analysis. I have assumed that the data are clustered but, for the sake of simplicity, that the relations are all Level 1 (i.e., I am estimating what Preacher et al., 2010, referred to as a 1-1-1 mediated model). Preacher et al. (2010) noted that estimating the hypothesized mediation only in the within model results in a conflated estimation; that is, between-group relationships may be detected as within-group relationships if only the within-group model is estimated. The solution to this conflation is to estimate the unconflated model (Preacher et al., 2010), estimating the same relationships on the within-group and between-group levels, as shown below.

```
Mplus VERSION 7 (Mac)
MUTHEN & MUTHEN

INPUT INSTRUCTIONS

TITLE:      Multilevel analysis;
DATA:       FILE IS ch9.dat;
VARIABLE:   NAMES ARE Leader TFL GHQ Trust MTFL;
            USEVARIABLES ARE GHQ TFL Trust;
            ! WITHIN IS TFL Trust;
            CLUSTER IS Leader;
DEFINE:     CENTER TFL Trust (GRANDMEAN);
ANALYSIS:   TYPE IS TWOLEVEL RANDOM;
MODEL:      %WITHIN%
```

```
    GHQ ON Trust (AW);
    Trust ON TFL (BW);
```

Note: The two effects constituting the mediated relationship are estimated at the within-group level and labeled AW and BW, respectively.

```
    GHQ ON TFL;
    %BETWEEN%
    GHQ Trust TFL;
```

Note: Naming the variables on the between-group level allows the estimation of residual variances on this level.

```
    GHQ ON Trust (AB);
    Trust ON TFL (BB);
```

Note: The two effects are estimated on the between-group level and labeled AB and BB, respectively.

```
    GHQ ON TFL;
    MODEL CONSTRAINT:
    NEW (INDW) (INDB);
```

Note: Two new terms (INDW and INDB) corresponding to the within-group indirect effect and the between-group indirect effect are introduced in the model.

```
    INDW = AW * BW;
    INDB = AB * BB;
```

Note: The indirect effects are calculated as the cross-products of their constituent direct effects.

```
OUTPUT: CINTERVAL;
```

Note: I am requesting that the confidence intervals (CIs) for these effects be estimated.

```
*** WARNING in DEFINE command
  The CENTER transformation is done after all other DEFINE transformations
  have been completed.
1 WARNING(S) FOUND IN THE INPUT INSTRUCTIONS

Multilevel analysis;

SUMMARY OF ANALYSIS

Number of groups                                                     1
Number of observations                                             236
```

```
Number of dependent variables                                   2
Number of independent variables                                 1
Number of continuous latent variables                           0

Observed dependent variables
  Continuous
     GHQ         TRUST

Observed independent variables
     TFL

Variables with special functions
  Cluster variable      LEADER

  Centering (GRANDMEAN)
     TFL         TRUST

Estimator       MLR

Information matrix                                       OBSERVED
Maximum number of iterations                                  100
Convergence criterion                                    0.100D-05
Maximum number of EM iterations                               500
Convergence criteria for the EM algorithm
  Loglikelihood change                                   0.100D-02
  Relative loglikelihood change                          0.100D-05
  Derivative                                             0.100D-03
Minimum variance                                         0.100D-03
Maximum number of steepest descent iterations                  20
Maximum number of iterations for H1                          2000
Convergence criterion for H1                             0.100D-03
Optimization algorithm                                        EMA

Input data file(s)
  ch9.dat
Input data format FREE

SUMMARY OF DATA

Number of clusters                                            121

Average cluster size                                        1.950

Estimated Intraclass Correlations for the Y Variables

            Intraclass            Intraclass            Intraclass
  Variable  Correlation Variable  Correlation Variable  Correlation

     GHQ      0.120       TRUST      0.025       TFL      0.179
```

Note: The input command and a description of the data are presented.

```
THE MODEL ESTIMATION TERMINATED NORMALLY

MODEL FIT INFORMATION

Number of Free Parameters                                      15

Loglikelihood
          H0 Value                                      -1198.559
          H0 Scaling Correction Factor                     1.0669
             for MLR
          H1 Value                                      -1198.590
          H1 Scaling Correction Factor                     1.0669
             for MLR

Information Criteria
          Akaike (AIC)                                   2427.118
          Bayesian (BIC)                                 2479.076
          Sample-Size Adjusted BIC                       2431.532
            (n* = (n + 2) / 24)

Chi-Square Test of Model Fit

          Value                                             0.000*
          Degrees of Freedom                                    0
          P-Value                                          1.0000
          Scaling Correction Factor                        1.0000
             for MLR

*    The chi-square value for MLM, MLMV, MLR, ULSMV, WLSM and
     WLSMV cannot be used for chi-square difference testing in
     the regular way. MLM, MLR and WLSM chi-square difference
     testing is described on the Mplus website. MLMV, WLSMV, and
     ULSMV difference testing is done using the DIFFTEST option.

RMSEA (Root Mean Square Error Of Approximation)
          Estimate                                          0.000

CFI/TLI
          CFI                                               1.000
          TLI                                               1.000

Chi-Square Test of Model Fit for the Baseline Model
          Value                                            62.388
          Degrees of Freedom                                    6
          P-Value                                          0.0000

SRMR (Standardized Root Mean Square Residual)
          Value for Within                                  0.001
          Value for Between                                 0.086
```

Note: The model provides a good fit (but is a saturated model).

MODEL RESULTS

	Estimate	S.E.	Est./S.E.	Two-Tailed P-Value
Within Level				
GHQ ON				
TRUST	-0.973	0.363	-2.677	0.007
TFL	-0.481	0.436	-1.104	0.270
TRUST ON				
TFL	0.495	0.110	4.502	0.000
Variances				
TFL	0.498	0.057	8.688	0.000
Residual Variances				
GHQ	13.945	2.319	6.012	0.000
TRUST	0.542	0.056	9.658	0.000
Between Level				
GHQ ON				
TRUST	-1.036	45.747	-0.023	0.982
TFL	-0.423	6.818	-0.062	0.951
TRUST ON				
TFL	0.147	0.343	0.427	0.669
Means				
TFL	0.010	0.056	0.186	0.852
Intercepts				
GHQ	22.154	0.278	79.752	0.000
TRUST	0.000	0.051	-0.001	0.999
Variances				
TFL	0.107	0.050	2.131	0.033
Residual Variances				
GHQ	1.972	1.492	1.321	0.186
TRUST	0.003	0.030	0.095	0.924
New/Additional Parameters				
INDW	-0.481	0.200	-2.409	0.016
INDB	0.152	6.682	-0.023	0.982

Note: The effects constituting the model are significant within groups but not between groups. As you would expect, the new parameter INDW (the within-group indirect effect) is significant; the corresponding between-group effect (INDB) is not.

QUALITY OF NUMERICAL RESULTS

Condition Number for the Information Matrix   0.621E-07
(ratio of smallest to largest eigenvalue)

CONFIDENCE INTERVALS OF MODEL RESULTS

	Lower .5%	Lower 2.5%	Lower 5%	Estimate	Upper 5%	Upper 2.5%	Upper .5%
Within Level							
GHQ ON							
TRUST	-1.908	-1.685	-1.570	-0.973	-0.375	-0.261	-0.037
TFL	-1.603	-1.334	-1.197	-0.481	0.236	0.373	0.641
TRUST ON							
TFL	0.212	0.279	0.314	0.495	0.675	0.710	0.777
Variances							
TFL	0.351	0.386	0.404	0.498	0.593	0.611	0.646
Residual Variances							
GHQ	7.970	9.399	10.129	13.945	17.760	18.490	19.919
TRUST	0.398	0.432	0.450	0.542	0.635	0.652	0.687
Between Level							
GHQ ON							
TRUST	-118.871	-90.700	-76.290	-1.036	74.218	88.628	116.799
TFL	-17.986	-13.787	-11.639	-0.423	10.793	12.941	17.140
TRUST ON							
TFL	-0.738	-0.527	-0.418	0.147	0.712	0.820	1.031
Means							
TFL	-0.135	-0.100	-0.082	0.010	0.103	0.121	0.156
Intercepts							
GHQ	21.439	21.610	21.697	22.154	22.611	22.698	22.870
TRUST	-0.131	-0.100	-0.084	0.000	0.084	0.100	0.131
Variances							
TFL	-0.022	0.009	0.024	0.107	0.190	0.206	0.237
Residual Variances							
GHQ	-1.872	-0.953	-0.483	1.972	4.427	4.897	5.815
TRUST	-0.074	-0.056	-0.047	0.003	0.052	0.062	0.080
New/Additional Parameters							
INDW	-0.995	-0.872	-0.810	-0.481	-0.152	-0.090	0.033
INDB	-17.363	-13.248	-11.144	-0.152	10.840	12.945	17.059

Note: The CIs for model parameters are estimated. The 95% CI for the effect INDW does not include zero (lower limit = −0.872, upper limit = −0.090). The between-group CI does include zero (lower limit = −13.248, upper limit = 12.945).

References

Akaike, H. (1987). Factor analysis and the AIC. *Psychometrika, 52,* 317-332.

Allen, N. J., & Meyer, J. P. (1990). The measurement, antecedents of affective, continuance and normative commitment to the organization. *Journal of Occupational Psychology, 63,* 1-18.

Anderson, J. C., & Gerbing, D. W. (1984). The effects of sampling error on convergence, improper solutions, and goodness-of-fit indices for maximum likelihood confirmatory factor analysis. *Psychometrika, 49,* 155-173.

Anderson, J. C., & Gerbing, D. W. (1988). Structural equation modelling in practice: A review and recommended two-step approach. *Psychological Bulletin, 103,* 411-423.

Antonakis, J., Bendahan, S., Jacquart, P., & Lalive, R. (2010). On making causal claims: A review and recommendations. *Leadership Quarterly, 21,* 1086-1120.

Asparouhov, T., & Muthén, B. (2009). Exploratory structural equation modeling. *Structural Equation Modeling, 16,* 397-438.

Bandura, A. (1977). *Social learning theory.* Englewood Cliffs, NJ: Prentice Hall.

Banks, M. J., Clegg, C. W., Jackson, P. R., Kemp, N. J., Stafford, E. M., & Wall, T. D. (1980). The use of the General Health Questionnaire as an indication of mental health in occupational settings. *Journal of Occupational Psychology, 53,* 187-194.

Barling, J., Kelloway, E. K., & Bremermann, E. H. (1991). Preemployment predictors of union attitudes: The role of family socialization and work beliefs. *Journal of Applied Psychology, 76,* 725-731.

Baron, R. M., & Kenny, D. A. (1986). The moderator-mediator variable distinction in social psychological research: Conceptual, strategic and statistical considerations. *Journal of Personality and Social Psychology, 51,* 1173-1182.

Bass, B. M., & Avolio, B. J. (Eds.). (1994). *Improving organizational effectiveness through transformational leadership.* Thousand Oaks, CA: Sage.

Bentler, P. M. (1980). Multivariate analysis with latent variables: Causal modelling. *Annual Review of Psychology, 31,* 419-456.

Bentler, P. M. (1990). Comparative fit indexes in structural models. *Psychological Bulletin, 107,* 238-246.

Bentler, P. M., & Bonett, D. G. (1980). Significance tests and goodness of fit in the analysis of covariance structures. *Psychological Bulletin, 88,* 588-606.

Bentler, P. M., & Chou, C. P. (1987). Practical issues in structural equation modeling. *Sociological Methods & Research, 16,* 78-117.

Blalock, H. M. (1964). *Causal inference in non-experimental research.* Chapel Hill: University of North Carolina Press.

Bollen, K. A. (1989). *Structural equations with latent variables.* New York: John Wiley.

Bollen, K., & Lennox, R. (1991). Conventional wisdom on measurement: A structural equation perspective. *Psychological Bulletin, 110,* 305-314.

Bollen, K. A., & Long, J. S. (1993). Introduction. In K. A. Bollen & J. S. Long (Eds.), *Testing structural equation models* (pp. 1-9). Beverly Hills, CA: Sage.

Boomsma, A. (1983). *On the robustness of LISREL (maximum likelihood estimation) against small sample size and nonnormality.* Unpublished doctoral dissertation, University of Groningen, Groningen, The Netherlands.

Boomsma, A., & Hoogland, J. J. (2001). The robustness of LISREL modeling revisited. In R. Cudeck, S. du Toit, & D. Sörbom (Eds.), *Structural equation models: Present and future. A Festschrift in honor of Karl Jöreskog* (pp. 139-168). Lincolnwood, IL: Scientific Software International.

Brannick, M. T. (1995). Critical comments on applying covariance structure modeling. *Journal of Organizational Behavior, 16,* 201-213.

Browne, M. W. (1982). Covariance structures. In D. M. Hawkins (Ed.), *Topics in multivariate analysis* (pp. 72-141). Cambridge, UK: Cambridge University Press.

Browne, M. W., & Cudeck, R. (1989). Single sample cross-validation indices for covariance structures. *Multivariate Behavioral Research, 24,* 445-455.

Browne, M. W., & Cudeck, R. (1993). Alternative ways of assessing model fit. In K. A. Bollen & J. S. Long (Eds.), *Testing structural equation models* (pp. 136-162). Newbury Park, CA: Sage.

Byrne, B. M. (2012). *Structural equation modeling with Mplus: Basic concepts, applications and programming.* New York: Routledge.

Cliff, N. (1983). Some cautions concerning the application of causal modeling methods. *Multivariate Behavioral Research, 18,* 115-116.

Cohen, J., Cohen, P., West, S. G., & Aikem, L. S. (2003). *Applied multiple regression/correlation analysis for the behavioral sciences.* Mahwah, NJ: Lawrence Erlbaum.

Cudeck, R., & Browne, M. W. (1983). Cross-validation of covariance structures. *Multivariate Behavioral Research, 18,* 147-167.

Enders, C. K., & Tofighi, D. (2007). Centering predictor variables in cross-sectional multilevel models: A new look at an old issue. *Psychological Methods, 12,* 121-138.

Fan, X., & Sivo, S. A. (2007). Sensitivity of fit indices to model misspecification and model types. *Multivariate Behavioral Research, 42,* 509-529.

Fishbein, M., & Ajzen, I. (1975). *Belief, attitude, intention and behavior: An introduction to theory and research.* Reading, MA: Addison-Wesley.

Fullagar, C., McCoy, D., & Shull, C. (1992). The socialization of union loyalty. *Journal of Organizational Behavior, 13,* 13-26.

Gerbing, D. A., & Anderson, J. C. (1992). Monte Carlo evaluations of goodness of fit indices for structural equation models. *Sociological Methods and Research, 21,* 132-160.

Glaser, B. G., & Strauss, A. L. (1967). *The discovery of grounded theory: Strategies for qualitative research.* Chicago: Aldine.

Glymour, C., Schienes, R., Spirtes, P., & Kelly, K. (1987). *Discovering causal structure: Artificial intelligence, philosophy of science, and statistical modeling.* San Diego, CA: Academic Press.

Graham, J. W. (2009). Missing data analysis: Making it work in the real world. *Annual Review of Psychology, 60,* 549-576.

Hershberger, S. L. (2003). The growth of structural equation modeling from 1994 to 2001. *Structural Equation Modeling, 10,* 35-47.

Hofmann, D. A., & Gavin, M. B. (1998). Centering decisions in hierarchical linear models: Implications for research in organizations. *Journal of Management, 24,* 623-641.

Hu, L., & Bentler, P. M. (1999). Cutoff criteria for fit indexes in covariance structure analysis: Conventional criteria versus new alternatives. *Structural Equation Modeling, 6,* 1-55.

James, L. R., & James, L. A. (1989). Causal modeling in organizational research. In C. L. Cooper & I. Robertson (Eds.), *International review of industrial and organizational psychology, 1989* (pp. 371-404). Chichester, UK: Wiley.

James, L. R., Mulaik, S. A., & Brett, J. M. (1982). *Causal analysis: Assumptions, models, and data.* Beverly Hills, CA: Sage.

James, L. R., Mulaik, S. A., & Brett, J. M. (2006). A tale of two methods. *Organizational Research Methods, 9,* 233-244.

Jöreskog, K. G., & Sörbom, D. (1992). *LISREL VIII: Analysis of linear structural relations.* Mooresville, IN: Scientific Software.

Kelloway, E. K. (1995). Structural equation modelling in perspective. *Journal of Organizational Behavior, 16,* 215-224.

Kelloway, E. K. (1996). Common practices in structural equation modeling. In C. L. Cooper & I. Robertson (Eds.), *International review of industrial and organizational psychology, 1996* (pp. 141-180). Chichester, UK: Wiley.

Kelloway, E. K. (1998). *Using LISREL for structural equation modeling: A researcher's guide.* Thousand Oaks, CA: Sage.

Kelloway, E. K., & Barling, J. (1993). Members' participation in local union activities: Measurement, prediction and replication. *Journal of Applied Psychology, 78,* 262-279.

Kelloway, E. K., & Francis, L. (2012). Longitudinal research methods. In M. Wang, R. Sinclair, & L. Tetrick (Eds.), *Research methods in occupational health psychology* (pp. 374-394). New York: Elsevier.

Kelloway, E. K., Gottlieb, B. H., & Barham, L. (1999). The source, nature, and direction of work and family conflict: A longitudinal investigation. *Journal of Occupational Health Psychology, 4,* 337-346.

Kelloway, E. K., Turner, N., Barling, J., & Loughlin, C. (2012). Transformational leadership and employee psychological well-being. *Work & Stress, 26,* 39-55.

Kelloway, E. K., Weigand, H., McKee, M., & Das, H. (2013). Positive leadership. *Journal of Leadership and Organizational Studies, 20,* 107-117.

Kim, K. H. (2005). The relation among fit indexes, power, and sample size in structural equation modeling. *Structural Equation Modeling, 12,* 368-390.

Klein, K. J., & Zedeck, S. (2004). Theory in applied psychology: Lessons (re)learned. *Journal of Applied Psychology, 89,* 931-933.

Little, R. J. A., & Rubin, D. B. (2002). *Statistical analysis with missing data.* Chichester, UK: Wiley.

Little, T. D., Cunningham, W. A., Shahar, G., & Widaman, K. F. (2002). To parcel or not to parcel: Exploring the question, weighing the merits. *Structural Equation Modeling: A Multidisciplinary Journal, 9,* 151-173.

Loehlin, J. C. (1987). *Latent variable models: An introduction to factor, path, and structural analysis.* Hillsdale, NJ: Lawrence Erlbaum.

Long, J. S. (1983a). *Confirmatory factor analysis: A preface to LISREL.* Beverly Hills, CA: Sage.

Long, J. S. (1983b). *Covariance structure models: An introduction to LISREL.* Beverly Hills, CA: Sage.

MacCallum, R. C. (1986). Specification searches in covariance structural modeling. *Psychological Bulletin, 100,* 107-120.

MacCallum, R. C., Browne, M. W., & Cai, L. (2006). Testing differences between nested covariance structure models: Power analysis and null hypotheses. *Psychological Methods, 11,* 19-35.

MacCallum, R. C., Browne, M. W., & Sugawara, H. M. (1996). Power analysis and determination of sample size for covariance structure modeling. *Psychological Methods, 1,* 130-149.

MacCallum, R. C., & Hong, S. (1997). Power analysis in covariance structure modeling using GFI and AGFI. *Multivariate Behavioral Research, 32,* 193-210.

MacCallum, R. C., Roznowski, M., & Necowitz, L. B. (1992). Model modifications in covariance structure analysis: The problem of capitalization on chance. *Psychological Bulletin, 111,* 490-504..

MacKenzie, S. B., Podsakoff, P. M., & Jarvis, C. (2005). The problem of measurement model misspecification in behavioral and organizational research and some recommended solutions. *Journal of Applied Psychology, 90,* 710-730.

MacKinnon, D. P., Fairchild, A. J., & Fritz, M. S. (2007). Mediation analysis. *Annual Review of Psychology, 58,* 593-614.

Marcoulides, G. A., & Ing, M. (2012). Automated structural equation modeling strategies. In R. Hoyle (Ed.), *Handbook of structural equation modeling* (pp. 690-704). New York: Guilford.

Marsh, H. W., Balla, J. R., & MacDonald, R. P. (1988). Goodness-of-fit indexes in confirmatory factor analysis: The effect of sample size. *Psychological Bulletin, 88,* 245-258.

Marsh, H. W., Muthén, B., Asparouhov, T., Lüdtke, O., Robitzsch, A., Morin, A.J.S., & Trautwein, U. (2009). Exploratory structural equation modeling, integrating CFA and EFA: Application to students' evaluations of university teaching. *Structural Equation Modeling, 16,* 439-476.

Maxwell, S. E., & Cole, D. A. (2007). Bias in the cross-sectional analysis of longitudinal mediation. *Psychological Methods, 12,* 23-44.

McArdle, J. J., & Hamagami, F. (1996). Multilevel models from a multiple group structural equation perspective. In G. Marcoulides & R. Schumaker (Eds.), *Advanced structural equation modeling techniques* (pp. 89-124). Hillsdale, NJ: Lawrence Erlbaum.

McGrath, J. E., Martin, J., & Kukla, R. A. (1982). *Judgment calls in research.* Beverly Hills, CA: Sage.

Medsker, G. J., Williams, L. J., & Holahan, P. J. (1994). A review of current practices for evaluating causal models in organizational behavior and human resources management research. *Journal of Management, 20,* 439-464.

Meyers, L. S., Gamst, G. C., & Guarino, A. J. (2006). *Applied multivariate research: Design and interpretation.* Thousand Oaks, CA: Sage.

Muthén, L. K., & Muthén, B. O. (1998-2013). *Mplus user's guide* (6th ed.). Los Angeles, CA: Muthén & Muthén.

Muthén, L. K., & Muthén, B. O. (2002). How to use a Monte Carlo study to decide on sample size and determine power. *Structural Equation Modeling, 4,* 599-620.

O'Keefe, D., Kelloway, E. K., & Francis, R. (2012). Introducing the OCEAN.20: A 20-item five-factor personality measure based on the Trait Self-Descriptive Inventory. *Military Psychology, 24,* 433-460.

Pedhazur, E. J. (1982). *Multiple regression in behavioral research: Explanation and prediction.* New York: Holt, Rinehart & Winston.

Pitariu, A. H., & Ployhart, R. E. (2010). Explaining change: Theorizing and testing dynamic mediated longitudinal relationships. *Journal of Management, 36,* 405-429.

Ployhart, R. E., & Vandenberg, R. K. (2010). Longitudinal research: The theory, design, and analysis of change. *Journal of Management, 36,* 94-120.

Podsakoff, N. P., Shen, W., & Podsakoff, P. M. (2006). The role of formative measurement models in strategic management research: Review, critique, and implications for future research. In D. J. Ketchen & D. D. Bergh (Eds.), *Research methods in strategy and management* (Vol. 3, pp. 201-256). Greenwich, CT: JAI.

Preacher, K. J., & Coffman, D. L. (2006, May). Computing power and minimum sample size for RMSEA [Computer software]. Retrieved February 10, 2014, from http://quantpsy.org/rmsea/rmsea.htm

Preacher, K. J., Zhang, Z., & Zyphur, M. J. (2011). Alternative methods for assessing mediation in multilevel data: The advantages of multilevel SEM. *Structural Equation Modeling, 18,* 161-182.

Preacher, K. J., Zyphur, M. J., & Zhang, Z. (2010). A general multilevel SEM framework for assessing multilevel mediation. *Psychological Methods, 15,* 209-233.

Raykov, T., Tomer, A., & Nesselroade, J. R. (1991). Reporting structural equation modeling results in *Psychology and Aging*: Some proposed guidelines. *Psychology and Aging, 6,* 499-503.

Rogers, W. M., & Schmitt, N. (2004). Parameter recovery and model fit using multidimensional composites: A comparison of four empirical parceling algorithms. *Multivariate Behavioral Research, 39,* 379-412.

Satorra, A., & Bentler, P. M. (2001). A scaled difference chi-square test statistic for moment structure analysis. *Psychometrika, 66,* 507-514.

Schoemann, A. M., Preacher, K. J., & Coffman, D. L. (2010, April). Plotting power curves for RMSEA [Computer software]. Retrieved February 10, 2014, from http://quantpsy.org/rmsea/rmseaplot.htm

Singer, J. D., & Willett, J. B. (2003). *Applied longitudinal data analysis: Modeling change and event occurrence.* New York: Oxford University Press.

Soper, D. (2013). A-priori sample size calculator for structural equation models [Computer software]. Retrieved February 10, 2014, from http://www.danielsoper.com/statcalc3/calc.aspx?id=89

Steiger, J. H. (1990). Structural model evaluation and modification: An interval estimation approach. *Multivariate Behavioral Research, 25,* 173-180.

Tabachnick, B. G., & Fidell, L. S. (1996). *Using multivariate statistics* (3rd ed.). New York: HarperCollins College.

Tanaka, J. S. (1993). Multifaceted conceptions of fit in structural equation models. In K. A. Bollen & J. S. Long (Eds.), *Testing structural equation models* (pp. 10-39). Newbury Park, CA: Sage.

Taris, T. (2003). Challenges in longitudinal designs in occupational health psychology. *Scandinavian Journal of Work and Environmental Health, 29,* 1-4.

Tepper, B. J. (2007). Abusive supervision in work organizations: Review, synthesis and research agenda. *Journal of Management, 33,* 261-289.

Tomarken, A. J., & Waller, N. G. (2005). Structural equation modeling: Strengths, limitations, and misconceptions. *Annual Review of Clinical Psychology, 1,* 31-65.

Ullman, J. B. (2006). Structural equation modeling: Reviewing the basics and moving forward. *Journal of Personality Assessment, 87,* 35-50.

Vandenberg, R. J., & Lance, C. E. (2000). A review and synthesis of the measurement invariance literature: Suggestions, practices and recommendations for organizational research. *Organizational Research Methods, 3,* 4-70.

Westland, J. C. (2010). Lower bounds on sample size in structural equation modeling. *Electronic Commerce Research and Applications, 9,* 476-487.

Williams, L. J. (1995). Covariance structure modeling in organizational research: Problems with the method vs. applications of the method. *Journal of Organizational Behavior, 16,* 225-233.

Williams, L. J., & O'Boyle, E. H. (2008). Measurement models for linking latent variables and indicators: A review of human resource management research using parcels. *Human Resource Management Review, 18,* 233-242.

Williams, L. J., Vandenberg, R. J., & Edwards, J. (2009). Structural equation modeling in management research: A guide for improved analysis. *Academy of Management Annals, 3,* 543-605.

Wright, S. (1934). The method of path coefficients. *Annals of Mathematical Statistics, 5,* 161-215.

Index

Absolute fit of model, 22–26
Academy of Management, Research Methods Division, 1
Adjusted goodness-of-fit (AGFI) test, 25
Affective commitment measure, 130
AGFI (adjusted goodness-of-fit) test, 25
Ajzen, I., 5, 23, 30
Akaike information criterion (AIC), 29
Allen, N. J., 130
Alternative fit indices, 24
ANALYSIS command, 41
Anderson, J. C., 24, 56, 131
Antonakis, J., 8
Approximation, root mean square error of (RMSEA), 17, 24–25, 132
Association, in causal inference, 8
Autoregressive models, 177–178

Balla, J. R., 28
Baron, R. M., 96, 106
Baseline model, 26
Batch processor, Mplus as, 1
Bayesian estimators, 16
Bayesian information criterion (BIC), 29
Bendahan, S., 8
Bentler, P. M., 17, 27–28, 129
Bias-corrected confidence intervals, 107–108, 113
BIC (Bayesian information criterion), 29
Bollen, K. A., 7, 13–14, 28, 56, 97, 130
Bonett, D. G., 28
Boomsma, A., 17
Bootstrapping confidence intervals, 107
Brett, J. M., 25

Browne, M. W., 17, 28
Byrne, B. M., 16

Causal inference, 8
Causality, direction of, 56
Centering predictors, 195–196
CFI (comparative fit index), 27, 132
Chi-square (χ^2) statistic:
  in absolute fit of model, 22–24
  in comparative fit of model, 27
  in parsimonious fit of model, 29, 33
Chou, C. P., 17
Cliff, N., 3
Close fit, test of (PCLOSE test), 25
Clustering of data, 185
Coffman, D. L., 17
Command file, Mplus, 39–42
Comparative fit index (CFI), 27, 132
Comparative fit of model, 26–28
Compound paths, 10–11, 106
Conditional models, 195–201
  code for, 196–197
  model fit information, 199–200
  model results, 200–201
  overview, 195–196
  summary of analysis, 197–198
  summary of data, 198–199
  See also Multilevel modeling
Condition 9 and Condition 10 tests, 25–26, 33
Confidence intervals, 107, 220
Confirmatory factor analysis, 52–93
  fit assessment for, 69–70
  measurement equivalence across time by, 152–153

231

model identification in, 56–57
model specification in, 52–55
nested model comparisons in, 30
path analysis with, 3
rigor of, 2
sample results section for, 89–93
Confirmatory factor analysis, estimation output for, 57–69
model fit information, 59
model modification indices, 67–69
model results, 59–61
quality of numerical results, 67
standardized model results, 61–63
STD standardization, 65–67
STDY standardization, 63–65
summary, 58–59
Confirmatory factor analysis, model modification from, 70–89
exploratory structural equation model output, 71–89
item parceling, 70–71
Correlation matrix:
absolute fit of model and, 22
decomposing, 11
just-identified model, 14
overview, 11–13
theory implications in, 6–7
Cost-benefit trade-off, in fit of model, 21
Covariance matrix, 13, 22, 24
Cross-lagged models, 176–184
Cross-validation index (CVI), 28
Cudeck, R., 28
CVI (cross-validation index), 28

DATA command, 39–40
Data file, in Mplus, 37–39
Data-mining techniques, 20
DEFINE command, 39, 41
Disaggregation strategies, in confirmatory factor analysis, 71–72
Distal relationships, strength of, 6

ECVI (expected value of the cross-validation index), 28
Edwards, J., 56
Effect size, 17

Endogenous variables, 8, 95
Equality constraints, 115–120, 153
Estimation and fit, 15–17. *See also* Fit of model
Estimators, choosing, 16
Exogenous variables, 8, 95
Expected value of the cross-validation index (ECVI), 28
Exploratory factor analysis, 2
Exploratory structural equation model output, 71–89

Factor analysis, path diagram as, 9–10
FIML (full information maximum likelihood) estimation, in Mplus, 37
Fishbein, M., 5, 23, 30
Fit of model, 21–36
absolute, 22–26
assessment strategy for, 35–36
comparative, 26–28
conditional models and, 199–200
confirmatory factor analysis assessment for, 59, 69–70
estimation and, 15–17
means-as-outcomes models and, 204–205
observed variable path analysis for, 103–104
overview, 21–22
parsimonious, 29–35
Five-factor model, 69–70
Formative indicators, 56
Four-step process, in mediation, 106–107
Francis, R., 52
Full information maximum likelihood (FIML) estimation, in Mplus, 37

Gerbing, D. W., 24, 56, 131
GFI (goodness-of-fit) test, 25, 29
Glymour, B. G., 20
Goodness-of-fit (GFI) test, 25
Graham, J. W., 37
"Grounded theory" approach, 19
Growth curves, latent, 170–176

Hypothesis testing approach, 19

ICC (intraclass correlation
    coefficient), 189
Identification of models:
    confirmatory factor analysis, 56–57
    observed variable path analysis, 97
    overview, 13–14
IFI (incremental fit index), 28
Incremental fit index (IFI), 28
Independence model, 26
Indirect effect, confidence intervals
    around, 107
Indirect relationships in models, 96–97
Ing, M., 20
Intraclass correlation coefficient
    (ICC), 189
Isolation, in causal inference, 8
Item parceling, 70–71
Iterative estimation, by Mplus, 15

Jacquart, P., 8
James, L. A., 3, 18
James, L. R., 3, 18, 25, 29
Just-identified models, 13, 96

Kelloway, E. K., 52
Kelly, K., 20
Kenny, D. A., 96, 106
Kim, K. H., 17
Known distributional characteristics, in
    alternative fit indices, 24

Lalive, R., 8
Latent growth curves, 170–176
Latent variable models, 3
Latent variable path analysis, model
    specification in, 129–148
    alternative, 130
    measurement model testing, 132–140
    partially mediated and nonmediated
        model testing, 147–148
    structural model testing, 140–147
    testing complications in, 130–132
Latent variable path analysis, sample
    results for, 148–151
Latent variables, 10
Lennox, R., 56

LISREL program, 25
Loehlin, J. C., 36
Logistic regression, in Mplus, 47–51
Long, J. S., 7
Longitudinal analysis, 151–184
    cross-lagged models, 176–184
    latent growth curves, 170–176
Longitudinal analysis, measurement
    equivalence across time, 151–169
    confirmatory factor analysis model
        for, 152–153
    equality constraints for, 153
    model modifications analysis in,
        161–169
    summary analysis of, 153–161

MacCallum, R. C., 17
MacDonald, R. P., 28
Manifest variables, 10
Marcoulides, G. A., 20
Marsh, H. W., 28
Maximum likelihood with robust errors
    (MLR) estimator, 16, 188, 194
Means-as-outcomes models:
    code for, 201–202
    model fit information, 204–205
    model results, 205–206
    sample statistics, 203–204
    summary analysis, 202–203
    summary of data, 203
    See also Multilevel modeling
Measurement, confirmatory factor
    analysis of, 2–3
Measurement equivalence across time,
    151–169
    confirmatory factor analysis model
        for, 152–153
    equality constraints for, 153
    model modifications analysis for,
        161–169
    summary analysis of, 153–161
Mediation, in observed variable path
    analysis, 106–114
    confidence intervals for, 107
    four-step process, 106–107
    Mplus MODEL INDIRECT
        subcommand for, 107–108
    Mplus output for, 108–114

Mediation, latent variable path analysis and, 147–148
Mediation, multilevel modeling and complications in, 217–219
    unconflated model estimation, 219–224
Meyer, J. P., 130
MIMIC (multiple indicators, multiple causes) model, 57
MLM estimators, 16
MLR (maximum likelihood with robust errors) estimator, 16, 188, 194
MODEL command, 41, 43, 55, 140, 211
MODEL INDIRECT subcommand, 107–108, 218
Modification of models:
    confirmatory factor analysis indices for, 67–69
    exploratory structural equation model output, 71–89
    item parceling, 70–71
    measurement equivalence across time, 161–169
    observed variable path analysis, 101–103, 106
    overview, 17–20
MODINDICES command, 42
Monte Carlo analysis, 17, 56
Mplus, 37–51
    absolute model fit indices in, 24–25
    command file, 39–42
    comparative model fit indices in, 27–28
    data file, 37–39
    logistic regression by, 47–51
    parsimonious model fit indices in, 29
    regression analysis by, 42–46
    standardized solution by, 47
    See also Confirmatory factor analysis; Latent variable path analysis; Longitudinal analysis; Multilevel modeling; Observed variable path analysis
Mulaik, S. A., 25
Multilevel modeling, 185–224
    overview, 185–186
    random-slope models, 211–217
    simultaneous, 206–211

Multilevel modeling, conditional models, 195–201
    code for, 196–197
    model fit information, 199–200
    model results, 200–201
    overview, 195–196
    summary analysis, 197–198
    summary of data, 198–199
Multilevel modeling, means-as-outcomes models:
    code for, 201–202
    model fit information, 204–205
    model results, 205–206
    sample statistics, 203–204
    summary analysis, 202–203
    summary of data, 203
Multilevel modeling, mediation and, 217–224
    complications in, 217–219
    unconflated model estimation, 219–224
Multilevel modeling, Mplus for, 187–195
    null model estimation in, 190–195
    TWOLEVEL BASIC option in, 187–190
Multiple indicators, multiple causes (MIMIC) model, 57
Multisample analysis, in observed variable path analysis, 120–128
Muthén, B. O., 17
Muthén, L. K., 17

Nesselroade, J. R., 89
Nested model comparisons, 30–34
NFI (normed fit index), 28
Nonmediated models, 97, 147–149
Non-normed fit index, 27
Normed fit index (NFI), 28
N2Mplus data translation program, 39
Null *B* rule, in model identification, 97
Null model, 26–27, 190–195

Observed variable path analysis, 94–128
    equality constraints, 115–120
    model identification in, 97

model specification in, 94–97
multisample analysis, 120–128
Observed variable path analysis,
    estimation output, 97–106
  model fit information, 103–104
  model modification indices,
      101–103, 106
  model results, 99–100, 104
  quality of numerical results, 101, 106
  standardized model results, 100–101,
      104–106
  summary, 98–99
Observed variable path analysis,
    mediation, 106–114
  confidence intervals for, 107
  four-step process, 106–107
  Mplus MODEL INDIRECT
      subcommand for, 107–108
  Mplus output for, 108–114
Observed variables, 10
OCEAN.20 measure. *See* Confirmatory
    factor analysis
O'Keefe, D., 52
OUTPUT command, 42, 44
Overidentified models, 14–15

Parsimonious fit of model, 29–35
Parsimonious goodness-of-fit
    (GFI) test, 29
Parsimonious normed fit index
    (PNFI), 29
Partially mediated models, 97, 147–149
Path analysis:
  correlations reproduced in, 7
  nested model comparisons in, 30, 33
  overview, 3
  relationships depicted in, 8–13
  See also Latent variable path analysis;
      Observed variable path analysis
PCLOSE test, 25
Ployhart, R. E., 176
PNFI (parsimonious normed fit
    index), 29
Post hoc model modification, 19
Power analysis, 17
Preacher, K. J., 17, 219
Prediction, path models for, 3
Proximal relationships, strength of, 6

Qualitative data analysis, 19
Quantitative grounded theory
    approach, 19

Random-slope models, 211–217
Rank-and-order conditions, in model
    identification, 97
Raykov, T., 89
Reasoned action, theory of (Fishbein
    and Ajzen), 5
Recursive rule, in model identification,
    14, 97
Reflective indicators, 56
Regression analysis, in Mplus, 42–46
Relative fit index (RFI), 28
Research Methods Division, Academy of
    Management, 1
Residuals, analysis of, 24–25
Respecification of models:
  Mplus guidelines for, 34–35
  process of, 17–20
RFI (relative fit index), 28
RMNET listserv, of Academy of
    Management, 1
RMSEA (root mean square error of
    approximation), 17, 24–25, 132
Root mean square error of
    approximation (RMSEA),
    17, 24–25, 132

SABIC (sample size-adjusted Bayesian
    information criterion), 29
Sample size, 16–17
Sample size-adjusted Bayesian
    information criterion
    (SABIC), 29
SAMPSTAT command, 42, 44–45
Satorra-Bentler χ^2 corrected value, 16
Saturated models, 13, 24, 96
Schienes, R., 20
Simple paths, 10–11
Soper, D., 17
Specification of models:
  confirmatory factor analysis for,
      52–55
  observed variable path analysis, 94–97
  structural equation model process
      for, 7–13

Specification of models, latent variable path analysis for, 129–148
  alternative, 130
  measurement model testing, 132–140
  partially mediated and nonmediated model testing, 147–148
  structural model testing, 140–147
  testing complications in, 130–132
Spirtes, P., 20
SPSS, Mplus vs., 37–38
SRMR (standardized root mean square residual), 24
Stability models, 177
STANDARDIZED command, 42
Standardized model results, 61–63, 104–106
Standardized root mean square residual (SRMR), 24
Standardized solution, in Mplus, 47
Stat/Transfer data translation program, 38–39
STD standardization, in Mplus, 47, 65–67
STDY standardization, in Mplus, 47, 63–65
STDYX standardization, in Mplus, 47
Steiger, J. H., 18, 25
Structural equation modeling:
  estimation and fit from, 15–17
  identification issues in, 13–14
  modification of models from, 17–20
  overview, 5–7
  specification of models from, 7–13
  value of, 2–4
Sugawara, H. M., 17

Temporal order, in causal inference, 8
TETRAD program, 19–20
Theory. *See* Structural equation modeling
Theory trimming, 18, 34–35
Time. *See* Longitudinal analysis
Tomarken, A. J., 16
Tomer, A., 89
t rule, in model identification, 56, 97
Tucker-Lewis index (TLI), 27
TWOLEVEL BASIC option in Mplus, 187–190
TWOLEVEL RANDOM analysis, 211
Type I errors, respecification of models and, 35

Ullman, J. B., 35
Unconstrained models, 24
Underidentified models, 13

Vandenberg, R. J., 56
Vandenberg, R. J., 176
VARIABLE command, 39–40, 120, 127
Variables:
  endogenous and exogenous, 8, 95
  in path analysis, 8–9
  latent and observed or manifest, 10
Waller, N. G., 16
"Wastebasket" parameters, 18, 161
Weighted least squared estimator, 16
Williams, L. J., 56
WLSMV estimator, in Mplus, 47
Wright, Sewall, 7, 11, 106

ⓈSAGE researchmethods

The essential online tool for researchers from the world's leading methods publisher

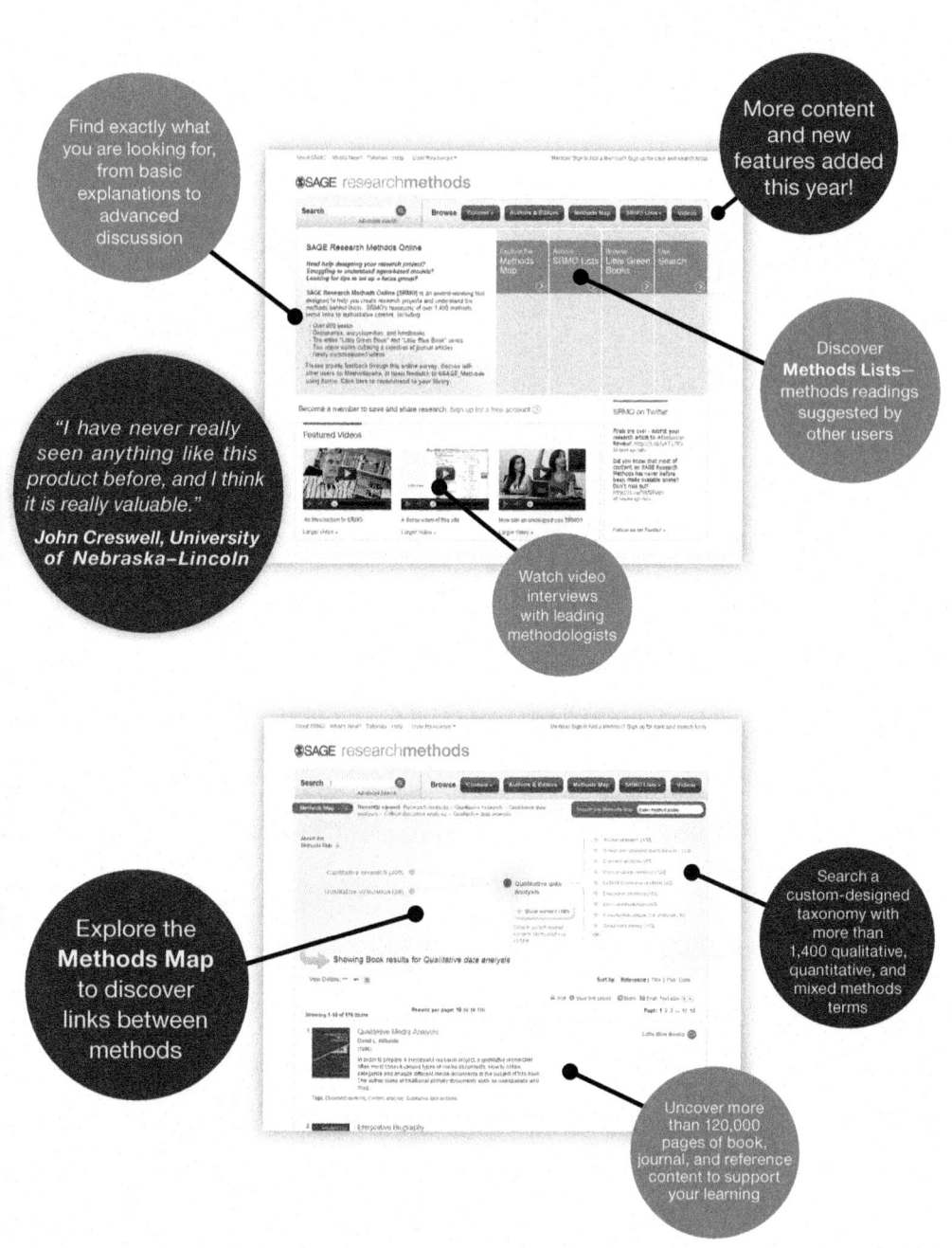

- Find exactly what you are looking for, from basic explanations to advanced discussion
- More content and new features added this year!
- Discover **Methods Lists**—methods readings suggested by other users
- "I have never really seen anything like this product before, and I think it is really valuable."
  John Creswell, University of Nebraska–Lincoln
- Watch video interviews with leading methodologists
- Explore the **Methods Map** to discover links between methods
- Search a custom-designed taxonomy with more than 1,400 qualitative, quantitative, and mixed methods terms
- Uncover more than 120,000 pages of book, journal, and reference content to support your learning

Find out more at
www.sageresearchmethods.com